Oracle SQL
The Essential Reference

Oracle SQL

The Essential Reference

David C. Kreines

Foreword by Ken Jacobs

O'REILLY®

Beijing · Cambridge · Farnham · Köln · Paris · Sebastopol · Taipei · Tokyo

Oracle SQL: The Essential Reference
by David C. Kreines

Published by O'Reilly & Associates, Inc., 101 Morris Street, Sebastopol, CA 95472.

Editors: Deborah Russell and Jonathan Gennick

Production Editor: Darren Kelly

Cover Designer: Ellie Volckhausen

Printing History:

> September 2000:   First Edition.

Library of Congress Cataloging-in-Publication Data

Kreines, David C.
    Oracle SQL : the essential reference / David Kreines.--1st ed.
        p. cm.
    Includes bibliographical references and index.
    ISBN 1-56592-697-8
    1. SQL (Computer program language) 2. Oracle (Computer file) I. Title.

QA76.73.S67 K74 2000
005.75'85—dc21   00-046520

[M]

For my children, Michael and Matthew.
You make me proud.
—David C. Kreines

Table of Contents

Foreword

SQL: A Venerable History and a Vital Future

The SQL language is the lingua franca of database management. Fluency in SQL is as important for a developer or a database administrator as is knowledge of a programming language or knowledge of the business needs of the application. The book you hold in your hands can be an indispensable guide to successfully exploiting the power of SQL as implemented in Oracle8*i*.

SQL has a long and venerable history, a critical role in today's e-commerce IT systems, and a bright future. I've described the origins, evolution, and future of SQL in this Foreword in the hope that it will deepen your appreciation of SQL as you read this excellent language reference.

Programming and Data Access Languages

General-purpose programmable computers were first developed during World War II for military applications. The UNIVAC I, the first commercial general-purpose machine, was delivered in 1951. Several generations of programming languages have been developed since that time. Each generation has improved the productivity of programmers by automating mechanical tasks, allowing a programmer to concentrate on the higher-level concepts related to the application.

The earliest programs were written in machine code—the numbers corresponding to the instructions the programmer wanted to store in the machine's memory.

Assembly language, which allowed the programmer to use names instead of numbers for instructions and memory locations, was developed in the early 1950s. The development of higher-level programming languages represented a significant step in raising the semantic level at which programmers work. A succession of such programming languages were invented, from Fortran (1957) to C (1972) to Java (1995), and their history is marked by a succession of growing and fading popularity. In addition to Fortran, C, and Java, Algol, COBOL, Ada, C++, and Basic are just a few of the important languages we have used to develop applications and systems programs.

In contrast to this plethora of procedural programming languages, today there is only one widely used data access language: SQL. SQL is a non-procedural data access language, as it leaves to the database management system the responsibility of determining how data will be processed to resolve a query. The application programmer needn't be concerned with the data access path and processing steps required to produce the desired result. Just as it was easier to write applications programs in higher-level procedural programming languages as compared to low-level machine code and assembly language, the SQL language makes it easier to access data in application programs or in an ad hoc, interactive fashion. SQL allows the application programmer to concentrate on business logic, rather than be concerned with the issues of using indexes or navigating through chains of pointers to retrieve or update data.

SQL was developed in the mid-to-late 1970s and is still evolving, but seems unlikely to be superseded. Unlike procedural programming languages, where no major language ever seems to fall into complete disuse, today the vast majority of database management systems implement a dialect of SQL. The Rosetta stone contained the data that unlocked the mystery of the ancient Egyptian language and hieroglyphics, and thus led to a better understanding of ancient Egyptian history and culture. Today, many would regard SQL as the language that unlocks the value of data and information in enterprise databases everywhere.

There are several dialects of SQL in different vendors' implementations, but most of the SQL language is common to most of the commercial database management systems now on the market. To be sure, there have been other data access languages, some developed in universities and others implemented in commercial products. But no data access language has been so successful or widely implemented as SQL. Professor Michael Stonebreaker of the University of California at Berkeley has even called SQL "intergalactic dataspeak."

The Origins of SQL

So, where did SQL come from, how has it evolved, and where is it going? The story of SQL begins at the IBM research laboratories near San Jose, California in the 1970s. Ted Codd, a mathematician and research fellow at IBM, created a formal theory of data management and wrote a seminal paper entitled "A Relational Model of Data for Large Shared Data Banks", published in the *Communications of the ACM* in June 1970. He defined the relational data model, consisting of data structures (tables of rows and columns); operations (like selection, projection, and joins) on that data; and integrity rules that ensure consistency of data (primary keys and referential integrity, for example).

Codd's rigorous mathematical definition of the relational model allowed him to define a procedure for designing databases that preserve data integrity and minimize redundancy. So-called *normalization theory* defines *third normal form*, where every table in the database has a *primary key* that can uniquely identify each row in the table, and where each column in the row is dependent on the primary key. A database designed in third normal form is especially able to support applications and queries that cannot be anticipated at database design time.

Codd also defined a mathematical data manipulation language, DSL/Alpha. This language was based on the mathematics of set theory, and could be used to express queries and manipulate the data tables that comprise a relational database. Codd proved that a relational database could be manipulated in any required way using the operations he defined, so that any result that is consistent with the database could be derived. He called this property *relational completeness*.

The language Codd defined was very powerful, as compared with the more traditional approach of writing a program that would navigate through complex chains of pointers linking records in the non-relational databases of the time. Codd's language could answer questions like "find the employees who make more than their managers" in just a few lines, as compared with the pages of programs it would otherwise take.

In the early 1970s a group was formed in the IBM Research Division to develop a prototype relational database management system based on Codd's ideas. A project called System R, led by Frank King, was started. The objective of the project was to develop a complete relational database prototype supporting SQL, while still delivering key attributes of existing non-relational databases, including multi-user support, transactions, security, and good performance.

The System R group recognized that Codd's mathematical DSL/Alpha language was too difficult for non-mathematicians to comprehend. So, they created a language called SQUARE, standing for Specifying Queries as Relational Expressions.

Although an improvement over DSL/Alpha, SQUARE was not suitable for keyboard entry, as it required subscripts which were not easy to represent at the time.

The group then decided to adapt the ideas of SQUARE to an approach based on English keywords, because it was easier to type. They extended and improved their new language and called it SEQUEL, standing for Structured English Query Language. The name was subsequently changed to SQL because of trademark issues. Most often pronounced "sequel," SQL is sometimes pronounced "ess-que-ell," but both are in common usage. In 1974, Don Chamberlin and Ray Boyce authored a paper entitled "SEQUEL: A Structured English Query Language" that was published in the *Proceedings of the May 1974 ACM SIGMOD Workshop on Data Description, Access, and Control.* This was the first widely circulated paper about the language that wasProceedings of the May 1974 ACM SIGMOD Workshop on Data Description, Access and Control to become SQL.

A group of the people involved in the early development of System R and SQL met for a twenty-fifth anniversary reunion in 1995. They reminisced about the people and the project, and provided valuable insights about how SQL was developed. A transcript of their discussion is available on the World Wide Web, at the following URL: *http://www.mcjones.org/System_R/SQL_Reunion_95/index.html.*

The SQL Language

A key aspect of SQL (and of Codd's original data manipulation language) is that it expresses operations against sets of data, in a non-procedural form, rather than requiring a program that retrieves records one by one, and specifies sequences of steps to process each record. Unlike programs written in most languages, which specify sequences of steps to be performed, a SQL statement expresses the result the user desires, and the database management system is responsible for producing that result as efficiently as possible. A SQL statement specifies the operations (like filtering, grouping,and sorting) to be performed on sets of rows, and the database system determines the precise ways in which the data will be accessed and the sequence of the various processing steps needed to produce the desired result. A very useful aspect of SQL is the "closure" property: a query result is generated in the form of a table. Therefore, the set of rows returned by a query can be inserted into another table, or used as part of a query expression in SQL, as a "subquery" or as part of a view definition.

Another important element of the original definition of SQL was that it included syntax for defining the content of the database. The database administrator defines its *schema*—the names of tables and the names and data types of their columns, among other things—using so-called DDL (Data Definition Language), which is, in fact, not a separate language, but a set of SQL commands (or "verbs") like CRE-

ATE, DROP and ALTER. This aspect of SQL is as much part of the SQL language as is DML (Data Manipulation Language), the part of SQL used to query and update the database. DDL is comprised of the verbs SELECT, INSERT, UPDATE, and DELETE and other SQL verbs such as GRANT and REVOKE, which are used to specify the privileges users have to access data.

Significantly, SQL specifies that the meta-data used to describe the contents of the database be itself stored in the database, in rows and columns of the tables in the *data dictionary*. The data dictionary (or catalog) tables can also be queried using SQL, so applications can be written that dynamically adjust to the shape and content of the database on which they are operating.

The inventors of SQL did not originally design it to be a complete programming language. The non-procedural set-oriented capabilities of SQL are ideal for data access and manipulation, but the business logic of an application requires a more traditional procedural language. The System R developers created Embedded SQL, a "sub-language" that permits application programmers to use SQL statements within host programming languages such as COBOL, Fortran, and C. SQL statements prefixed by the words "EXEC SQL" can be embedded in the source code of programs and can reference variables of the host programming language ("host variables"). A program called a precompiler replaces the embedded SQL statements with calls to a DBMS-specific program library.

While many aspects of SQL conform to the original definitions of Codd's relational theory, many concessions were also made in its definition to facilitate performance, ease of use, or ease of implementation. For example, in Codd's language, a query result always consisted of distinct rows because, by definition, the "projection" operation eliminates duplicates. In SQL, duplicates can appear in the set of rows returned by a query unless the keyword DISTINCT appears in the query's SELECT list.

Furthermore, as a computer language, SQL has its quirks and shortcomings. An ideal language perhaps would be more orthogonal and regular, with fewer restrictions on which language elements can appear in which contexts. Some critics of SQL find fault with SQL's treatment of missing information (nulls), or with the fact that SQL often supports several ways to write the same query.

Chris Date, an author and lecturer who has done much to popularize relational technology and SQL, has often been one of the most vocal critics of the SQL language. In fact, Date and Codd disagree vehemently about the proper way to treat missing data. But, for all its critics and all its faults, and those of the database management systems that implement it, SQL has proven to be immensely valuable, and has become successful far beyond its inventors' expectations.

The Commercial Development of SQL through the 1980s

In 1977, Larry Ellison and two others founded what became Relational Software Incorporated (RSI) with the expressed purpose of bringing to market the world's first commercial relational database management system. They were inspired by Codd's 1970 paper describing the relational model and the 1974 paper describing SQL, and they decided to develop from scratch a commercial product that was as compatible as possible with the prototype being developed at IBM's research facilities. Ellison's vision was to implement a SQL system on small minicomputers, and he correctly anticipated that in addition to the novelty of a relational database, IBM compatibility would be attractive to the market. Indeed, so complete was their commitment to strict compatibility with System R that Larry Ellison himself called Don Chamberlin at IBM to request the error numbers that the system used. Early demonstrations of ORACLE often included the "underpaid managers" query used to illustrate the power of the IBM System R prototype. ORACLE was small in size and lean in resource requirements compared to System R, which ran on large, water-cooled mainframe computers.

In 1979, RSI released the first commercially available relational database, ORACLE. The name ORACLE was taken from a project Ellison and his colleagues had worked on for the U.S. Government. Version 1 of ORACLE was an internal prototype, so the first commercial release was ORACLE Version 2. The SQL implementation in ORACLE V2 was reasonably complete for its time, as it included joins, subqueries, and views, as well as a unique language extension for processing hierarchies, the CONNECT BY clause. The next major version added innovations like an outer join, a date/time datatype and numerous built-in functions.

The system's first customers were successful in deploying simple departmental applications, mostly for decision support rather than for mission-critical transaction processing requirements. Many of these early users of ORACLE were so impressed with the power of the relational model and the ease of use SQL provided that they often overlooked many of the reliability shortcomings of the early releases of ORACLE. RSI, which changed its name in 1982 to Oracle Corporation, began to grow very rapidly, doubling each year for 10 years. Oracle established its present headquarters campus in Redwood Shores, California in 1989. One of the small ironies of the database world is that the closest airport to Oracle's headquarters is in San Carlos, and it sports the three-letter code SQL!

There have been many implementations of SQL since the introduction of ORACLE back in 1979, and the commercial success of relational technology is extraordinary. Perhaps surprisingly, it took a while for IBM to benefit from its research on relational database management and its development of SQL. Although Codd's work was published in 1970 and the SQL language was first described in 1974, IBM took many years to bring to market its first SQL product. It wasn't until 1981 that IBM introduced SQL/DS (which used much of the original System R prototype code) for the DOS/VSE and VM operating systems. In 1985, IBM released the first version of DB2 for mainframes running MVS, though it was careful to position it as suitable only for departmental applications with predominantly decision support requirements, so as not to compete with its flagship hierarchical system IMS. But because of IBM's dominance in the IT industry at the time, these announcements greatly accelerated the acceptance of SQL and relational systems, as it became clear that SQL would become a de facto industry standard.

The IBM researchers were not the only visionaries who anticipated the great potential of relational databases, nor was Larry Ellison the only one to see the significant commercial opportunity at hand for the companies that brought the technology to market. Professor Michael Stonebreaker and his computer science students at the University of California at Berkeley had, since the early 1970s, been developing a relational database prototype called INGRES for the then very new Unix operating system. The Berkeley team was building on Codd's ideas, but there was a definite spirit of competition, at least for academic recognition, between the INGRES group and the IBM researchers. In 1980, Stonebreaker formed a company called Relational Technology Incorporated (RTI), to bring INGRES to market. Eventually, RTI changed its name to Ingres Corporation. The company was later bought by Ask, Inc., and subsequently by Computer Associates, which now market the OpenIngres product.

INGRES implemented a data access language called QUEL, which was similar to SEQUEL. Some people argued that QUEL was a "better" language than SQL, since it had fewer arbitrary restrictions (it was more "orthogonal"), and had some capabilities SQL lacked. Whatever its technical merits, QUEL did not have the market momentum SQL did, as it was seen as a proprietary language. The perception was that SQL was likely to become a de facto industry standard, with implementations likely to be available from several vendors. As a result, to remain competitive, in about 1986 Ingres Corporation implemented a subset dialect of SQL, layered above the existing QUEL interface, but missing some key features like nulls and subqueries. Later releases of INGRES supported a native SQL implementation.

In the early days of the relational database market, staunch defenders of existing non-relational databases dismissed SQL and relational databases as mere toys, never to be suitable for significant business applications. The advocates of SQL and relational systems praised the productivity of their systems, and claimed that theoretical performance obstacles could be overcome.

Some people argued that the high-level relational interface of SQL could not compete with low-level navigational interfaces called by application programmers.

Others argued that the physical storage organization of relational tables and the required access by data values through indexes could never perform as well as direct access through pointers embedded in record structures. The System R developers claimed that automatic compilation of SQL statements and query optimization would overcome these problems. Over the years, of course, improvements in relational technology (along with dramatic improvements in hardware performance) made SQL systems suitable for even the most demanding transaction processing systems. Relational database systems have also been able to take advantage of the set-oriented nature of SQL to support parallel execution of SQL statements across multiple CPUs, providing highly scalable performance for complex queries against large data warehouse databases.

During the 1980s, several other vendors introduced SQL systems. Relational Data Systems, later renamed Informix Corporation, introduced its namesake database management system with a SQL interface in 1984. Among other hardware vendors, Digital Equipment Corporation released Rdb in 1985. Rdb implemented not SQL, but a competing relational language, called RDML. RDML was fairly popular with Digital customers, but Digital never attempted to make it more popular, much less standardize it. Recognizing the need to comply with the industry standard, Digital released Rdb Version 5 in 1988 with a full native SQL implementation. In 1994, Digital Equipment sold Rdb to Oracle Corporation, which still markets and supports the product.

The introduction, in 1985, of the Teradata parallel query machine was a notable milestone in the evolution of SQL. The Teradata system used a special-purpose hardware platform comprised of Intel 8086 processors connected with a proprietary tree network, and was the first commercial database product that could automatically execute SQL statements in parallel. Teradata's SQL dialect, however, was limited, initially lacking support for views and referential integrity. The Teradata system was oriented toward the query processing needs of data warehouse applications, and was not generally regarded as applicable to transaction processing systems.

Britton-Lee, a spin-off from Ingres, also designed and sold a "relational database machine" that found limited market success, was soon bought by Teradata, and eventually disappeared from the market. Teradata was acquired by NCR (which itself was later bought and spun off by AT&T). Today, NCR/Teradata has abandoned the approach of specialized hardware, and it runs on general-purpose platforms using the Windows NT and Unix operating systems. Teradata has been quite successful in the data warehouse market, especially with large retailers having multiple terabytes of data in their data warehouses. Teradata and Britton-Lee both found it difficult to keep pace with the innovations in hardware and software design and achieve the economies of commodity hardware with a proprietary approach that requires specialized hardware.

Another notable milestone was the introduction of NonStop SQL from Tandem in 1987. NonStop SQL was optimized for excellent transaction processing performance and high availability. Tandem supported its performance claims by running a workload that simulated simple banking transactions. A derivative of this benchmark eventually became the basis of the first industry-standard benchmarks developed by the Transaction Processing Performance Council (TPC). The introduction of NonStop SQL put to rest the myth that relational systems could not deliver the performance required for high-end transaction processing applications.

Sybase was an important but relative latecomer to the SQL market; the first version of SQL introduced by Sybase Inc. in 1987. Microsoft acquired the rights to the source code of the Sybase product and in 1993 introduced SQL Server for Windows NT.

Sybase was designed for the client/server architecture, where the application runs on a PC or workstation and accesses a database server across the network. As in the case of parallel execution, we see an unexpected benefit of the high-level nature of the SQL language and interface. Invoked by just a few network messages, a single SQL statement can iterate over large sets of rows, or join tables together, for example. In general, with lower-level navigational interfaces such operations would incur excessive network traffic.

Sybase was the first programmable SQL database system, and this had considerable market impact. With Sybase, DBAs or application developers could implement business logic and enforce data integrity rules with triggers and stored procedures written in Transact-SQL, the company's proprietary procedural language. DBAs and application developers could write programs that contained embedded SQL statements to retrieve or update database data to perform a complete business transaction. Triggers could be associated with database tables to execute after INSERT, UPDATE, or DELETE operations to validate the transactions, do auditing, or perform other transformations. This approach reduces network traffic because an entire business transaction can be executed with a stored procedure, invoked efficiently across the network. With stored procedures, which are stored within the database and executed within the database server, the application program need not communicate with the server for each record access, nor indeed for each SQL statement required to complete the business transaction.

Another important benefit of programmability is the ability of the database server to protect the integrity of the data from malicious or errant ad hoc users and applications accessing the database across a network. While basic relational integrity rules such as referential integrity are generally best defined declaratively, as part of the database schema, database triggers make it possible for the server to actively enforce arbitrary business rules that require a procedural definition. By centralizing business logic in the database, it need not be coded in every application that accesses the database, thus avoiding redundancy and errors, and making it feasible to provide end users with direct access to the data.

For its part, Oracle Corporation used the Ada programming language as a model for PL/SQL, its own proprietary procedural language. Like Ada, PL/SQL includes language features like exception handling and parameter type declarations that facilitate the development of reliable, large-scale, and complex systems. The procedural language eventually added to the SQL standard resembles PL/SQL in many respects. PL/SQL first appeared for client-side use (in Oracle's SQL*Forms) in 1988, and with Oracle7 in 1992 for triggers and stored procedures that execute within the database.

The Evolution of SQL: the 1990s and Beyond

If the 1970s was the decade of SQL invention, and the 1980s was the decade of SQL commercialization, then the 1990s was the decade of SQL evolution. During this period, the various vendors with SQL products raced to bring to market the features needed to support new and demanding applications. Commercial SQL products and the SQL standards have both been extended, in recent years, with new features to support object-oriented programming languages and multimedia data, integration with Java and XML, and the requirements of data warehouse applications. SQL is clearly a living language, with new capabilities developed in response to market demands.

In the early 1990s, the object-oriented programming paradigm became popular for commercial application development, because programmers found they could write complex applications more quickly and reliably using the object approach. An object-oriented language permits the programmer to define types (or classes) that describe not only the structure of data, but its behavior as well. Types can have complex structures and can include procedures (methods) as part of their definition. Types can be derived from other types, inheriting attributes from parent types. A fundamental concept of the object paradigm is that every object has a distinct identifier, and one object can refer directly to another via its object identifier.

Although it was not until the late 1990s that object technology had an influence on the direction of SQL, the ideas of object programming are not new, having originated in the 1960s with the Simula and Smalltalk programming languages. Many object-oriented programming languages have been developed, but the first such language to attract a wide following for commercial use was C++, an upward-compatible extension of C. Part of the success of C++ was due to its interoperability with existing C programs, and the fact that programmers of C need not learn an all-new language.

The object model stands in stark contrast to the relational model, with its simple data structures (tables, rows, and columns) and non-navigational approach to data access. Very fundamentally, the relational model relies on value-based addressing, where rows are located by the values of data stored in the (primary) key column(s). In a SQL database, a join operation matches rows from multiple tables by comparing the values of their columns. This approach is very much the antithesis of object references that directly point from one object to another.

Because of the strong differences in their type systems, much has been made of the so-called "impedance mismatch" between SQL and object-oriented programming languages. Some people have argued that SQL and the relational database model is obsolete, and that only database systems designed to make programming language objects seamlessly persistent can meet the needs of modern applications. Others have developed products that perform mappings of the simple data types and structures of the database to the types defined in applications.

In recent years, relational database vendors such as Oracle, IBM, and Informix have added object capabilities to the SQL language. These object-relational products, and the most recent SQL standard, permit the definition of types that are similar to those of the object languages, but not identical with any of them. These extended SQL types can have multiple values per column, may have methods or functions as part of their definition, may inherit attributes from higher-level types, and may contain attributes whose value is a reference (a pointer!) to instances of objects of a particular type. This enhanced SQL of the extended relational model provides the database designer with the ability to more directly model the real world, and makes it possible for a system to directly map database types to types of object-oriented programming languages such as C++ and Java.

A key goal of the approach to extending SQL is to preserve the benefits of the relational model, including non-procedural query capability over sets of objects (which are generally stored in tables). New object-oriented applications can co-exist with existing relational applications, and the database system can synthesize objects from traditional relational data through a new feature called an *object view*. The object-oriented SQL extensions were added in an upward-compatible way, much the way C++ was developed from C. Although there are some efforts to define new database languages that are more purely object-oriented, SQL, with these new object capabilities, has until now successfully defended its role as the "universal dataspeak."

The vendors of object-relational databases have used extended SQL to provide support within their products for datatypes that were previously difficult to manage in a relational database, including text, video, and audio data. Users of these products can also define application-specific datatypes and index types using extended SQL.

Emerging Internet technologies have also made new demands on SQL. Java is a portable object-oriented language that is particularly suitable for developing applications designed for Internet deployment. SQL has evolved quickly in recent years to accommodate the quickly growing community of Java developers. Database vendors have rapidly agreed upon and introduced in their products interfaces that integrate Java with SQL. The JDBC call interface permits Java programs to send SQL statements to a database server for execution. The SQLJ specification allows SQL to be embedded in Java programs in a way that is similar to other host programming languages such as COBOL and Fortran. Oracle8*i*, for example, supports the execution of both JDBC and SQLJ programs within the database server. Thus, SQLJ and JDBC programs can execute on the client, at the application server tier, or within the database server itself as stored procedures, database triggers, or methods for object types. The SQL language will continue to evolve to even better integrate with Java—for example, by supporting the use of Java classes as the definitions of data types of columns.

XML, the Extended Markup Language, is another Internet technology that is influencing the evolution of SQL. Because XML makes data self-describing, it is especially suitable for information exchange between independently developed applications and between enterprises. Electronic commerce applications, for example, can use XML to exchange data such as orders, payments, and customer information. Naturally, since most business applications use relational databases, it becomes important for SQL data and XML data to coexist.

Just as SQL has grown to accommodate Java and its object model, it has already begun to be extended to facilitate use of XML data. The rich object extensions of today's SQL language are well suited to support convenient representations or mappings of XML data, bringing database manipulation and query to static XML data structures. Vendors such as Oracle have moved aggressively to implement capabilities that can map XML data structures to database data, and to produce XML-formatted results from SQL queries. The integration of SQL with emerging XML-based query languages is also an area of active development within vendor, standards and academic communities.

Although SQL is extremely powerful in many areas, it has never provided strong support for analytic tasks, despite the importance of SQL for data warehouse applications. Many basic business intelligence calculations have required extensive programming outside of standard SQL, often with significant performance challenges.

While some proprietary SQL extensions designed to address these requirements have existed in a few specialized products, only recently has the vendor community agreed on standardized SQL extensions to meet these needs.

The CUBE and ROLLUP extensions to the GROUP BY clause have been added to the SQL standard and to several SQL products. These operators fill in totals and subtotals across values of the grouping columns, and facilitate generation of aggregates for "cross-tab" reports. Data warehouse and business intelligence users have had a long-standing need for SQL to support rankings and moving averages, and to perform period-to-period comparisons. However, queries like "show the top 10 and bottom 10 salespeople in each region," or "compute the 13-week moving average of a stock price" have been difficult or impossible to express in standard SQL. Recently, Oracle and IBM have jointly designed and submitted for standardization new capabilities that address these requirements. Oracle8*i* Release 2 introduced a set of powerful analytic functions that supports ranking, moving averages, comparison of values at different levels of aggregation, and period-to-period comparisons.

Standardization of the SQL Language

Because of IBM's dominance in the 1980s, SQL was destined to be an important language for database management. Oracle closely followed the IBM definition of SQL, the first of several vendors to do so, making it a de facto standard. However, SQL would not be such a universal data access language without the efforts of national and international standards bodies to develop a public specification of the language.

If the SQL language is the Rosetta stone that unlocks access to the world's information, then the SQL standard document is something of a Rosetta stone itself. Other than vendor documentation, the SQL standard provides the only formal, complete definition of the syntax and semantics of the SQL language.

The history of the standards process is interesting. In the 1950s, the U.S. Department of Defense established the Conference on Data Systems Languages (CODA-SYL) to develop a standardized computer programming language for business applications. CODASYL developed the COBOL language and was the parent organization of the Data Base Task Group (DBTG), which in 1971 published a set of specifications by which COBOL programs might navigate databases that implemented the pointer-based "network model." It is from these origins that the efforts to formally standardize the SQL language arose.

Commonly known as the ANSI SQL Committee, the H2 Technical Committee on Database is chartered by the National Committee for Information Technology Standards (NCITS) to develop American National Standards for database languages and for representing the United States in related international standardization activities. The committee was originally established in 1978 to formally standardize the recommendations of the CODASYL committee. While it maintained responsibility for the standard for network databases, the committee also began work on a standard for relational databases in 1982.

Although the SQL committee started its work on relational databases with a formal specification of IBM's SQL, initial efforts were devoted to addressing the many perceived deficiencies in SQL. The engineers working on this effort were pleased with the resulting "improved" language (which they named RDL for Relational Database Language). However, RDL was quite different from the emerging de facto standard SQL represented by DB2. Reconsidering the value of a new database language that diverged from commercially available implementations, in 1984 the committee abandoned its previous efforts, and reset its document to the original IBM SQL contribution as the basis for the ANSI and ISO de jure standards.

The first formal SQL standard was published in 1986, and comprised approximately 100 pages. This standard defined a bare bones language that represented the common features of the most important SQL implementations of the time, including many of their arbitrary restrictions. The document defined the basic SQL language, including the ability to CREATE tables and views, but not the ability to DROP or ALTER them, nor to GRANT or REVOKE access privileges.

The lack of referential integrity capabilities in SQL-86 was a glaring omission, from the viewpoint of relational database advocates. Because of the heated criticism, the SQL standards committee quickly released a specification called the "Integrity Enhancement Feature" to address this shortcoming. This feature included the ability to define primary and foreign keys as part of the database schema, with the requirement that inserts, updates, and deletes not result in rows for which a foreign key did not match the primary key of another table. This basic feature meant that a very fundamental data integrity rule could be enforced automatically by systems implementing the standard. The Integrity Enhancement Feature was incorporated into the 1989 revision of the SQL standard that also included a specification for embedding SQL in COBOL, Fortran, and C.

The next standard was adopted in 1992 and is known as SQL-92. SQL-92 added numerous capabilities to the SQL language, including outer joins, date-time and other datatypes, standardized error reporting, a set of standardized catalog tables, dynamic schema manipulation (DROP, ALTER, GRANT, and REVOKE), and the ability for host programs to execute SQL statements not defined at compile time (dynamic SQL). Other features new with SQL-92 included cascaded update and delete referential actions, transaction consistency levels, scrolled cursors, and deferred constraint checking. The standard comprised nearly 600 pages, and was divided into three levels:

- Entry SQL-92 contained only features from SQL-89.

- Intermediate SQL-92 added about half of the new features.

- Full SQL-92 represented the complete standard.

Both the SQL-86 and SQL-89 standards defined a subset of the SQL language as it was implemented in commercial database products. In contrast, when it was defined, the SQL-92 standard anticipated developments in SQL products, and still serves as a guide to software development. Vendors typically follow the specification when they implement the new features it defines, but SQL-92 also contains features that no vendor has ever implemented.

The current standard, SQL-1999, was published in July 1999, and comprises nearly 2000 pages in all its parts. Work actually began on this standard in 1990, as the SQL committee deferred many features from SQL-92 to the next standard, known during its development as SQL3. The long development period of SQL3 was due to its wide-ranging scope and, in particular, to the incorporation of object capabilities in SQL. There were many opinions and false starts to reconcile before consensus was achieved. Many debates involved the subtle distinctions between abstract data types (ADTs) defined as referenceable "object ADTs" and those defined as embedded "value ADTs," with many proposals considered, adopted, and replaced in various drafts of SQL. Eventually, the committee members resolved their differences by compromising on a single model of abstract types that unified their properties.

The powerful set of object oriented extensions incorporated in the new SQL standard constitute an object model very similar to that of Java, easing the task of using the two languages together. SQL-1999 adds facilities for user-defined types (ADTs) with both behavior (methods) and an encapsulated internal structure (including arrays and named row types). The definition of an ADT can be derived from a more general type (single inheritance). SQL-1999 supports strong typing with compile-time checking and dynamic method dispatch (polymorphism). Instances of object data types can be stored in a column in an ordinary table. However, each instance of such types that is stored as a row (in a typed table) has a persistent object ID that can be referenced from SQL statements, and can be persistently stored as an attribute of another object.

The core SQL functionality, or SQL/Foundation, contains many other features in addition to object functionality, some anticipating commercial implementation, and others long present in a variety of commercial products. SQL-1999 includes the following new features, among many others:

- User-defined procedures and functions, including those defined externally

- Row-level and statement-level database triggers that fire before or after INSERT, UPDATE, or DELETE

- A Boolean datatype and large objects (binary and character LOBs)

- Support for character sets, translations, and collations (orderings)

- New WHERE predicates (for all, for some, similar to)

- Updateable views

- Roles for defining security profiles

- Savepoints to which a partly complete transaction can roll back

- Recursive queries, which permit processing bills of materials

In addition to the core functionality of SQL/Foundation, the SQL committee has developed other parts of the SQL specification, including some that utilize the object model now part of SQL. Briefly, these include the following parts of SQL-1999:

- SQL/PSM (persistent stored modules): procedural language capabilities for looping, branching, procedure invocation, and dynamic exception handling

- SQL/OLB (object language bindings) defining the way the Java language interfaces with the SQL language and accesses SQL data

- SQL/MED (management of external data) specifying interfaces that permit SQL to access data stored in operating system or non-SQL sources

- SQL/CLI (call level interface) specifying an application programming interface for SQL and database services

- SQL/Temporal, defining features that support time-varying views of database content

Also, separate from the standard itself, but layered upon the new ADT capabilities, the SQL committee is developing the SQL/MM (multimedia data) specification, defining functionality for managing text, spatial, and image data.

Clearly, SQL is no longer a simple language for defining, accessing, and managing tables containing rows of columns each with a single value. With SQL-1999, the language that had its origins in the mathematics of the formal relational model has gone beyond its original pragmatic deviations from that model. Like the network data model defined by CODASYL, SQL-1999 now supports complex data record structures with arrays, groups, repeating groups, and nested repeating groups. With this power and complexity, the database design process moves beyond the database normalization principles defined by Ted Codd. Database designers will need a strong understanding of the processing requirements of the application, as well as knowledge of data dependencies, to fully benefit from the power of the data structures and hierarchies now possible with SQL-1999.

The SQL standard is large, and a complete detailed understanding of every aspect of the language is perhaps beyond human understanding. Today no commercial products implement the entire standard, and, given the size of the standard, it seems unlikely that they ever will. Further, different products implement different sets of features and there is no certification test of compliance to the standard. What, then, are the benefits of this specification?

Generally speaking, vendors do look to the standard specification for design guidance when implementing new features. Thus, product interoperability and portability of applications from one implementation to another is facilitated, at least for most mainstream features. Further, vendors frequently cooperate on designs for SQL features within the standards process to prevent divergence of new capabilities in future products. Also, companies choosing SQL products can evaluate a vendor's commitment to compatibility and to technology leadership by comparing the features within a product against the standard. A DBA or developer who has experience with one SQL implementation can leverage that knowledge with other products, because the various dialects of SQL differ from one another in a way that's more like regional accents than entire languages.

SQL: A Success Story

The unparalleled success of relational database technology and the SQL language is one of the great achievements of the IT industry. A number of factors have contributed to that success.

The strong foundation of SQL as a non-procedural data access language, and its relational theoretical underpinnings, have proven to be a powerful starting point, despite the evolution of SQL beyond those beginnings. Improvements in hardware and software technology have overcome the initial concerns about performance of relational databases. The high-level nature of the SQL interface has turned out to be particularly suitable to parallelism for data warehousing and to programmatic database extensions needed in client/server and Internet environments. SQL and relational databases have been a critical success factor for a wide range of customer applications, from the simplest department application to mission-critical transaction processing systems and enormous data warehouses that support business intelligence. Responding to competitive pressure, database vendors have continually innovated and extended their SQL implementations, at the same time being forced by the market to conform to and contribute to the standards process. The standards process has given SQL legitimacy and a roadmap for further development. SQL has proven its ability to adapt to changing market

requirements, such as the rise of give a sense ofdata warehousing and new technologies like objects, Java, and XML.

One look at the classified ads for IT professionals should provide an appreciation
of the value of a good working understanding of SQL. Knowledge of the history of
SQL, and some sense of its future can help those familiar with the language and
the technology appreciate its value even more.

—Ken Jacobs, VP Product Strategy, Server Technologies,
Oracle Corporation

Preface

The roots of relational database systems extend back to 1970, when Dr. E. F. Codd published a paper entitled "A Relational Model of Data for Large Shared Data Banks."* The paper appeared in the June 1970 issue of *Communications of the ACM,* the journal of the Association of Computer Machinery (ACM). That paper changed the world of computing forever; the model for a relational database management system (RDBMS) that Codd proposed ultimately became the definitive standard for relational databases, and relational databases are the predominant database type in use today.

Codd's model required a new language to access the database, so IBM developed *Structured English Query Language* and first gave it the name SEQUEL in 1974. Unfortunately, a trademark already existed for SEQUEL, so "English" was dropped from the name and the new language was renamed SQL, or *Structured Query Language*. (However, it is still pronounced "sequel.")

In 1979 Larry Ellison and Bob Miner founded Relational Software, Inc. (RSI) and began developing the first commercially viable implementation of Codd's model, along with the SQL language, and the company released Oracle V.2 as the world's first relational database. Relational Software soon changed its name to Oracle Systems, and subsequently to Oracle Corporation. The rest is history.

SQL soon grew in popularity, but each vendor implemented it in different ways and with different features. A standard was finally developed by ANSI and ISO; the most recent standards are:

---

* E.F. Codd, "A Relational Model of Data for Large Shared Data Banks," *Communications of the ACM* 13, 6 (June 1970) 377–387.

- ANSI X3.135-1992, "Database Language SQL"

- ISO/IEC 9075:1992, "Database Language SQL"

Today, virtually all vendors of database systems claim to have implemented a relational model, and all use SQL as their access language. SQL-92 defines four levels of compliance: Entry, Transitional, Intermediate, and Full. A conforming SQL implementation must support at least Entry SQL. Oracle8 fully supports Entry SQL and has many features that conform to Transitional, Intermediate, and Full SQL.

Audience for This Book

This book was written for Oracle developers and database administrators (DBAs) who use SQL. The book is designed as a reference; the material is intentionally presented as concisely as possible. Since I assume that you are already somewhat familiar with relational concepts and the basics of the SQL language, I have attempted to provide you with the information you need in a location and format that allows you to access it quickly, as required. If you are looking for clear, concise information about Oracle's implementation of SQL, with plenty of summary tables and quick reference to syntax and usage, then you have come to the right place. However, if you are trying to learn SQL, and want a tutorial that will teach you about it from start to finish, you will probably want to start with an introductory text. Hang on to this book, however — you'll find it very useful later on!

I certainly don't want to deter you from buying and using this book, but I want you to know that my approach is to cram as much concise and fast-moving material as possible into these pages.

Versions of Oracle

This book was written using Oracle Version 8.1.6, and all information presented is accurate for that version. Most of the material applies to Oracle Versions 7.3 and 8.0 as well, but some new features were added to SQL in Version 8.1 (Oracle8*i*).

Beginning with Oracle Version 8.0, a new option called the Object Option became available. Effective with Oracle Version 8.1.6 (Oracle8*i* Release 2), the Object Option is included in the base release of all Oracle server products. In my experience, this option is not yet widely used; it is, however, tremendously complex and it adds a significant amount of syntax to the SQL language. In fact, Oracle's Object Database would require an entire book to cover properly. Consequently, I decided to omit the Object features from the hardcopy version of this book. If you do use the Object Option, you will find the full syntax available on the O'Reilly web site at *www.oreilly.com/catalog/orsqlter* and in Oracle's *SQL Reference Manual*. If you, like most current Oracle users, don't use the Object features, I think you will find the hardcopy book much easier to use without the extra material. Once the option is in wider use, I'll include it in a later edition of this book. Let me know what you think about this decision!

Contents of This Book

This book contains the following chapters:

Chapter 1, *Elements of SQL*, outlines general elements and requirements of the SQL language, including: structure, naming standards, characteristics of various datatypes, relational operators, and so on.

Chapter 2, *Data Definition Statements*, presents each of the SQL statements used for definition or modification of database objects. I have included a brief explanation of what each statement does, along with structured syntax, definitions of syntax elements as required, and a short example illustrating use.

Chapter 3, *Data Manipulation and Control Statements*, is similar in structure to Chapter 2, but lists the SQL statements used to manipulate data and control sessions in the database.

Chapter 4, *Common SQL Elements*, presents portions of the SQL language that are applicable to multiple types of SQL statements. The clauses shown in this chapter are referenced by the statements presented in Chapters 2 and 3.

Chapter 5, *SQL Functions*, summarizes the rich array of SQL functions available for use in Oracle. For convenience they are grouped by purpose; for example, all character string manipulation functions are presented together.

Chapter 6, *SQL*Plus*, presents Oracle's standard interface to the SQL language. SQL*Plus is such an integral part of Oracle that no programmer can do without it. This chapter provides a summary of the use of this product that I hope conveys the power of SQL*Plus.*

Chapter 7, *PL/SQL*, provides a concise definition of the structure and syntax for the basic elements of PL/SQL, as well as the basic syntax for creating and using Oracle procedures, functions, packages, and triggers.†

---

* The information presented in this chapter is only the tip of the iceberg. For more information about SQL*Plus, see Jonathan Gennick's *Oracle SQL*Plus: The Definitive Guide* (O'Reilly & Associates, 1999) and *Oracle SQL*Plus Pocket Reference* (O'Reilly & Associates, 2000).

† Speaking of icebergs, PL/SQL is a monumental one. For more information about PL/SQL, see Steven Feuerstein and Bill Pribye's *Oracle PL/SQL Programming*, 2nd Edition (O'Reilly & Associates, 1998) and the other PL/SQL books in the Feuerstein series.

Chapter 8, *SQL Statement Tuning*, explains how the Oracle kernel actually executes the SQL statements presented in this book and provides invaluable information on how to make SQL statements and programs perform well.

Appendix A, *SQL Resources*, provides listings of SQL-related books, other publications, organizations, and web sites that may be useful.

Conventions Used in This Book

This book uses a number of standard conventions that let me clearly display the detailed syntax of SQL statements:

Constant width

Used to show syntax diagrams and the output of commands.

Contant width bold

Used to represent user input in examples that show user interaction.

Initial_Cap_Italics

Indicates a common element of SQL that is documented in Chapter 4. These elements usually end in "Clause," as in *Storage_Clause*.

lowercase italics

Indicates items that are replaced by actual values in a SQL statement.

UPPERCASE

Indicates keywords or components of SQL syntax.

Braces { }

Indicate that one item is required from the list provided within the braces. Items in the list are separated by vertical bars (|). Note that this list may be quite extensive and that a single item may include several keywords.

Ellipses (…)

Indicate that the previous keyword or group of keywords may be repeated as required.

Square brackets [ ]

Indicate that the item(s) enclosed within the square brackets are optional. Multiple optional items are separated by a vertical bar (|).

Underline

Indicates that the underlined keyword or value is the default.

column

The name of a column in a table.

column_list

The name of one or more columns in a table, separated by commas.

filename

    The valid operating system name for a file, normally enclosed in single quotes.

integer

    A whole number, such as 0, 1, 2, etc.

schema

    The name of a collection of objects in the database, also called the user, username, or owner.

string

    One or more characters enclosed in single quotes, such as 'this is a string'.

table

    The name of a table.

tablespace

    The name of a tablespace in the database.

 Indicates a tip, suggestion, or general note.

 Indicates a warning or caution.

Comments and Questions

I have tested and verified the information in this book to the best of my ability, but you may find that features have changed or that I have made mistakes. If so, please notify me by writing to:

O'Reilly & Associates
101 Morris Street
Sebastopol, CA 95472
(800) 998-9938 (in the United States or Canada)
(707) 829-0515 (international/local)
(707) 829-0104 (fax)

You can also send O'Reilly messages electronically. To be put on the mailing list or request a catalog, send email to:

info@oreilly.com

To ask technical questions or comment on the book, send email to:

bookquestions@oreilly.com

There is a web site for this book, where you can find examples and errata. (Previously reported errors and corrections are available for public view there.) You can access this page at:

http://www.oreilly.com/catalog/orsqlter

For more information about this book and others, see the O'Reilly web site:

http://www.oreilly.com

You can also contact me directly; send email to:

dkreines@usa.net

Acknowledgments

I am indebted to a great many people who have contributed in large and small ways to the creation of this book.

This book began with a conversation with my editor at O'Reilly, Deborah Russell, who agreed that there was a real need for a book like this, and pushed me to get it done. I would like to thank her for providing invaluable comments on content, structure, and style. She is probably even happier than I am that this book is done!

The first Oracle employee I ever met was Ken Jacobs, who at the time was serving as our technical sales support liaison. Over the following 15-plus years I have had many interactions with Ken, who is known to the Oracle community for his remarkable expertise and quiet competence. Ken is a technical genius, an excellent scuba diver, and a really great person. I am honored that he agreed to write the Foreword for this book. Ken, I am forever in your debt!

I am grateful beyond words to Jonathan Gennick, who not only provided a detailed technical review and editorial assistance, but also supplied massive amounts of material and helped rescue me from the brink of disaster! It suffices to say that, for me, backups have taken on a new level of importance!

Special thanks go to John Beresniewicz, Steven Feuerstein, and Brian Laskey, as well as to Richard Sarwal and Sandy Venning from Oracle Corporation, who generously gave up their time to provide a technical review for this book.

I am also immensely grateful to my loving and supportive wife, Suzanne, who once again tolerated my nightly retreats to my basement "cave," not to mention my spending a significant portion of our vacation at the beach hunched over a laptop in the corner.

I would like to thank my colleagues at Rhodia, including Brian McMahon, Dave Flood, Bin Pan, Deb Irwin, Joaquin Lucero, Paul Mars, Nick Palmer, and Frank Foley, for doing early reads of the "work in progress" and for putting up with me in general!

This book certainly would not have been possible without a lot of hard work and support from the staff at O'Reilly & Associates: Darren Kelly, who managed the production process; Ann Schirmer, who copyedited the book; Maureen Dempsey, who proofread the book; Ellie Volckhausen who found the scorpion and created the cover; Rob Romano who developed the figures; David Chu, the editorial assistant who helped prepare the book for production; and James Carter, Deborah Smith, and Nancy Williams who provided production support.

1

Elements of SQL

SQL was developed to provide easy access to relational databases, so it is able to perform the following kinds of actions:

- Querying data from a database
- Inserting data into a database
- Deleting data from a database
- Creating and manipulating database objects
- Controlling access to the database

Strictly speaking, SQL is not a language at all, but rather a means of conveying instructions to the Oracle database. It differs from traditional programming languages in several important ways:

- SQL provides automatic navigation to data.
- SQL operates on sets of data, rather than on individual data elements.
- SQL is declarative, not procedural, and does not provide procedural control.
- SQL programming is done at the logical level; there is little need to deal with the details of implementation.

Simply put, when programming in SQL you tell Oracle *what* you want to do, but not *how* it should be done. However, this approach can be both a blessing and a curse. Consider the following SQL statement:

```
SELECT ename, deptno, sal, comm
FROM scott.emp
WHERE hiredate > '01-JAN-00';
```

This simple SQL statement tells the database to display a list consisting of name (ename), department number (deptno), salary (sal), and commission (comm) for each employee hired after January 1, 2000. Such a program might have taken hundreds of lines of code in an "old style" procedural language, but takes only three lines in SQL. At the same time, however, Oracle is not always too smart about how it retrieves data. Although Oracle's internal "query optimizer" has steadily improved, there are still many ways to improve SQL performance, and Chapter 8, *SQL Statement Tuning*, is dedicated to this subject.

 The lack of procedural control was viewed by some as a disadvantage of SQL, so Oracle Corporation developed PL/SQL (Procedural Language/SQL), which is discussed in Chapter 7, *PL/SQL*.

SQL statements, also known as SQL commands, are combinations of the following:

Keywords
Reserved words with specific operational meaning to Oracle.

Variables
Data elements, which may be dynamically replaced with text or numeric values. In SQL these are the names of objects such as columns, tables, or views.

Literals
Constant data, including text strings and numbers.

Operators
Symbols or words that operate on one or more variables or literals.

Lexical Conventions

SQL statements are composed of commands, variables, and operators, which are described in detail in this and subsequent chapters. A SQL statement is constructed from:

- Characters A through Z (or the equivalent from your database character set)
- Numbers 0 through 9
- Spaces
- The following special characters: + - * = ? ! @ ( ) _ . , < > | $ #

Oracle strongly discourages the use of # and $.

Other characters, such as &, are also used in SQL statements, but may be intercepted and interpreted by SQL*Plus if you are using that tool. See Chapter 6, *SQL*Plus*, for more information.

A SQL statement can contain one or more of the following items anywhere a single space can occur:

- Tab
- Carriage return
- Multiple spaces
- Comments

Certain components of SQL statements (such as variable names and strings) may contain other characters, as long as they are enclosed in double quotes.

The following two SELECT statements, for example, are evaluated in exactly the same way by Oracle and both return the same result set:

```
SELECT ename,empno,sal FROM scott.emp WHERE sal>500;

SELECT ename,
       empno, sal
FROM   scott.emp
WHERE  sal > 500;
```

SQL is generally not case-sensitive, so case is not significant except in literals, which are enclosed in quotes.

Be aware that a variable name enclosed in double quotes will be case-sensitive. This fact is especially important if you access your Oracle database using Microsoft Access, which creates objects using lowercase names.

Naming in SQL

Most naming requirements in SQL are actually requirements of the Oracle database; names that are acceptable for schema objects (defined in the next section) in the Oracle database are acceptable in SQL, and vice versa. The following rules apply to the names of schema objects in Oracle:

- They may comprise 1 to 30 alphanumeric characters.

- They must begin with a letter.

- They may include an underscore (_).

- They may include a dollar ($) or pound sign (#), although Oracle discourages the use of these characters.

- They may not be a reserved word.

- They may not be the name of a SQL command.

 A name may begin with and/or contain any characters if it is enclosed in double quotes.

Schema Objects

A schema object is a logical collection of data or other objects that are owned by a user and stored in the database. The following types of objects are considered schema objects:

- Clusters
- Database links
- Database triggers
- Dimensions
- External procedure libraries
- Index-organized tables
- Indexes
- Index types
- Materialized views/snapshots
- Materialized view logs/snapshot logs
- Nested table types
- Object types
- Operators
- Packages

- Sequences
- Stored functions
- Stored procedures
- Synonyms
- Tables
- Varying array types
- Views
- Database links

General Syntax

Generally, you reference schema objects in SQL statements using the following syntax:

```
schema.object_name.object_part@dblink
```

These syntax elements have the following meaning:

schema
> The name of the schema that owns the object. In Oracle, a schema corresponds one-to-one with a username; if the schema is omitted from a reference to a schema object, then the username that is currently logged in is used by default.

object_name
> The name of the object being referenced, such as a table.

object_part
> The name of a part of an object, for those schema objects that have a part, such as a column of a table.

dblink
> The name of a database link referencing a remote database.

The syntax shown here, with a schema name followed by a period, then followed by an object name (for example, scott.emp) is commonly referred to as *dot notation*. Generally, if the *schema.* portion of a name is omitted; the schema of the user currently connected to the database will be used by default.

For example, the following SQL statement queries data from a table, which is a schema object named emp in the schema scott. This schema is located in a remote database and is referenced by the database link test:

```
SELECT ename, empno, sal
FROM scott.emp@test
WHERE sal > 500;
```

Partition Syntax

When referencing a specific partition or subpartition of a partitioned table, use the following syntax:

```
schema.table_name {PARTITION (partition) |
                   SUBPARTITION (subpartition)
                                 )
```

These syntax elements have the following meaning:

schema
> The name of the schema that owns the object. In Oracle, a schema corresponds one-to-one with a username, and if the schema is omitted from a reference to a schema object, then the username that is currently logged in is used by default.

table_name
> The name of the table being referenced.

partition
> The name of a partition of the table.

subpartition
> The name of a subpartition of the table.

This construct is known as a *partition-extended table name*. A partition-extended table name may not have a database link associated with it. Therefore, if you want to access this object on a remote database, you must create a view that can be accessed using the general schema object syntax described previously.

Datatypes

Oracle stores data in the database in any of three basic families of datatypes: character, numeric, and date. Both the character and numeric families have several distinct datatypes associated with them, which are described in the following sections.

Character Data

Character data is any string of one or more bytes of data that will not be the direct target of an arithmetic operation. Oracle (and SQL) supports several types of character data, which are listed below with their usage syntax:

```
CHAR [(length)]
```

Fixed-length character data, with a maximum length of 2000 bytes. *length* specifies the maximum length of the character string to be stored.

`VARCHAR2 [(length)]`

Variable-length character data, with a maximum length of 4000 bytes. *length* specifies the maximum length of the character string to be stored.

`NCHAR [(length)]`

Fixed-length character data consisting of characters from a National Character Language (NLS) supported character set. Since a character may require more than one byte, the maximum length is 2000 bytes (which may allow fewer than 2000 characters). *length* specifies the maximum length of the character string to be stored.

`NVARCHAR2 [(length)]`

Variable-length character data consisting of characters from a National Language Support (NLS) character set. Since a character may require more than one byte, the maximum length is 4000 bytes (which may allow fewer than 4000 characters). *length* specifies the maximum length of the character string to be stored.

`LONG`

Variable-length character data with a maximum length of 2 gigabytes.

`RAW`

Raw binary data with a maximum length of 2000 bytes. RAW data will not be converted by Oracle when moving between systems with different character sets.

`LONG RAW`

Raw binary data with a maximum length of 2 gigabytes. LONG RAW data will not be converted by Oracle when moving between systems with different character sets.

The following character datatypes are also recognized for compatibility with ANSI SQL:

```
CHARACTER
CHARACTER VARYING
CHAR VARYING
NATIONAL CHARACTER
NATIONAL CHAR
NATIONAL CHARACTER VARYING
NATIONAL CHAR VARYING
NCHAR VARYING
```

Large Objects

Oracle provides several datatypes that support storage of large amounts of data in a single column. These datatypes are often used to store images, sound, and other large objects:

BLOB

Large, raw binary data with a maximum length of 4 gigabytes. BLOB data will not be converted by Oracle when moving between systems with different character sets. When a BLOB column is referenced, a LOB locator is returned.

CLOB

Large character data with a maximum length of 4 gigabytes.

NCLOB

Large character data consisting of characters from a National Language Support (NLS) character set with a maximum length of 4 gigabytes. NCLOB data will not be converted by Oracle when moving between systems with different character sets.

BFILE

Provides access to a binary file stored in an operating system file external to the Oracle database. The file can have a maximum size of 4 gigabytes.

Numeric Data

Numeric data is data that can participate in an arithmetic operation directly without data conversion. Oracle has only a single type of numeric data: the NUMBER type.

NUMBER data can hold values between 10^{-130} and $9.99999...x\ 10^{125}$, but the number will be accurate only to 38 positions.

A NUMBER data element can be expressed as:

```
NUMBER [(precision[,scale])]
```

precision

The number of digits in the number, which can range from 1 to 38.

scale

The number of digits to the right of the decimal point, which can range from -84 to 127.

If *scale* is omitted, the number is treated as an integer number, and no decimal portion is stored. If both *scale* and *precision* are omitted, the number is treated as a floating-point number.

It is a good idea to always specify a precision for a number datatype. If you do not, some ODBC drivers will assume a precision of 0, as opposed to the Oracle default of 38. In such cases, the ODBC-compliant client tool will not be able to insert or update rows where the column value is not 0.

Although all numeric data is stored by Oracle as a NUMBER, the following datatypes are also recognized for compatibility with ANSI SQL:

```
FLOAT
NUMERIC
DECIMAL
NUMBER
INTEGER
INT
SMALLINT
DOUBLE PRECISION
REAL
```

Dates

The DATE datatype is used by Oracle to store date and time information. Oracle DATE data is stored in a proprietary format that contains the following information:

- Century
- Year
- Month
- Day
- Hour
- Minute
- Second

To store data in a DATE datatype, the date and/or time information must be converted into Oracle's internal format. If the character representation of a date matches the default format (as specified by the NLS_DATE_FORMAT parameter in the initialization file, *INIT.ORA*), then Oracle can perform this conversion automatically. For example, if the default NLS_DATE_FORMAT of DD-MON-YY is in effect, then the following SQL statement will insert the date July 4, 2076 into a table column called T_DATE:

```
INSERT INTO sample_table (t_date)
VALUES ('07-JUL-76');
```

If the date and/or time information is available in another format, you can use one of Oracle's built-in TO_DATE functions to perform the conversion. For example, if the same date is presented as 07/04/76, then the SQL statement shown here, which uses Oracle's TO_DATE function, inserts the following row of data:

```
INSERT INTO sample_table (t_date)
VALUES (TO_DATE('07-JUL-76','MM/DD/YY'));
```

See Chapter 5, *SQL Functions*, for more information on TO_DATE and other conversion functions.

NULL

One sometimes confusing aspect of SQL is the concept of a NULL. NULL is the absence of data; it is neither character nor numeric. Both character and numeric data elements can be set to NULL, which indicates that the element contains no value whatsoever.

NULL is not the same as zero. In fact, any arithmetic operation involving a data element containing NULL will evaluate to NULL. For example, if the current value of a is NULL, then the following expression will evaluate to NULL:

```
(a+10)*20
```

 This feature of Oracle can make life difficult for a programmer if arithmetic will be performed involving a column that could contain a NULL. Luckily, Oracle provides the NVL function to take care of this problem. See Chapter 5 for more information.

Similarly, when using comparisons, a NULL will never match a condition, even though it may logically seem that it should. If col1 contains the value NULL, then the following clause:

```
WHERE col1 <> 1
```

will not resolve to TRUE.

You can test for the presence or absence of NULL in a data element. The condition IS NULL evaluates to TRUE if the expression evaluates to NULL, and to FALSE if it does not.

Locators

Oracle provides several datatypes whose primary purpose is to provide efficient reference to objects stored both within and outside the database.

ROWID

ROWID returns a string that represents the physical location of a row of data and contains all the information Oracle needs to locate a row of data, including:

- The data file containing the row
- The block of the file containing the row
- The position of the row in the data block
- The object number of the object (Oracle8 only)

Except in the case of tables stored in clusters, a ROWID will uniquely identify any single row of data.

ROWID is always returned as an 18-character string and may be used in a Data Manipulation Language (DML) statement just like any other Oracle column.

While ROWID can be stored in a table column, you should never rely on a row retaining its ROWID value. Since the ROWID represents a physical location, the value can change if the row is stored differently. For example, an export followed by an import will almost certainly invalidate any stored ROWID.

UROWID

Because some types of Oracle objects may not have physical locations that are fixed or generated by Oracle (such as objects accessed via a Transparent Gateway), Oracle has developed the *Universal ROWID* (UROWID) datatype, which can contain the physical ROWID when it is available; otherwise, it contains the logical ROWID. Oracle strongly recommends that you use the UROWID datatype in place of ROWID so either type of location information can be accommodated.

Pseudo-Columns

While not actual datatypes, Oracle supports several special-purpose data elements. These elements are not actually contained in a table, but are available for use in SQL statements as though they were part of the table.

ROWNUM

For each row of data returned by a SQL query, ROWNUM will contain a number indicating the order in which the row was retrieved. For example, the first row retrieved will have a ROWNUM of 1, the second row will have a ROWNUM of 2, and so on. This approach can be useful for limiting the number of rows returned

by a query. To display only ten rows of the emp table, the following SQL statement makes use of the ROWNUM pseudo-column:

```
SELECT *
FROM emp
WHERE ROWNUM < 11;
```

 ROWNUM returns a number indicating the order in which the row
was retrieved from the table, but this is not always the order in
which a row is displayed. For example, if a SQL statement includes
an ORDER BY clause, rows will not be displayed in ROWNUM
sequence, since ROWNUM is assigned before the sort operation.

CURRVAL

When using Oracle SEQUENCE values, (see "CREATE/ALTER/DROP SEQUENCE"
in Chapter 2, *Data Definition Statements*), the pseudo-column CURRVAL returns
the current value of the sequence. To reference CURRVAL, it must be associated
with a sequence:

[*schema.*]*sequence_name*.CURRVAL

schema
> The owner of the sequence. If *schema* is omitted, Oracle assumes the user-
> name under which you are currently connected to the database.

sequence_name
> The name of an Oracle sequence.

CURRVAL
> The current value of the sequence.

NEXTVAL

When using Oracle SEQUENCE values, the pseudo-column NEXTVAL returns the
next value of the sequence and causes the sequence to increment by one. You can
only reference NEXTVAL if it is associated with a sequence:

[*schema.*]*sequence_name*.NEXTVAL

schema
> The owner of the sequence. If omitted, the userid under which you are cur-
> rently logged in is used.

sequence_name
> The name of an Oracle sequence.

NEXTVAL
> The next value of the sequence.

Oracle will only increment the sequence once in a given SQL statement, so if a statement contains multiple references to NEXTVAL, the second and subsequent reference will return the same value as CURRVAL.

LEVEL

For each row returned by a hierarchical query (using the CONNECT BY clause), LEVEL returns 1 for a root node, 2 for a child of a root, and so on. A root node is the highest node within an inverted tree. A child node is any nonroot node, a parent node is any node that has children, and a leaf node is any node without children.

USER

This pseudo-column will always contain the Oracle username under which you are connected to the database.

SYSDATE

This pseudo-column will contain the current date and time. This column is a standard Oracle DATE datatype.

The date and time contained in SYSDATE comes from the server that processes the query, not the client from which the query is run. So if you connect to a server in Tokyo from a client workstation in London, the date and time will be that of the server in Tokyo (and the date will probably be a day ahead!).

If you return a SYSDATE column via a database link (for example, SELECT SYSDATE FROM *dual@london*), the date and time will be returned from the server you are connected to, not the remote server referenced by the database link.

Data Conversion

There are multiple ways to represent data in a database. For example, a salary, which is normally considered a numeric value such as 25,000 can be represented easily as a character string such as "25000". Likewise, an employee ID can be represented as a number (500) or a string ("500"). If you attempt to perform an arithmetic operation on a character value in most computer languages, an error will occur. Not so with SQL. Oracle automatically performs a data conversion when it is necessary (and possible) to complete a requested operation. In the following SQL statement, assume that sal is defined in the database as CHAR(6)—a character string with a fixed length of six bytes:

```
SELECT ename, SAL * 1.1
FROM scott.emp;
```

The character string (sal) is multiplied by a numeric constant (1.1). To perform this operation, Oracle first converts the string into a number, and then performs the multiplication. This type of automatic conversion is an *implicit data conversion.*

While convenient, implicit data conversion also has a cost in CPU utilization, so be careful when deciding how to store data elements in the database.

Implicit data conversion can have an unexpected negative impact on performance, since it can dramatically affect the way the Oracle query optimizer generates an execution plan. For example, use of an index may be suppressed due to implicit data conversion, resulting in a full table scan.

SQL also provides several functions that perform explicit data conversion:

TO_CHAR
Performs numeric-to-character and date-to-character conversions

TO_NUMBER
Performs character-to-numeric conversion

TO_DATE
Performs character-to-date conversion

See Chapter 5 for more information.

Relational Operators

An operator manipulates data elements and returns a result. The data elements that are operated upon are called *operands* or *arguments,* and a special character or keyword represents the actual operator. Oracle SQL supports several types of operators, listed in this section.

Arithmetic Operators

Arithmetic operators perform arithmetical calculations on a pair of data elements and/or constants. Table 1-1 lists the arithmetic operators available in SQL.

Table 1-1. SQL's Arithmetic Operators

Operator	Description	Example
+	Addition	sal + comm
−	Subtraction	sal − comm
*	Multiplication	sal * 1.1
/	Division	sal / 12
−	Negation	−sal
+	Identity	+sal

Concatenation Operator

The concatenation operator (| |) combines two character strings. Consider the following SQL statement:

```
SELECT fname || ' ' || lname
FROM employee_master;
```

This statement returns (for each row) a single string consisting of the first name, a space, and the last name.

 Although most Oracle platforms use solid vertical bars (| |) as the concatenation operator, some platforms, most notably IBM platforms using the EBCDIC character set, use the broken vertical bars (¦ ¦). When converting between ASCII and EBCDIC character sets, the conversion of these characters may not be correct.

If one of two concatenated strings is NULL, the result is a non-NULL string. The NULL string is treated as an empty string. If both strings being concatenated are NULL, then the resulting string is NULL. If either of the operands is a VARCHAR2 datatype, the resulting string is a VARCHAR2 datatype as well.

 A concatenated string may not be longer than 2000 characters if the operands are CHAR datatypes, or 4000 characters otherwise. Other character types, like LONG and CLOB, cannot be concatenated.

Comparison Operators

Comparison operators are used to compare two data elements (or a data element and a constant) and return a result that is TRUE, FALSE, or NULL, depending on how the values in the two elements relate to each other. Table 1-2 lists the comparison operators available in SQL.

Table 1-2. SQL's Comparison Operators

Operator	Use	Description	Example
=	*a = b*	Tests for equality of two operands.	SELECT * FROM emp WHERE sal =500
!=	*a != b*	Tests for inequality of two operands.	SELECT * FROM emp WHERE sal !=500
^=	*a ^= b*	Tests for inequality of two operands.	SELECT * FROM emp WHERE sal ^=500
<>	*a <> b*	Tests for inequality of two operands.	SELECT * FROM emp WHERE sal <>500
<	*a < b*	Tests that operand *a* is less than operand *b*.	SELECT * FROM emp WHERE sal <500
!<	*a !< b*	Tests that operand *a* is not less than operand *b*. This is the same as >=.	SELECT * FROM emp WHERE sal !<500
>	*a > b*	Tests that operand *a* is greater than operand *b*.	SELECT * FROM emp WHERE sal >500
!>	*a !> b*	Tests that operand *a* is not greater than operand *b*. This is the same as <=.	SELECT * FROM emp WHERE sal !>500
<=	*a <= b*	Tests that operand *a* is less than or equal to operand *b*. This is the same as !>.	SELECT * FROM emp WHERE sal <=500
>=	*a >= b*	Tests that operand *a* is greater than or equal to operand *b*. This is the same as !<.	SELECT * FROM emp WHERE sal >=500
IN	*a* IN (*b,c...*)	Tests that operand *a* matches at least one element of the list provided (operand *b*, operand *c*, etc.).	SELECT * FROM emp WHERE sal IN (500,600,700)
NOT IN	*a* NOT IN (*b,c...*)	Tests that operand *a* does not match any element of the list provided (operand *b*, operand *c*, etc.).	SELECT * FROM emp WHERE sal NOT IN (500,600,700)

Table 1-2. SQL's Comparison Operators (continued)

Operator	Use	Description	Example
ANY	a = ANY ($b,c...$) a < ANY ($b,c...$) a > ANY ($b,c...$), etc.	Tests that the relation-ship specified (e.g., =, <>, <, >, etc.) is true for at least one element of the list provided (oper-and b, operand c, etc.). When testing for equal-ity, this is equivalent to IN.	SELECT * FROM emp WHERE sal = ANY (500,600,700)
SOME	a = SOME ($b,c...$) a < SOME ($b,c...$) a > SOME ($b,c...$), etc.	Tests that the relation-ship specified (e.g., =, <>, <, >, etc.) is true for at least one element of the list provided (oper-and b, operand c, etc.). When testing for equal-ity, this is equivalent to IN.	SELECT * FROM emp WHERE sal = SOME (500,600,700)
ALL	a = ALL ($b,c...$) a < ALL ($b,c...$) a < ALL ($b,c...$), etc.	Tests that the relation-ship specified (e.g., =, <>, <, >, etc.) is true for every element of the list provided (operand b, operand c, etc.).	SELECT * FROM emp WHERE sal > ALL (500,600,700)
BETWEEN	a BETWEEN b and c	Tests that operand a is greater than or equal to operand b and less than or equal to operand c.	SELECT * FROM emp WHERE sal BETWEEN 400 AND 600
NOT BETWEEN	a NOT BETWEEN b and c	Tests that operand a is less than operand b or greater than operand c.	SELECT * FROM emp WHERE sal NOT BETWEEN 400 and 600
EXISTS	EXISTS (*query*)	Tests that the query returns at least one row.	SELECT * FROM emp e WHERE EXISTS (SELECT deptno FROM dept d WHERE deptno= e.deptno)
NOT EXISTS	NOT EXISTS (*query*)	Tests that the query does not return a row.	SELECT * FROM emp e WHERE NOT EXISTS (SELECT deptno FROM dept d WHERE deptno= e.deptno)

Table 1-2. SQL's Comparison Operators (continued)

Operator	Use	Description	Example
LIKE	*a* LIKE *b*	Tests that operand *a* matches pattern operand *b*. The pattern may contain _, which matches a single character in that position, or %, which matches all characters.	SELECT * FROM emp WHERE ename LIKE 'SMI%'
NOT LIKE	*a* NOT LIKE *b*	Tests that operand *a* does not match pattern operand *b*. The pattern may contain _, which matches a single character in that position, or %, which matches all characters.	SELECT * FROM emp WHERE ename NOT LIKE 'SMI%'
IS NULL	*a* IS NULL	Tests that operand *a* is NULL.	SELECT * FROM emp WHERE comm IS NULL
IS NOT NULL	*a* IS NOT NULL	Tests that operand *a* is not NULL.	SELECT * FROM emp WHERE comm IS NOT NULL

Logical Operators

SQL provides logical operators that are similar to those available in most other programming languages. The logical operators AND and OR combine the results of two Boolean values to produce a single result based on them, while the logical operator NOT inverts a result. The Boolean values may be any expression that can be evaluated to TRUE or FALSE. Usually the values come from comparison expressions. Table 1-3 presents the logical operators available in SQL, along with the possible results from each.

Table 1-3. SQL's Logical Operators

Operator	Operand 1	Operand 2	Result
AND	TRUE	TRUE	TRUE
	FALSE	FALSE	FALSE
	TRUE	FALSE	FALSE
	FALSE	TRUE	FALSE
	TRUE	NULL	NULL
	FALSE	NULL	FALSE

Table 1-3. SQL's Logical Operators (continued)

Operator	Operand 1	Operand 2	Result
	NULL	TRUE	NULL
	NULL	FALSE	FALSE
	NULL	NULL	NULL
OR	TRUE	TRUE	TRUE
	FALSE	FALSE	FALSE
	TRUE	FALSE	TRUE
	FALSE	TRUE	TRUE
	TRUE	NULL	TRUE
	FALSE	NULL	NULL
	NULL	TRUE	TRUE
	NULL	FALSE	NULL
	NULL	NULL	NULL
NOT	TRUE		FALSE
	FALSE		TRUE
	NULL		NULL

Set Operators

Unlike other relational operators that operate on one or more individual data elements, set operators work on the entire set of data returned by two queries. Table 1-4 describes the set operators available in SQL.

Table 1-4. SQL's Set Operators

Operator	Description	Example
UNION	Combines all rows returned by both queries and eliminates duplicate rows.	SELECT * FROM emp WHERE deptno=10 UNION SELECT * FROM emp WHERE sal > 500
UNION ALL	Combines all rows returned by both queries and includes duplicate rows.	SELECT * FROM emp WHERE deptno=10 UNION ALL SELECT * FROM emp WHERE sal > 500

Table 1-4. SQL's Set Operators (continued)

Operator	Description	Example
MINUS	Takes the rows returned by the first query, removes rows that are also returned by the second query, and returns the rows that remain.	SELECT * FROM emp MINUS SELECT * FROM emp WHERE sal > 500
INTERSECT	Returns only the rows returned by both queries.	SELECT * FROM emp WHERE deptno = 10 INTERSECT SELECT * FROM emp WHERE SAL>500

Structure of a SQL Statement

A SQL statement can be broken into three major components:

- The SQL operation
- The target
- The condition

Only the first two components are required; the condition is optional or may not apply, depending on the SQL operation being performed.

The SQL Operation

There are four basic operations performed by a SQL DML statement. Each of these is discussed in this section. Each operation is also the name of a SQL statement, and the detailed syntax for each statement can be found in Chapter 3, *Data Manipulation and Control Statements.*

SELECT

The SELECT statement is probably the most common and widely used of all SQL statements. The purpose of a SELECT statement is to retrieve data from the database. The statement may return data elements from one or more database tables or views, from expressions involving data elements from at least one database table or view and/or constant, or from constants. A SELECT statement always has a target component, and often has a condition component. The target of a SELECT statement is the set of tables and views listed in the FROM clause (the tables and views from which data is retrieved). The condition is the expression in the WHERE clause, and possibly in the HAVING clause as well, that restricts the rows that will be returned. If no condition is specified, all rows of the target table(s) and/or view(s) are returned.

INSERT

The INSERT statement creates new rows of data in a target database table or view. The statement provides a list of columns that will receive the data provided (all columns of the table or view are implied if no list is provided) and a corresponding list containing the data elements to be placed in each column. The condition component does not apply to an INSERT.

UPDATE

The UPDATE statement modifies data already in a database table or view. The UPDATE statement always has an associated target, and usually has a condition as well. If no condition is specified, all rows of the target table are updated.

DELETE

The DELETE statement removes rows from a database table or view. This statement will always have an associated target, and usually has a condition as well. If no condition is specified, all rows of the target table or view are removed.

The Target

All SQL DML statements operate on one or more database tables or views. The purpose of the target component is to identify those tables or views. This component takes a different form depending on the statement with which it's being used. For example, the SELECT and DELETE statements have similar target structures:

```
SELECT *
FROM emp          --This is the target component
WHERE depno = 10

DELETE
FROM emp          --This is the target component
WHERE deptno = 10
```

The INSERT and UPDATE statements, however, use the target differently:

```
INSERT INTO emp   --This is the target component
   (empno, ename, sal, hiredate)
VALUES ('1234','Dave Kreines',500,'06-01-00')

UPDATE emp        --This is the target component
SET sal = 600
WHERE empno = '1234'
```

Joins

When two or more tables or views are referenced as the target of a SELECT statement, this is called a *join*. One of the fundamental concepts of a relational database is the ability to combine two or more tables into a single result set by specifying how the tables are related (thus the term *relational*). Two or more tables or views are typically related to each other by one or more columns that share common data. Such a column is called a *key column*. An example of a key column might be a department number. Figure 1-1 illustrates such a relationship.

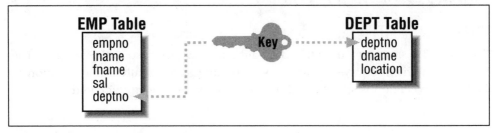

Figure 1-1. Two tables related through a common key

The target component specifies the tables or views to be included in a join, and the condition component tells Oracle how to relate the tables or views to each other.

The following example joins the emp and dept tables:

```
SELECT ename, location
FROM emp, dept
WHERE emp.deptno = dept.deptno
```

This statement instructs Oracle to return the name and location for each employee from the database by first forming all possible combinations of data rows from the two tables, and then returning all rows where the two department numbers match. Note that the number of rows in each table can be different; it is the data value that is used for the match. One row from the dept table can, and probably will, match multiple rows of the emp table.

The idea of forming all possible combinations of all rows by joining two tables is conceptual. Oracle almost always finds a more optimal way to generate the join results.

If no condition is specified for a join, all possible combinations of rows from the two tables are returned as the result. In other words, every row of the first table is matched with every row of the second table (assuming that two tables are joined).

This result is known as a *Cartesian product*, and it is usually something you want to avoid. The number of rows returned is equivalent to the number of rows in the first table multiplied by the number of rows in the second. If your tables are large to begin with, the number of rows in the Cartesian product can become extremely large. Performance will suffer greatly by having to generate those rows, and they are not likely be of much use anyway. Cartesian products usually represent a mistake in writing a query.

The existence of two or more tables or views in the FROM clause, with no corresponding set of join conditions in the WHERE clause, always results in a Cartesian product.

Outer join

In the standard join, rows are only returned when there are corresponding rows in each of the joined tables or views. An *outer join* allows data to be returned even if no matching row exists in one of the tables. The outer join is specified by adding (+) to the end of the column names for the table that you want to make optional. In other words, (+) means "add a phantom row to this table that contains NULL values for all columns if a matching row does not exist." Here is an example of an outer join that displays a NULL location if there is no matching department number in the dept table:

```
SELECT ename, location
FROM emp, dept
WHERE emp.deptno = dept.deptno(+)
```

Normally, a query joining the emp and dept tables would return rows for only the employees who had been assigned to a valid department. By adding (+) to the end of the dept.deptno column name, we make the join into an outer join. Rows are now returned for all employees, whether or not they have a valid department assignment.

The Condition

The condition component, which is specified using the WHERE clause, identifies the specific rows to be operated on by a SELECT, UPDATE, or DELETE statement. While a WHERE clause may be very complex, it ultimately evaluates to either TRUE or FALSE for each row of data, and that action controls whether or not the operation takes place for each row. Consider the following query:

```
SELECT *
```

```
FROM emp
WHERE sal > 500
```

Oracle will look at each row of data in the emp table and evaluate the condition sal > 500. Rows for which this expression evaluates to TRUE will be returned, while those for which this condition evaluates to FALSE or unknown (those with values of sal that are less than or equal to 500 or that contain NULL) will not be returned.

Another important use for the WHERE clause is to identify the columns that relate one table to another to perform a join. Here is a query that includes a simple join:

```
SELECT ename, loc
FROM emp, dept
WHERE emp.deptno = dept.deptno
```

Both the emp and dept tables have a column called deptno, which contains the department number. The columns do not need to have the same name, but they do have to contain data with the same meaning. In this example, each emp row contains a department number in a column named deptno. The department number also exists in the deptno column of the dept table. Since we know that a department number in the emp table has the same meaning as one in the dept table, these columns can be used to specify a join condition.

In the example, the column name (deptno) was prefixed by the name of the table (emp or dept). This prefix occurs because both tables in the join have identically named columns. As a result, you need to qualify the column names with the table names so Oracle knows which column you are referring to. Oracle would return an error if you failed to do this because the column names would then be ambiguous. What is intended may be obvious to you, but not to Oracle!

SQL Statements

There are a large number of SQL statements supported for Oracle and described in subsequent chapters of this book. As an aid to identifying the particular SQL statement you might need and helping you find it in the book, Table 1-5 presents a list of SQL commands in alphabetical order, along with a short description, and the chapter number and heading where you can find the full syntax and description of that statement.

Table 1-5. SQL Statements Covered in This Book

SQL Statement	Description	Found in Chapter	Under This Heading
ALTER CLUSTER	Redefines future storage allocations or allocates an extent for a cluster	2	"CREATE/ALTER/ DROP CLUSTER"
ALTER DATABASE	Changes one or more characteristics of an existing database	2	"CREATE/ALTER DATABASE"
ALTER FUNCTION	Recompiles a stored PL/SQL function	7	"ALTER FUNCTION"
ALTER INDEX	Changes the characteristics of an index	2	"CREATE/ALTER/ DROP INDEX"
ALTER MATERIALIZED VIEW	Changes the storage characteristics or automatic refresh characteristics of a materialized view or snapshot	2	"CREATE/ALTER/ DROP MATERIAL- IZED VIEW"
ALTER MATERIAL- IZED VIEW LOG	Changes the storage characteristics of a materialized view log	2	"CREATE/ALTER/ DROP MATERIAL- IZED VIEW LOG"
ALTER PACKAGE	Recompiles a PL/SQL package	7	"ALTER PACKAGE"
ALTER PROCEDURE	Recompiles a PL/SQL stored procedure	7	"ALTER PROCE- DURE"
ALTER PROFILE	Adds, changes, or removes a resource limit from an existing profile	2	"CREATE/ALTER/ DROP PROFILE"
ALTER RESOURCE COST	Modifies the formula calculating the total resource cost used in a session	2	"ALTER RESOURCE COST"
ALTER ROLE	Changes the authorization level required to enable a role	2	"CREATE/ALTER/ DROP ROLE"
ALTER ROLLBACK SEGMENT	Changes the online status of a rollback segment or modifies its storage characteristics	2	"CREATE/ALTER/ DROP ROLLBACK SEGMENT"
ALTER SEQUENCE	Changes the characteristics of an Oracle sequence	2	"CREATE/ALTER/ DROP SEQUENCE"
ALTER SESSION	Changes the functional characteristics of the current database session	2	"ALTER SESSION"
ALTER SNAPSHOT	Changes the storage characteristics or automatic refresh characteristics of a snapshot	2	"CREATE/ALTER/ DROP SNAPSHOT"

Table 1-5. SQL Statements Covered in This Book (continued)

SQL Statement	Description	Found in Chapter	Under This Heading
ALTER SNAPSHOT LOG	Changes the storage characteristics of a snapshot log	2	"CREATE/ALTER/ DROP SNAPSHOT LOG"
ALTER SYSTEM	Makes dynamic changes to the database instance	2	"ALTER SYSTEM"
ALTER TABLE	Modifies the characteristics of a table	2	"CREATE/ALTER/ DROP TABLE"
ALTER TABLESPACE	Changes the characteristics of an existing tablespace	2	"CREATE/ALTER/ DROP TABLESPACE"
ALTER TRIGGER	Recompiles a PL/SQL trigger	7	"ALTER TRIGGER"
ALTER USER	Changes the security and storage characteristics of a user	2	"CREATE/ALTER/ DROP USER"
ALTER VIEW	Recompiles a view	2	"CREATE/ALTER/ DROP VIEW"
ANALYZE	Collects or deletes statistics about an object in the database	2	"ANALYZE"
ASSOCIATE STATISTICS	Associates a method of statistics computation with database objects	2	"ASSOCIATE STATISTICS"
AUDIT	Sets up auditing for specific SQL statements in subsequent user sessions	2	"AUDIT (SQL Statements)"
AUDIT	Sets up auditing for a specific schema object	2	"AUDIT (Schema Objects)"
CALL	Executes a stored PL/SQL procedure	2	"CALL"
COMMENT	Adds a comment about a table, view, snapshot, or column	2	"COMMENT"
CREATE CLUSTER	Creates a cluster that contains at least one table with one or more columns in common	2	"CREATE/ALTER/ DROP CLUSTER"
CREATE CONTROLFILE	Recreates a control file, allowing changes to some parameters	2	"CREATE CONTROL-FILE"
CREATE DATABASE	Creates a database and specifies parameters associated with it	2	"CREATE/ALTER DATABASE"

Table 1-5. SQL Statements Covered in This Book (continued)

SQL Statement	Description	Found in Chapter	Under This Heading
CREATE DATABASE LINK	Creates a database link to provide access to objects on a remote database	2	"CREATE/DROP DATABASE LINK"
CREATE DIMENSION	Creates a dimension that defines a parent-child relationship between pairs of column sets	2	"CREATE/DROP DIMENSION"
CREATE DIRECTORY	Creates a directory object that specifies an operating system directory for storing BFILE objects	2	"CREATE/DROP DIRECTORY"
CREATE FUNCTION	Creates a stored PL/SQL function	7	"CREATE FUNCTION"
CREATE INDEX	Creates an index on at least one column of a table or cluster	2	"CREATE/ALTER/ DROP INDEX"
CREATE MATERIALIZED VIEW	Creates a materialized view, also called a snapshot	2	"CREATE/ALTER/ DROP MATERIALIZED VIEW"
CREATE MATERIALIZED VIEW LOG	Creates a materialized view log	2	"CREATE/ALTER/ DROP MATERIALIZED VIEW LOG"
CREATE PACKAGE	Creates a PL/SQL package	7	"CREATE PACKAGE"
CREATE PROCEDURE	Creates a PL/SQL stored procedure	7	"CREATE PROCEDURE"
CREATE PROFILE	Creates a profile to set limits on database resources	2	"CREATE/ALTER/ DROP PROFILE"
CREATE ROLE	Creates a role, which is a set of privileges that can be granted to users	2	"CREATE/ALTER/ DROP ROLE"
CREATE ROLLBACK SEGMENT	Creates a rollback segment, which is used by Oracle to store data necessary to roll back changes made by transactions	2	"CREATE/ALTER/ DROP ROLLBACK SEGMENT"
CREATE SCHEMA	Creates multiple tables and/or views, and issues grants in a single statement	2	"CREATE SCHEMA"

Table 1-5. SQL Statements Covered in This Book (continued)

SQL Statement	Description	Found in Chapter	Under This Heading
CREATE SEQUENCE	Creates an Oracle sequence used to automatically generate sequential numbers	2	"CREATE/ALTER/DROP SEQUENCE"
CREATE SNAPSHOT	Creates a snapshot (or materialized view)	2	"CREATE/ALTER/DROP SNAPSHOT"
CREATE SNAPSHOT LOG	Creates a snapshot log	2	"CREATE/ALTER/DROP SNAPSHOT LOG"
CREATE TABLE	Creates a table by specifying the structure or referencing an existing table	2	"CREATE/ALTER/DROP TABLE"
CREATE TABLESPACE	Creates a new tablespace, optionally specifying default storage characteristics for objects subsequently created in the tablespace	2	"CREATE/ALTER/DROP TABLESPACE"
CREATE TRIGGER	Creates a PL/SQL trigger	7	"CREATE TRIGGER"
CREATE TEMPORARY TABLESPACE	Creates a temporary tablespace	2	"CREATE TEMPORARY TABLESPACE"
CREATE USER	Creates a new database user and assigns security and storage properties	2	"CREATE/ALTER/DROP USER"
CREATE VIEW	Create a view	2	"CREATE/ALTER/DROP VIEW"
CREATE SYNONYM	Creates a public or private synonym for a database object	2	"CREATE/DROP SYNONYM"
DROP SYNONYM	Removes a public or private synonym from the database	2	"CREATE/DROP SYNONYM
DELETE	Deletes one or more rows from a table, view, or snapshot	3	"DELETE"
DISASSOCIATE STATISTICS	Disassociates a method of statistics computation from database objects	2	"DISASSOCIATE STATISTICS"
DROP CLUSTER	Removes a cluster from the database	2	"CREATE/ALTER/DROP CLUSTER"
DROP DATABASE LINK	Removes a database link from the database	2	"CREATE/DROP DATABASE LINK"

Table 1-5. SQL Statements Covered in This Book (continued)

SQL Statement	Description	Found in Chapter	Under This Heading
DROP DIMENSION	Removes a dimension from the database	2	"CREATE/DROP DIMENSION"
DROP DIRECTORY	Removes a directory object from the database	2	"CREATE/DROP DIRECTORY"
DROP FUNCTION	Removes a stored PL/SQL function	7	"DROP FUNCTION"
DROP INDEX	Removes an index from the database	2	"CREATE/ALTER/ DROP INDEX"
DROP MATERIAL- IZED VIEW	Removes a materialized view (or snapshot) from the database	2	"CREATE/ALTER/ DROP MATERIAL- IZED VIEW"
DROP MATERIAL- IZED VIEW LOG	Removes a materialized view log from the data- base	2	"CREATE/ALTER/ DROP MATERIAL- IZED VIEW LOG"
DROP PACKAGE	Removes a PL/SQL pack- age from the database	7	"DROP PACKAGE"
DROP PROCEDURE	Removes a PL/SQL stored procedure from the data- base	7	"DROP PROCEDURE"
DROP PROFILE	Removes a profile from the database	2	"CREATE/ALTER/ DROP PROFILE"
DROP ROLE	Removes a role from the database	2	"CREATE/ALTER/ DROP ROLE"
DROP ROLLBACK SEGMENT	Removes a rollback seg- ment from the database	2	"CREATE/ALTER/ DROP ROLLBACK SEGMENT"
DROP SEQUENCE	Removes a sequence from the database	2	"CREATE/ALTER/ DROP SEQUENCE"
DROP SNAPSHOT	Removes a snapshot from the database	2	"CREATE/ALTER/ DROP SNAPSHOT"
DROP SNAPSHOT LOG	Removes a snapshot log from the database	2	"CREATE/ALTER/ DROP SNAPSHOT LOG"
DROP TABLE	Removes a table from the database	2	"CREATE/ALTER/ DROP TABLE"
DROP TABLESPACE	Removes a tablespace from the database	2	"CREATE/ALTER/ DROP TABLESPACE"
DROP TRIGGER	Removes a PL/SQL trigger from the database	7	"DROP TRIGGER"
DROP USER	Removes a user from the database	2	"CREATE/ALTER/ DROP USER"

Table 1-5. SQL Statements Covered in This Book (continued)

SQL Statement	Description	Found in Chapter	Under This Heading
DROP VIEW	Remove a view from the database	2	"CREATE/ALTER/ DROP VIEW"
EXPLAIN PLAN	Creates an explanation of the execution plan for a SQL statement	2	"EXPLAIN PLAN"
GRANT	Grants a system privilege or role to one or more users and/or roles	2	"GRANT (System Privilege or Role)"
GRANT	Grants privileges on a database object to one or more users or roles	2	"GRANT (Object Privileges)"
INSERT	Inserts a row of data into a table or view	3	"INSERT"
NOAUDIT	Stops auditing defined by a prior AUDIT statement for schema objects	2	"NOAUDIT (Schema Objects)"
NOAUDIT	Stops auditing defined by a prior AUDIT statement for SQL statements	2	"NOAUDIT (SQL Statements)"
RENAME	Changes the name of an existing table, view, sequence, or private synonym	2	"RENAME"
REVOKE	Removes a system privilege or role from one or more users and/or roles	2	"REVOKE (System Privilege or Role)"
REVOKE	Revokes privileges on a database object from one or more users or roles	2	"REVOKE (Object Privileges)"
SAVEPOINT	Identifies a point in a transaction to which you can roll back using the ROLLBACK command	3	"SAVEPOINT"
SELECT	Retrieves data from a table, view, or snapshot	3	"SELECT"
SET CONSTRAINT	Specifies at the transaction level how constraints are checked	3	"SET CONSTRAINT"
SET ROLE	Enables or disables roles for the current session	3	"SET ROLE"

Table 1-5. SQL Statements Covered in This Book (continued)

SQL Statement	Description	Found in Chapter	Under This Heading
SET TRANSACTION	Establishes the current transaction as read-only or read-write, or specifies the rollback segment to be used by the transaction	3	"SET TRANSACTION"
TRUNCATE	Removes all rows from a table or cluster	3	"TRUNCATE"
UPDATE	Changes the value stored in column of data in one or more tables, views, or snapshots	3	"UPDATE"

2

Data Definition Statements

SQL statements fall into two categories: Data Definition Language (DDL) and Data Manipulation Language (DML). You invoke DDL statements when you need to manipulate the structure of your Oracle database. You can use DDL statements to define, modify, and remove every type of object that can exist in an Oracle database. For this reason, it is critically important that you understand DDL statements and know how to use them properly. Many of the DDL statements require special database privileges and are normally executed by the DBA; for DBAs, of course, knowledge of DDL is a requirement. But Oracle developers and designers will also find knowledge of these statements to be very useful. Because DDL statements can perform so many different functions, there are a large number of them, and many have a wide range of options and syntax choices. This chapter provides a quick reference to what these SQL statements do and how you issue them.

SQL statements in the second category, DML, are used to manipulate the actual data contained in an Oracle database. DML statements are covered in Chapter 3, *Data Manipulation and Control Statements.*

SQL DDL Statements by Task

Often one of the most frustrating and time-consuming aspects of working with an Oracle database is simply finding the proper statement to accomplish a particular task. Table 2-1 lists most common data definition tasks, along with the appropriate SQL statements used to accomplish each task. You will find the detailed syntax of each statement later in this chapter.

Table 2-1. Common DDL Tasks and Their Corresponding SQL Statements

If you want to	Use this statement
Add a column/integrity constraint to a table	ALTER TABLE
Add a comment about a table, view, snapshot, or column into the data dictionary	COMMENT
Add a resource limit from an existing profile	ALTER PROFILE
Add datafiles to an existing tablespace	ALTER TABLESPACE
Add/rename data files	ALTER TABLESPACE
Allocate an extent for a cluster	ALTER CLUSTER
Allocate an extent for the table	ALTER TABLE
Allow/disallow access to a table	GRANT/REVOKE ROLE
Allow/disallow writing to a table	ALTER TABLE
Allow/disallow writing to a tablespace	ALTER TABLESPACE
Associate a method of statistics computation with database objects	ASSOCIATE STATISTICS
Audit a specific schema object	AUDIT
Audit specific SQL statements	AUDIT
Back up the current control file	ALTER DATABASE
Begin/end a backup by putting a tablespace in backup or normal mode	ALTER TABLESPACE
Bring a rollback segment online/offline	ALTER ROLLBACK SEGMENT
Change a resource limit from an existing profile	ALTER PROFILE
Change a user's default role	ALTER USER
Change a user's default table space	ALTER USER
Change a user's password	ALTER USER
Change a user's profile	ALTER USER
Change a user's tablespace quotas	ALTER USER
Change a user's temporary tablespace	ALTER USER
Change an existing tablespace	ALTER TABLESPACE
Change database control file parameters	CREATE CONTROLFILE
Change parameters for a database	ALTER DATABASE
Change storage parameters for an existing tablespace	ALTER TABLESPACE
Change the authorization level required to enable a role	ALTER ROLE
Change the characteristics of an index	ALTER INDEX
Change the characteristics of an Oracle sequence	ALTER SEQUENCE
Change the dynamically modifiable characteristics of the running database instance	ALTER SYSTEM
Change the formula used to calculate the total resource cost used in a session	ALTER RESOURCE COST

Table 2-1. Common DDL Tasks and Their Corresponding SQL Statements (continued)

If you want to	Use this statement
Change the functional characteristics of the current database session, including several National Language Support (NLS) characteristics	ALTER SESSION
Change the name of a database	CREATE CONTROLFILE
Change the name of a schema object	RENAME
Change the name of an existing table, view, sequence, or private synonym	RENAME
Change the online status of a rollback segment	ALTER ROLLBACK SEGMENT
Change the security and storage characteristics of a user	ALTER USER
Change the storage characteristics of a materialized view log	ALTER MATERIALIZED VIEW LOG
Change the storage characteristics of a snapshot log	ALTER SNAPSHOT LOG
Change the storage characteristics or automatic refresh characteristics of a materialized view (or snapshot)	ALTER MATERIALIZED VIEW
Change the storage characteristics or automatic refresh characteristics of a snapshot	ALTER SNAPSHOT
Choose archivelog/noarchivelog mode	ALTER DATABASE
Collect statistics about an object in the database	ANALYZE
Copy a new table from an existing table	CREATE TABLE AS
Create a cluster	CREATE CLUSTER
Create a database	CREATE DATABASE
Create a database link to access objects on a remote database	CREATE DATABASE LINK
Create a dimension that defines a parent-child relationship between pairs of column sets	CREATE DIMENSION
Create a directory object that specifies an operating system directory for storing BFILE objects	CREATE DIRECTORY
Create a materialized view (also called a snapshot)	CREATE MATERIALIZED VIEW
Create a materialized view log	CREATE MATERIALIZED VIEW LOG
Create a new database user	CREATE USER
Create a new tablespace	CREATE TABLESPACE
Create a PL/SQL package	CREATE PACKAGE
Create a PL/SQL package body	CREATE PACKAGE BODY
Create a PL/SQL trigger that is automatically executed when a particular SQL statement is executed against a table	CREATE TRIGGER
Create a profile to set limits on database resources	CREATE PROFILE
Create a public or private synonym for a database object	CREATE SYNONYM

Table 2-1. Common DDL Tasks and Their Corresponding SQL Statements (continued)

If you want to	Use this statement
Create a role	CREATE ROLE
Create a rollback segment	CREATE ROLLBACK SEGMENT
Create a snapshot	CREATE SNAPSHOT
Create a snapshot log	CREATE SNAPSHOT LOG
Create a standalone function	CREATE FUNCTION
Create a table by either specifying the structure or referencing an existing table	CREATE TABLE
Create a temporary tablespace	CREATE TEMPORARY TABLESPACE
Create a view	CREATE VIEW
Create an explanation of the execution plan for a SQL statement	EXPLAIN PLAN
Create an index for one or more columns of a table or cluster	CREATE INDEX
Create an Oracle sequence used to automatically generate sequential numbers	CREATE SEQUENCE
Delete a cluster from the database	DROP CLUSTER
Delete a database link from the database	DROP DATABASE LINK
Delete a dimension from the database	DROP DIMENSION
Delete a directory object from the database	DROP DIRECTORY
Delete a function from the database	DROP FUNCTION
Delete a materialized view (or snapshot) from the database	DROP MATERIALIZED VIEW
Delete a materialized view log from the database	DROP MATERIALIZED VIEW LOG
Delete a PL/SQL package from the database	DROP PACKAGE
Delete a profile from the database	DROP PROFILE
Delete a public or private synonym from the database	DROP SYNONYM
Delete a resource limit from an existing profile	ALTER PROFILE
Delete a role from the database	DROP ROLE
Delete a rollback segment from the database	DROP ROLLBACK SEGMENT
Delete a sequence from the database	DROP SEQUENCE
Delete a snapshot from the database	DROP SNAPSHOT
Delete a snapshot log from the database	DROP SNAPSHOT LOG
Delete a system privilege or role from one or more users and/or roles	REVOKE
Delete a tablespace from the database	DROP TABLESPACE
Delete a trigger from the database	DROP TRIGGER

Table 2-1. Common DDL Tasks and Their Corresponding SQL Statements (continued)

If you want to	Use this statement
Delete a user from the database	DROP USER
Delete a view from the database	DROP VIEW
Delete an index from the database	DROP INDEX
Delete privileges on a database object from one or more users or roles	REVOKE
Delete statistics about an object in the database	ANALYZE
Delete a table from the database	DROP TABLE
Disable a database trigger	ALTER TRIGGER
Disable a role for the current session	SET ROLE
Disable auditing by reversing the effect of a prior audit statement	NOAUDIT
Disassociate a method of statistics computation from database objects	DISASSOCIATE STATISTICS
Enable a database trigger	ALTER TRIGGER
Enable a role for the current session	SET ROLE
Enable/disable all triggers on a table	ALTER TABLE
Enable/disable autoextending the size of data files	ALTER DATABASE
Enable/disable table locks on a table	ALTER TABLE
Grant a system privilege or role to one or more users and/ or roles	GRANT
Grant privileges on a database object to one or more users or roles	GRANT
Identify migrated and chained rows in a table or cluster	ANALYZE
Issue multiple CREATE TABLE, CREATE VIEW, and GRANT statements	CREATE SCHEMA
Modify the column characteristics of a table	ALTER TABLE
Modify the degree of parallelism for a table	ALTER TABLE
Modify the integrity constraints associated with a table and/or its columns	ALTER TABLE
Modify the storage characteristics of a rollback segment	ALTER ROLLBACK SEGMENT
Modify the storage characteristics of a table	ALTER TABLE
Open/mount the database	ALTER DATABASE
Perform media recovery	ALTER DATABASE
Place a tablespace online	ALTER TABLESPACE
Recompile a PL/SQL package	ALTER PACKAGE
Recompile a standalone function	ALTER FUNCTION
Recompile a stored function	ALTER FUNCTION
Recompile a stored package	ALTER PACKAGE

Table 2-1. Common DDL Tasks and Their Corresponding SQL Statements (continued)

If you want to	Use this statement
Recompile a stored procedure	ALTER PROCEDURE
Recompile a view	ALTER VIEW
Recreate a control file	CREATE CONTROLFILE
Recreate SQL commands to build the database to the trace file	ALTER DATABASE
Remove a cluster from the database	DROP CLUSTER
Remove a database link from the database	DROP DATABASE LINK
Remove a dimension from the database	DROP DIMENSION
Remove a directory object from the database	DROP DIRECTORY
Remove a function from the database	DROP FUNCTION
Remove a materialized view (or snapshot) from the database	DROP MATERIALIZED VIEW
Remove a materialized view log from the database	DROP MATERIALIZED VIEW LOG
Remove a PL/SQL package from the database	DROP PACKAGE
Remove a profile from the database	DROP PROFILE
Remove a public or private synonym from the database	DROP SYNONYM
Remove a resource limit from an existing profile	ALTER PROFILE
Remove a role from the database	DROP ROLE
Remove a rollback segment from the database	DROP ROLLBACK SEGMENT
Remove a sequence from the database	DROP SEQUENCE
Remove a snapshot from the database	DROP SNAPSHOT
Remove a snapshot log from the database	DROP SNAPSHOT LOG
Remove a system privilege or role from one or more users and/or roles	REVOKE
Remove a tablespace from the database	DROP TABLESPACE
Remove a trigger from the database	DROP TRIGGER
Remove a user from the database	DROP USER
Remove a view from the database	DROP VIEW
Remove an index from the database	DROP INDEX
Remove privileges on a database object from one or more users or roles	REVOKE
Remove statistics about an object in the database	ANALYZE
Remove a table from the database	DROP TABLE
Rename an existing table, view, sequence, or private synonym	RENAME
Shrink a rollback segment to an optimal or given size	ALTER ROLLBACK SEGMENT

Table 2-1. Common DDL Tasks and Their Corresponding SQL Statements (continued)

If you want to	Use this statement
Specify a formula to calculate the total cost of resources used by a session	ALTER RESOURCE COST
Start backup of a tablespace by placing it in backup mode	ALTER TABLESPACE
Stop auditing defined by a prior AUDIT statement	NOAUDIT
Stop backup of a tablespace	ALTER TABLESPACE
Take a data file online/offline	ALTER DATABASE
Take a tablespace online/offline	ALTER TABLESPACE
Validate the structure of a table, index, or cluster	ANALYZE
Validate the structure of an object in the database	ANALYZE

SQL Statement Syntax

This section provides a detailed reference to each of the SQL statements used to create and maintain database objects. Each statement is listed in at least one of its forms, with a short explanation of the statement's purposes, its exact syntax and associated parameters, an example, and usage notes when applicable.

 Many of these statements are normally used only for administration of a database and are typically issued by a DBA. For this reason, many statements require specific privileges. Some statements also apply only when specific Oracle options, such as the Partition Option or the Object Option, are installed.

ALTER RESOURCE COST

```
ALTER RESOURCE COST
    [CPU_PER_SESSION weight]
    [CONNECT_TIME weight]
    [LOGICAL_READS_PER_SESSION weight]
    [PRIVATE_SGA weight]
```

Modifies the formula used to calculate the session's total resource cost. This cost may then be limited by the COMPOSITE_LIMIT parameter in a user's profile.

Keywords

CPU_PER_SESSION
    Specifies the amount of CPU time used in a session (in hundredths of a second).

CONNECT_TIME
    Specifies the total elapsed time for a session (in minutes).

LOGICAL_READS_PER_SESSION

Specifies the number of database blocks read in a session, including those read from memory and disk.

PRIVATE_SGA

Specifies the amount of memory a session can allocate in the shared pool of the System Global Area (SGA) (in bytes). Only applies when using the multi-threaded server and allocating private space in the SGA for the session.

weight

Integer weight of each resource.

The total resource cost is calculated by multiplying the amount of each resource used in the session by the weight assigned to that resource, and adding the products for all four resources. The result is expressed in service units. You must activate the ALTER RESOURCE COST privilege to issue this statement.

Example

Assign weights to CPU_PER_SESSION and CONNECT_TIME:

```
ALTER RESOURCE COST
      CPU_PER_SESSION 100
      CONNECT_TIME 2
```

The resulting cost in service units (SU) is calculated as:

```
SU = (CPU_Time*100) + Connect_Time*2;
```

ALTER SESSION

See Chapter 3 for a full description of this statement.

ALTER SYSTEM

```
ALTER SYSTEM
 {[SET
   {[RESOURCE_LIMIT = TRUE | FALSE] |
    [GLOBAL_NAMES = TRUE | FALSE] |
    [MTS_SERVERS = integer] |
    [MTS_DISPATCHERS = 'protocol, integer'] |
    [LICENSE_MAX_SESSIONS = integer] |
    [LICENSE_SESSIONS_WARNING = integer] |
    [LICENSE_MAX_USERS = integer]
   }] |
  [ENABLE RESTRICTED SESSION] |
  [DISABLE RESTRICTED SESSION] |
```

```
[FLUSH SHARED POOL] |
[CHECKPOINT [GLOBAL | LOCAL]] |
[CHECK DATAFILES GLOBAL | LOCAL] |
[SWITCH LOGFILE] |
[ENABLE DISTRIBUTED RECOVERY] |
[DISABLE DISTRIBUTED RECOVERY] |
[DISCONNECT SESSION 'sid_integer, session_integer' [POST_TRANSACTION] [IMMEDIATE]] |
[SUSPEND | RESUME]
[KILL SESSION 'sid_integer, session_integer' [IMMEDIATE]] |
[ARCHIVE_LOG [THREAD integer]
  {[START [TO 'destination']]
   [STOP]
   [SEQUENCE integer [TO 'destination']]
   [CHANGE integer [TO 'destination']]
   [CURRENT [TO 'destination']]
   [GROUP integer [TO 'destination']]
   [LOGFILE 'filename' [TO 'destination']]
   [NEXT [TO 'destination']]
   [ALL [TO 'destination']]
  }
}
```

Makes dynamic changes to a database instance.

Keywords

RESOURCE_LIMIT

Specifies whether resource limits will be enforced (TRUE) or not enforced (FALSE).

GLOBAL_NAMES

Specifies whether global naming will be enforced (TRUE) or not enforced (FALSE).

MTS_SERVERS

Changes the minimum number of shared multithreaded server (MTS) processes.

MTS_DISPATCHERS

Changes the number of dispatcher processes for the named protocol. The database must be open to issue this statement.

LICENSE_MAX_SESSIONS

Specifies the maximum number of sessions permitted on this instance. A value of 0 indicates no limit.

LICENSE_SESSIONS_WARNING

Specifies the maximum number of sessions permitted on this instance before a warning message is written to the alert log file. A value of 0 indicates no limit.

LICENSE_MAX_USERS

Specifies the maximum number of users in this database. A value of 0 indicates no limit.

ENABLE RESTRICTED SESSION

Allows only users with the RESTRICTED SESSION privilege to log on to the instance. The database may be dismounted, mounted, open, or closed when issuing this statement.

DISABLE RESTRICTED SESSION

Allows any user with the CREATE SESSION privilege to log on to the instance. The database may be dismounted, mounted, open, or closed when issuing this statement.

FLUSH SHARED POOL

Clears all data from the instance's shared pool. The database may be dismounted, mounted, open, or closed when issuing this statement.

CHECKPOINT

Causes Oracle to perform a GLOBAL or LOCAL checkpoint. GLOBAL performs a checkpoint for all instances that have opened the database; LOCAL performs a checkpoint only for the instance to which you are connected. The database may be open or closed when issuing this statement.

CHECK DATAFILES

Verifies access to online data files. GLOBAL verifies that all instances that have opened the database can access the datafiles, while LOCAL verifies that the instance to which you are connected can access the datafiles. The database may be open or closed when issuing this statement.

SWITCH LOGFILE

Causes Oracle to switch redo log file groups.

ENABLE DISTRIBUTED RECOVERY

Specifies that distributed recovery is to be enabled and, in a single-process environment, is used to initiate distributed recovery.

DISABLE DISTRIBUTED RECOVERY

Specifies that distributed recovery is to be disabled.

DISCONNECT SESSION

Disconnects the specified session from the database by killing the dedicated server process or the MTS virtual circuit.

POST_TRANSACTION

Specifies that ongoing transactions be completed before the session is disconnected.

IMMEDIATE

Specifies that the session be disconnected immediately, without waiting for transactions to complete. If POST_TRANSACTION is specified, this keyword will be ignored.

KILL SESSION

Terminates a session using SID and SERIAL# from the V$SESSION view. If the session is waiting for an activity, such as an operation on a remote database, to complete, Oracle will wait until this activity is complete unless IMMEDIATE is specified.

SUSPEND

Specifies that all I/O activity for all instances should be suspended until an ALTER SYSTEM RESUME command is issued. All tablespaces should be in hot backup mode before issuing this statement.

RESUME

Specifies that normal I/O operations should be resumed following an ALTER SYSTEM SUSPEND statement.

ARCHIVE_LOG

Manually archives redo log file groups or enables/disables automatic archiving.

THREAD

Specifies the thread containing the redo log file group to be archived. This parameter is required only when running the Oracle Parallel Server option in parallel mode.

START

Enables automatic archiving of redo log groups.

STOP

Disables automatic archiving of redo log groups.

SEQUENCE

Specifies the log sequence number of the redo log file group to be manually archived. The database must be mounted, but may be open or closed to issue this statement.

CHANGE

Manually archives the online redo log file group containing the redo log entry with the system change number (SCN) specified by the *integer*. If the SCN is the current log group, a log switch is performed. The database must be open to use this parameter.

CURRENT

Manually forces a log switch and archives the current redo log file group. The database must be open to use this parameter.

GROUP

Manually archives the online redo log file group with the specified GROUP value, which can be found in the DBA_LOG_FILES parameter in the *INIT.ORA* file. The database must be mounted, but may be open or closed when issuing this statement.

LOGFILE

Manually archives the online redo log file group containing the log file member identified by *filename*. The database must be mounted, but may be open or closed when issuing this statement.

NEXT

Manually archives the next online redo log file group that is full but has not yet been archived. The database must be mounted, but may be open or closed when issuing this statement.

ALL

Manually archives all online redo log file groups that are full, but that have not yet been archived. The database must be mounted, but may be open or closed when issuing this statement.

 Except as noted, the database must be mounted and open to issue these statements.

Examples

Change the number of dispatcher processes to 10 for TCP and 8 for DECNet:

```
ALTER SYSTEM
    SET MTS_DISPATCHERS = 'TCP,10'
        MTS_DISPATCHERS = 'DECnet,8';
```

Enforce Oracle licensing by setting the maximum number of sessions to 100 and the warning threshold to 80:

```
ALTER SYSTEM
    SET LICENSE_MAX_SESSIONS = 100
        LICENSE_SESSIONS_WARNING = 80;
```

Archive log sequence number 123 to the specified location:

```
ALTER SYSTEM
    ARCHIVE LOG SEQ 123 TO '/disk09/oracle/archive';
```

ANALYZE

See Chapter 3 for a complete description of this statement.

ASSOCIATE STATISTICS

```
ASSOCIATE STATISTICS WITH
 {COLUMNS [schema.]table.column[, [schema.]table.column...] |
  FUNCTIONS [schema.]function[,[schema.]function...] |
  PACKAGES [schema.]package[,[schema.]package...] |
  INDEXES [schema.]index[,[schema.]index...] |
 }
 {USING [schema.]statistics_type |
  DEFAULT COST (cpu_cost,io_cost,network_cost) |
  DEFAULT SELECTIVITY default_selectivity
 }
```

Associates a method of statistics computation with database objects.

Keywords

COLUMNS

Specifies that a list of columns will be provided.

schema

The schema containing the specified table.

table

The name of the table containing the specified column.

column

The column name for which an association is defined.

FUNCTIONS

Specifies that one or more functions will be associated.

PACKAGES

Specifies that one or more packages will be associated.

INDEXES

Specifies that one or more indexes will be associated.

USING statistics_type

Specifies the statistics type being associated.

DEFAULT COST

Specifies that default costs will be provided for CPU, I/O, and the network. This keyword is not valid if the COLUMNS keyword is used.

cpu_cost

Integer representing the CPU cost of a single execution or access.

io_cost

Integer representing the I/O cost of a single execution or access.

network_cost

Integer representing the network cost of a single execution or access.

DEFAULT SELECTIVITY default_selectivity

Specifies an integer between 1 and 100, representing the default selectivity as a percentage. This keyword is not valid if the COLUMNS keyword is used.

 To remove or disassociate statistics from an object, use the DISASSO-CIATE STATISTICS command.

Example

Create an associate for the emp_sal function using the cost function cost_funct:

```
ASSOCIATE STATISTICS WITH FUNCTIONS emp_sal USING cost_funct;
```

AUDIT (Schema Objects)

```
AUDIT {object_option[,object_option ...] | ALL}
ON {[schema.]objectname | DIRECTORY directory_name | DEFAULT}
[BY SESSION [WHENEVER [NOT] SUCCESSFUL]
[BY ACCESS [WHENEVER [NOT] SUCCESSFUL]
```

Sets up auditing for a specific schema object.

Keywords

object_option

Indicates that a particular operation will be audited. The following operations are valid: ALTER, AUDIT, COMMENT, DELETE, EXECUTE, GRANT, INDEX, INSERT, LOCK, RENAME, SELECT, and UPDATE. The keyword ALL specifies all the operations.

object_name

Specifies the name of the schema object to be audited.

DIRECTORY directory_name

Specifies the name of a directory to audit.

DEFAULT

Establishes the specified object option as the default for objects that have not yet been created.

BY SESSION

Causes Oracle to write a single record for all SQL statements of the same type issued in the same session.

BY ACCESS

Causes Oracle to write a single record for each audited statement.

WHENEVER SUCCESSFUL

Chooses auditing only for SQL statements that complete successfully.

WHENEVER NOT SUCCESSFUL

Chooses auditing only for SQL statements that fail or result in errors.

Examples

Audit for any UPDATE statement issued for scott's bonus table:

```
AUDIT UPDATE ON scott.bonus;
```

Audit for any unsuccessful operation on scott's emp table:

```
AUDIT ALL ON scott.emp WHENEVER NOT SUCCESSFUL;
```

AUDIT (SQL Statements)

```
AUDIT {system_option | sql_option}[,{system_option | sql_option ...}]
{[BY username[,username ...]] |
 [BY PROXY [ON BEHALF OF {ANY|username[,username]]}
}
{[BY SESSION] [WHENEVER [NOT] SUCCESSFUL] |
 [BY ACCESS] [WHENEVER [NOT] SUCCESSFUL]
}
```

Sets up auditing for specific SQL statements in subsequent user sessions.

Keywords

system_option

Specifies that SQL statements authorized by the named system privilege be audited.

sql_option

Specifies a set of SQL statements to be audited.

BY username

Specifies that SQL statements issued by the named user be audited.

BY proxy

Specifies that SQL statements issued by the specified proxy be audited.

ON BEHALF OF ANY

Specifies that SQL statements issued on behalf of any user be audited.

ON BEHALF OF user

Specifies the user on whose behalf the proxy executes the specified statement.

BY SESSION

Causes Oracle to write a single record for all SQL statements of the same type issued in the same session.

BY ACCESS

Causes Oracle to write a single record for each audited statement.

WHENEVER SUCCESSFUL

Chooses auditing only for SQL statements that complete successfully.

WHENEVER NOT SUCCESSFUL

Chooses auditing only for SQL statements that fail or result in errors.

Audit records are written to the audit trail, which is a database table containing audit records that can be accessed through data dictionary views. Auditing must be enabled using the AUDIT_TRAIL parameter in the *INIT.ORA* file.

Example

Audit for any unsuccessful SELECT statement (which may indicate an attempt to read a table for which a user has not been granted access):

```
AUDIT SELECT TABLE
    WHENEVER NOT SUCCESSFUL;
```

CALL

```
CALL [schema.][package.]{function | procedure}[@dblink]
    (expression[,expression…]) [INTO :host_variable [[INDICATOR] :indicator_variable]]
```

Executes a stored PL/SQL function or procedure.

Keywords

schema

Specifies the name of the schema that contains the package, function, or procedure.

package

Specifies the name of the package that contains the function or procedure.

function

Specifies the name of a function to be executed.

procedure

Specifies the name of a procedure to be executed.

dblink

Specifies the name of a database link.

expression

Specifies an argument to the function or procedure.

INTO

Specifies for a function the name of the host variable that will hold the return value.

INDICATOR

Specifies the name of a variable that will indicate the condition of the host variable.

COMMENT

```
COMMENT ON {TABLE [schema.]{table | view | snapshot} |
         COLUMN [schema.]{table | view | snapshot}.column
         }
IS 'text'
```

Adds a comment about a table, view, snapshot, or column into the data dictionary.

Keywords

schema

Specifies the name of a schema containing the table, view, or snapshot that will have a comment associated with it. If *schema* is omitted, the current schema is assumed.

TABLE

Specifies that the comment be associated with a table, view, or snapshot.

table

Specifies the name of a table with which the comment will be associated.

view

Specifies the name of a view with which the comment will be associated.

snapshot

Specifies the name of a snapshot with which the comment will be associated.

COLUMN

Specifies that the comment be associated with a column.

column

Specifies the name of the column to be commented.

text

The actual text of the comment. This text will be recorded in the data dictionary.

You can use the COMMENT ON COLUMN command to drop a comment. Simply set the comment to a null string ('').

Example

Add a comment to the ename column of scott's emp table:

```
COMMENT ON COLUMN scott.emp.ename IS 'Last name from personnel records';
```

CREATE/ALTER/DROP CLUSTER

```
CREATE CLUSTER [schema.]clustername
  (column  datatype[, column  datatype ...])
  [Physical_Attributes_Clause]
  [SIZE integer [K | M]]
  [TABLESPACE tsname]
  [STORAGE Storage_Clause]
  [INDEX]
  [[SINGLE TABLE] HASHKEYS integer HASH IS expression]
  [{PARALLEL [integer] | NOPARALLEL}]
  [CACHE | NOCACHE]
```

Creates a cluster, which is a schema object containing one or more tables with one or more columns in common.

```
ALTER CLUSTER [schema.]clustername
[SIZE integer[K | M]]
[Physical_Attributes_Clause]
[STORAGE Storage_Clause]
[{PARALLEL [integer] | NOPARALLEL}]
[ALLOCATE EXTENT
  (EXTSIZE integer[K | M] [DATAFILE 'filename'] [INSTANCE integer])]
```

Redefines future storage allocations or allocates an extent for a cluster.

```
DROP CLUSTER [schema.]clustername
[INCLUDING TABLES]
[CASCADE CONSTRAINTS]
```

Removes a cluster from the database.

Keywords

cluster_name

Specifies the name of the cluster.

column

Specifies the name of the column that defines the cluster key.

datatype

Specifies the datatype of the column.

PCTUSED

Changes the minimum percentage of used space that Oracle will maintain in each block. Values can range from 0 to 99, and the default is 40.

PCTFREE

Changes the percentage of space kept free for future updates to the rows contained in this cluster. Values can range from 0 to 99, and the default is 10.

INITTRANS

Changes the number of transaction entries allocated to each block in the cluster. Values can range from 1 to 255, but should not normally be changed from the default of 2.

MAXTRANS

Changes the maximum number of concurrent transactions that can update a block of the cluster. Values can range from 1 to 255, but should not normally be changed from the default, which is a function of the Oracle block size.

SIZE

Determines how much space is allocated to store rows with the same cluster key. The value should be a divisor of the Oracle block size, and will be rounded up to the next larger divisor if necessary.

TABLESPACE

Specifies the name of the tablespace where this cluster will be stored. If omitted, the default tablespace for the schema owner will be used.

STORAGE Storage_Clause

Specifies the physical storage characteristics. See Chapter 4, *Common SQL Elements*, for detailed information.

INDEX

Specifies that an indexed cluster be created. This keyword is not valid for a hash cluster.

SINGLE TABLE

Specifies that this cluster is a special type containing only one table.

HASHKEYS integer

Specifies that a hash cluster be created with *integer* hash keys.

HASH IS expression

Specifies an expression to be used as the hash function for the hash cluster.

NOPARALLEL

Specifies that the cluster be created serially. This is the default.

PARALLEL [integer]

Specifies that Oracle will select a degree of parallelism equal to the number of CPUs available on all participating instances, multiplied by the value of the PARALLEL_THREADS_PER_CPU initialization parameter. If *integer* is specified, it indicates the degree of parallelism.

CACHE

Specifies that the blocks retrieved for this table are placed at the most recently used end of the buffer cache when a full table scan is performed.

NOCACHE

Specifies that the blocks retrieved for this table are placed at the least recently used end of the buffer cache when a full table scan is performed. This is the default.

EXTSIZE integer

Specifies the size of the new extent in bytes, kilobytes, or megabytes.

DATAFILE

Specifies the name of the operating system datafile in the tablespace containing this cluster that is to hold the new extent. If omitted, Oracle will select a datafile.

INSTANCE

Makes the new extent available to the specified instance, which is identified by the initialization parameter INSTANCE_NUMBER. This parameter can only be used when running in parallel mode.

INCLUDING TABLES

Specifies that all tables belonging to the cluster be dropped.

CASCADE CONSTRAINTS

Specifies that all referential integrity constraints from tables outside the cluster referring to primary and unique keys in the cluster's tables will be dropped.

 Clustering can improve database performance and efficiency. Common columns are stored only once, and the data from all tables is normally stored contiguously.

Examples

Create a cluster in scott's schema that will allocate 512 bytes per block to cluster keys and allow a maximum of 20 extents for the cluster. All other values will be defaults:

```
CREATE CLUSTER demo.employee
    SIZE 512K
    STORAGE (MAXEXTENTS 20);
```

Alter an existing cluster to allocate 512 bytes per block to cluster keys and allow a maximum of 20 extents for the cluster:

```
ALTER CLUSTER demo.employee
    SIZE 512K
    STORAGE (MAXEXTENTS 20);
```

Remove a cluster and all the tables it contains from the database:

```
DROP CLUSTER demo.employee INCLUDING TABLES;
```

CREATE CONTROLFILE

```
CREATE CONTROLFILE [REUSE] [SET] DATABASE dbname
LOGFILE [GROUP integer] filespec[,[GROUP integer] filespec ...]
{RESETLOGS | NORESETLOGS}
[MAXLOGFILES integer]
[MAXLOGMEMBERS integer]
[MAXLOGHISTORY integer]
[MAXDATAFILES integer]
[MAXINSTANCES integer]
[ARCHIVELOG | NOARCHIVELOG]
DATAFILE (filespec[,filespec ...])
CHARACTER SET character_set
```

Recreates a control file, allowing changes to some parameters.

Keywords

REUSE

> Specifies that one or more existing control files specified in *INIT.ORA* can be reused and overwritten. If this keyword is omitted and if any of the control files named in *INIT.ORA* exists, an error will result.

SET

> Specifies that the supplied *dbname* will be a new name for the database. Valid names are one to eight characters long.

DATABASE

> Specifies the name of the database. Unless you use the SET command, this must be the current name of the database.

LOGFILE

> Specifies members of all redo log file groups, which must all exist.

RESETLOGS

> Specifies that the contents of the log files listed in the LOGFILE clause should be ignored. Each file listed in the LOGFILE clause must have a SIZE specified.

NORESETLOGS

> Specifies that all files listed in the LOGFILE clause (which must be current redo log files and not restored from backups) should be reused with their original sizes.

MAXLOGFILES

> Specifies the maximum number of redo log file groups that can ever be created for the database. The default and maximum values are operating system-dependent. This value must be at least 2, and should be at least 3.

MAXLOGMEMBERS

Specifies the maximum number of redo log group copies that may exist in the database. The minimum is 1, and the default and maximum are operating system-dependent.

MAXLOGHISTORY

Specifies the maximum number of archived redo log file groups for automatic media recovery of the Parallel Server. The minimum value is 1, and the default and maximum are operating system-dependent.

MAXDATAFILES

Specifies the maximum number of datafiles that can ever be created for the database. The minimum is 1, but it should never be set lower than the largest number of datafiles ever created in the database.

MAXINSTANCES

Specifies the maximum number of instances that can have the database mounted and open. This parameter applies only to the Parallel Server.

ARCHIVELOG

Specifies that the database will be run in archivelog mode.

NOARCHIVELOG

Specifies that the database will not be run in archivelog mode and that online redo log files will be reused. This option is the default.

DATAFILE

Specifies the names of all datafiles in the database, which must all exist.

character_set

Specifies the name of the character set used to create the database, if different from the default.

 I strongly recommend that you back up the entire database, including control files and redo log files, before you issue this command.

Example

Recreate a control file for a database called TEST:

```
CREATE CONTROLFILE REUSE DATABASE TEST
    LOGFILE GROUP 1 ('/disk01/oracle/log1.log','/disk02/oracle/log1.log')
            GROUP 2 ('/disk03/oracle/log2.log','/disk04/oracle/log2.log')
    NORESETLOGS
    DATAFILE '/disk10/oradata/db01.dbs'
    MAXLOGFILES 6
    MAXDATAFILES 128
    ARCHIVELOG;
```

CREATE/ALTER DATABASE

```
CREATE DATABASE [dbname]
CONTROLFILE [REUSE]
LOGFILE [GROUP integer] (filespec[,[GROUP integer] filespec ...])
[MAXLOGFILES integer]
[MAXLOGMEMBERS integer]
[MAXLOGHISTORY integer]
[MAXDATAFILES integer]
[MAXINSTANCES integer]
[ARCHIVELOG | NOARCHIVELOG]
[CHARACTER SET charset
[NATIONAL CHARACTER SET charset
DATAFILE (filespec[,filespec ...])[Autoextend_Clause]
```

Creates a database and specifies parameters associated with it.

```
ALTER DATABASE [dbname]
  {ARCHIVELOG | NOARCHIVELOG |
   MOUNT [[STANDBY | CLONE] DATABASE] |
   CONVERT |
   OPEN [READ WRITE [RESETLOGS | NORESETLOGS] | READ ONLY] |
   ACTIVATE STANDBY DATABASE |
   RENAME FILE 'filename` [,'filename' ...] TO 'filename` [,'filename' ...]  |
   RENAME GLOBAL_NAME TO database[.domain[.domain ...]] |
   RESET COMPATIBILITY |
   ENABLE [PUBLIC] THREAD integer |
   DISABLE THREAD integer |
   CHARACTER SET character_set |
   NATIONAL CHARACTER SET character_set |
   CREATE DATAFILE 'filename'[,'filename' ...] [AS filespec] |
   DATAFILE 'filename'[,'filename' ...]
     {ONLINE |
      OFFLINE [DROP} |
      RESIZE integer[K | M] |
      END BACKUP |
      Autoextend_Clause
     } |
   TEMPFILE 'filename'[,'filename' ...]
     {ONLINE |
      OFFLINE
      DROP |
      RESIZE integer[K | M] |
      Autoextend_Clause
     } |
   ADD LOGFILE [THREAD integer]
    [GROUP integer] filespec[,[GROUP integer] filespec ...] |
   ADD LOGFILE MEMBER 'filename' [RESUSE] [,'filename' [RESUSE] ...]
    TO logfile_descriptor[,logfile_descriptor ...] |
   DROP {GROUP integer | 'filename` | ('filename','filename'[,'filename' ...])} |
   DROP LOGFILE MEMBER 'filename'[,'filename' ...] |
   CREATE STANDBY CONTROLFILE AS 'filename' [REUSE] |
   BACKUP CONTROLFILE TO {'filename' [REUSE] | TRACE {RESETLOGS | NORESETLOGS]} |
   RECOVER [AUTOMATIC FROM 'location']
```

```
RECOVER [STANDBY] DATABASE [UNTIL {CANCEL | TIME date | CHANGE integer}] |
RECOVER [STANDBY] DATABASE USING BACKUP CONTROLFILE |
RECOVER [STANDBY] TABLESPACE {tablespace | DATAFILE 'filename'}
  UNTIL [CONSISTENT WITH] CONTROLFILE |
RECOVER TABLESPACE tablespace[,tablespace ...] |
RECOVER DATAFILE filename[,filename] |
RECOVER LOGFILE filename[,filename] |
RECOVER CONTINUE [DEFAULT] |
RECOVER CANCEL |
RECOVER MANAGED STANDBY DATABASE {TIMEOUT integer | CANCEL [IMMEDIATE]}
```

Changes one or more characteristics of an existing database.

Keywords

dbname

Specifies the name of the database. May be one to eight characters long and must not be a reserved word.

CONTROL FILE REUSE

Specifies that one or more existing control files specified in *INIT.ORA* can be reused and overwritten. If this keyword is omitted and any of the control files named in *INIT.ORA* exists, an error will result. If the parameters specified require that the control file be larger than the current size, the command will fail. Note that this option is not normally used for a new database creation.

LOGFILE

Specifies the names of one or more redo log files to be created.

MAXLOGFILES

Specifies the maximum number of redo log file groups that can ever be created for the database. The default and maximum value are operating system-dependent. This value must be at least 2, and should be at least 3.

MAXLOGMEMBERS

Specifies the maximum number of copies of a redo log group that may exist in the database. The minimum is 1, and the default and maximum are operating system-dependent.

MAXLOGHISTORY

Specifies the maximum number of archived redo log file groups for automatic media recovery of the Parallel Server. The minimum value is 1, and the default and maximum are operating system-dependent.

MAXDATAFILES

Specifies the maximum number of datafiles that can ever be created for the database. The minimum is 1, but it should never be set lower than the largest number of datafiles ever created in the database.

MAXINSTANCES

Specifies the maximum number of instances that can have the database mounted and open. This parameter applies only to the Parallel Server.

ARCHIVELOG

Specifies that the database will be run in archivelog mode, which means that a redo log group must be archived before the redo log group can be reused. If the group has not been archived, the database will halt until archiving occurs successfully. This mode is required to perform media recovery.

NOARCHIVELOG

Specifies that redo log groups will not be archived and may be reused immediately by Oracle. This option is the default.

CHARACTER SET

Specifies the character set that the database will use to store data. This character set cannot be changed after database creation. The choices and default are operating system-dependent.

NATIONAL CHARACTER SET

Specifies the national character set that will be used for specifically designated columns. If omitted, the default database character set is used.

DATAFILE

Specifies the names of all datafiles in the database. If omitted, a single datafile will be created by default for the SYSTEM tablespace.

Autoextend_Clause

Specifies whether a data file will be extended automatically. See Chapter 4 for more details.

MOUNT STANDBY DATABASE

Specifies that the standby database be mounted.

MOUNT CLONE DATABASE

Specifies that the clone database be mounted.

CONVERT

Specifies that the database data dictionary be converted from Oracle7 to Oracle8 or Oracle8*i*.

OPEN READ WRITE

Specifies that the database be opened in read/write mode. This option is the default.

RESETLOGS

Resets the log sequence number to 1 and invalidates all redo entries in the existing online and archived log files. This option should only be specified after performing incomplete media recovery or when opening the database after performing media recovery with a backup control file; otherwise, NORE-SETLOGS should be used. If the database is opened with the RESETLOGS keyword, you should immediately perform a complete backup of the database.

NORESETLOGS

Makes no change to the status of the current log sequence number and redo log entries.

OPEN READ ONLY

Specifies that the database be opened in read-only mode, which makes queries possible but disables write operations.

ACTIVATE STANDBY DATABASE

Specifies that the state of the database be changed from standby to active.

RENAME FILE filename1 TO filename2

Specifies that the name of a datafile, temporary file, or log file be changed in the control file. Note that this keyword does not affect the name of the operating system file.

RENAME GLOBAL NAME TO

Specifies that the global name of the database be changed to the supplied value, which may be up to eight characters.

RESET COMPATIBILITY

Specifies that the compatibility of the database be reset to the version specified. This change is effective the next time the database is started.

ENABLE THREAD

Specifies that the thread of redo log files is enabled in a Parallel Server environment. If the keyword PUBLIC is specified, the enabled thread is available to any instance. Otherwise, the thread is available only to an instance that specifically requests it.

DISABLE THREAD

Specifies that the thread of redo log files is disabled and made unavailable to all instance of a Parallel Server environment.

CREATE DATAFILE

Specifies that a new empty datafile be created in place of an old one (which may have been lost without backup). Media recovery must be performed before the datafile is usable.

ONLINE

Specifies that the datafile is to be brought online.

OFFLINE

Specifies that the datafile is to be brought offline.

RESIZE

Specifies that the size of the datafile is to be increased or decreased to the indicated size.

END BACKUP

Specifies that media recovery will not be performed when the database starts after a hot backup was interrupted.

TEMPFILE

Specifies that changes be made to a temporary datafile.

DROP

Specifies that the temporary datafile be removed from the database.

ADD LOGFILE

Specifies that one or more redo log file groups be added. THREAD may be indicated in a Parallel Server environment.

ADD LOGFILE MEMBER

Specifies that a new member *filename* be added to an existing redo log file group. REUSE may be used to indicate that *filename* already exists.

logfile_descriptor

Specifies an existing redo log file group either as GROUP *integer* or as a list of *filenames.*

DROP GROUP

Specifies that the entire redo log file group is to be dropped after an ALTER SYSTEM SWITCH LOGFILE statement has been issued. The dropped group may be specified either as GROUP *integer* or as a list of *filenames.*

DROP LOGFILE MEMBER filename

Specifies that one or more individual redo log file members be dropped.

CREATE STANDBY CONTROL FILE

Specifies that a control file be created to maintain a standby database.

BACKUP CONTROL FILE TO

Specifies that the current control file be backed up to the indicated *filename.* If the keywords TO TRACE are specified, a set of SQL statements will be written to the trace file instead of creating a backup of the control file. If RESET-LOGS is specified, the SQL statements written will include ALTER DATABASE OPEN RESETLOGS. If NORESETLOGS is specified, the SQL statement ALTER DATABASE OPEN NORESETLOGS will be written.

RECOVER FROM

Specifies the location from which archived redo log files required for recovery will be read. If the keyword AUTOMATIC is specified, the name of the next archived redo log file required for recovery will be generated, using the LOG_ ARCHIVE_DEST and LOG_ARCHIVE_FORMAT initialization parameters.

RECOVER DATABASE

Specifies that the entire database be recovered. If the STANDBY keyword is supplied, the standby database will be recovered using the control file and archived redo log files from the primary database. The keywords UNTIL CANCELLED may be supplied, specifying that the database be recovered until the operation is canceled using the RECOVER CANCEL clause. The TIME keyword specifies that time-based recovery be performed up to the supplied time. The CHANGE keyword indicates that recovery will be performed to just before the specified system change number.

RECOVER DATABASE USING BACKUP CONTROL FILE

Specifies that a backup control file (instead of the current control file) be used.

RECOVER STANDBY TABLESPACE UNTIL CONSISTENT WITH CONTROL FILE

Specifies that *tablespace* on an old standby database be recovered using the control file from the current standby database.

RECOVER STANDBY DATAFILE UNTIL CONSISTENT WITH CONTROL FILE

Specifies that *datafile* on an old standby database be recovered using the control file from the current standby database.

RECOVER TABLESPACE

Specifies one or more tablespaces (which must be offline) to be recovered.

RECOVER DATAFILE

Specifies one or more datafiles (which must be offline) to be recovered.

RECOVER LOGFILE

Specifies that media recovery should continue using the log file(s) supplied.

RECOVER CONTINUE DEFAULT

Specifies that recovery will continue using the redo log file that would be automatically generated. This keyword is equivalent to RECOVER AUTOMATIC, except that no prompt for filenames exists.

RECOVER CONTINUE

Specifies that recovery of multiple instances should continue after it was interrupted to disable a thread.

RECOVER CANCEL

Specifies that cancel-based recovery be ended.

RECOVER MANAGED STANDBY DATABASE

Specifies that recovery should occur using sustained standby recovery mode, which assumes the standby database as an active component.

TIMEOUT

Specifies the number of minutes to wait for a requested archived redo log file to become available for writing to the standby database.

CANCEL

Specifies that sustained recovery be ended after the current archived redo file has been applied, unless the IMMEDIATE keyword, which terminates after applying the next redo log file read is specified.

Example

Create a new database called TEST:

```
CREATE DATABASE TEST
LOGFILE GROUP 1 ('/disk01/oracle/log1.log','/disk02/oracle/log2.log')
             SIZE 50K,
         GROUP 2 ('/disk03/oracle/log2.log','/disk04/oracle/log2.log')
             SIZE 50K
MAXLOGIFLES 5
DATAFILE '/disk10/oradata/system01.dbf' SIZE 50M
MAXDATAFILES 100
ACHIVELOG;
```

CREATE/DROP DATABASE LINK

```
CREATE [SHARED] [PUBLIC] DATABASE LINK dblink
   [CONNECT TO {CURRENT USER |
              username IDENTIFIED BY password
                [AUTHENTICATED BY username IDENTIFIED BY password]
          }]
   [USING 'connect string']
```

Creates a database link, which allows access to objects on a remote database.

```
DROP [PUBLIC] DATABASE LINK dblink
```

Removes a database link from the database.

Keywords

dblink

Specifies the name of the database link being created. Must be a valid Oracle object name.

SHARED

Specifies that a single network connection be shared across users when the multithreaded server is configured.

PUBLIC

Specifies that the database link will be available to all users. If omitted, the database link is private and available only to you.

CONNECT TO CURRENT USER

Specifies that a current user database link be created, which requires a global user with a valid account on the remote database.

CONNECT TO username

Specifies the username and password used to connect to the remote database.

AUTHENTICATED BY

Specifies a *username* and *password* on the remote database to be used for authentication when the SHARED keyword is used.

USING

Specifies the Net8 database specification for the remote database.

 If the CONNECT TO clause is omitted, the account username and password currently logged in, not the username and password of the creator, will be used when the database link is invoked.

Examples

Create a public database link to scott's account on the TEST database:

```
CREATE PUBLIC DATABASE LINK testscott
CONNECT TO scott IDENTIFIED BY tiger
USING 'TEST';
```

Users on the local database may now access any of scott's objects for which they have privileges on the TEST database. For example, to select from the emp table on the remote database, you can use a SQL statement such as the following:

```
SELECT * FROM emp@testscott;
```

Remove the public database link named testscott from the database:

```
DROP PUBLIC DATABASE LINK empscott;
```

CREATE/DROP DIMENSION

```
CREATE [FORCE | NOFORCE] DIMENSION [schema.]dimension
LEVEL level IS {level_table.level_column |
               (level_table.level_column,level_table.level_column ...)}
HIERARCHY hierarchy (child_level CHILD OF parent_level
   [JOIN KEY {child_key_column | (child_key_column,child_key_column ...)}
    REFERENCES parent_level] |
ATTRIBUTE level DETERMINES {dependent_column | (dependent_column,
               dependent_column ...)}
```

Creates a dimension, which defines a parent-child relationship between pairs of column sets.

```
DROP DIMENSION [schema.]dimension
```

Removes a dimension from the database.

Keywords

FORCE

Specifies that the dimension be created, even if the referenced tables do not exist.

NOFORCE

Specifies that the dimension be created only if the referenced objects exist (default).

schema

Name of the schema in which this dimension will be created.

dimension

Name of the dimension.

LEVEL

Defines a level with a name that defines dimension hierarchies and attributes.

level_table.level_column

Specifies the columns (up to 32) for the level.

HIERARCHY

Specifies the name of a hierarchy.

child_level

Name of a level that has an *n*-to-1 relationship with a parent level.

CHILD OF

Specifies the name of a parent level.

JOIN KEY

Specifies the name of a column in the JOIN condition with a parent table.

REFERENCES

Specifies the name of the parent level.

ATTRIBUTE

Specifies the name of a level or hierarchy.

DETERMINES dependent_column

Specifies the name of a column that is dependent on an attribute level.

Examples

Create a dimension on the city, state, and country tables:

```
CREATE DIMENSION location
   LEVEL city_code     IS (city.city, city.state)
   LEVEL state_code    IS state.state
```

```
    LEVEL country_code  IS country.country
HIERARCHY region (
  City_code      CHILD OF
  State_code     CHILD OF
  Country_code
    JOIN KEY city.state REFERENCES state_code
    JOIN KEY state.country REFERENCES country_code;
```

Remove the dimension named location from the database:

```
DROP DIMENSION location;
```

CREATE/DROP DIRECTORY

```
CREATE [OR REPLACE] DIRECTORY directory_name AS 'path_name'
```

Creates a directory object that specifies an operating system directory for storing BFILE objects.

```
DROP DIRECTORY directory_name
```

Removes a directory object from the database.

Keywords

OR REPLACE

Specifies that this directory object should replace any existing directory object with the same name.

directory_name

Name of the directory object.

path_name

The operating system directory's full case-sensitive pathname.

Oracle does not check to see if the directory actually exists on the host operating system, so be sure to check the path you provide carefully.

Examples

Create a directory object graphic_home on the host disk storage system that an Oracle application will use for storing graphical images:

```
CREATE DIRECTORY graphic_home AS '/disk13/data/graphics';
```

Remove the directory object graphic_home:

```
DROP DIRECTORY graphic_home;
```

CREATE/ALTER/DROP FUNCTION

See Chapter 7, *PL/SQL*, for a complete description of these statements.

CREATE/ALTER/DROP INDEX

```
CREATE [UNIQUE | BITMAP] INDEX [schema.]indexname
ON {[[schema.]TABLE [alias] ({column|col_expr} [ASC | DESC]
                             [,{column|col_expr} [ASC | DESC] ...]) |
    CLUSTER [schema.]cluster
    }
[{[GLOBAL PARTITION BY RANGE (column_list)
     (Global_Partition_Clause[,Global_Partition_Clause...])
    [TABLESPACE {tablespace | DEFAULT}]
    [Physical_Attributes_Clause]
    [STORAGE Storage_Clause]
    [NOSORT | REVERSE]
    [UNRECOVERABLE | LOGGING | NOLOGGING]
    [ONLINE]
    [COMPUTE STATISTICS]
    [COMPRESS integer | NOCOMPRESS]
    [PARALLEL integer | NOPARALLEL] ] |
    [LOCAL (PARTITION partition
    [Physical_Attributes_Clause] [TABLESPACE tablespace] [LOGGING | NOLOGGING]
    [,PARTITION partition
    [Physical_Attributes_Clause] [TABLESPACE tablespace] [LOGGING | NOLOGGING] ...])
    [TABLESPACE {tablespace | DEFAULT}
    [Physical_Attributes_Clause]
    [STORAGE Storage_Clause]
    [NOSORT | REVERSE]
    [UNRECOVERABLE | LOGGING | NOLOGGING]
    [ONLINE]
    [COMPUTE STATISTICS]
    [COMPRESS integer | NOCOMPRESS]
    [PARALLEL integer | NOPARALLEL] ] |
[LOCAL {STORE IN {tablespace[,tablespace..]|DEFAULT) |
                 (PARTITION [partition] [TABLESPACE tablespace]
                   [,PARTITION [partition] [TABLESPACE tablespace] ...])
       }
   [TABLESPACE {tablespace | DEFAULT}
   [Physical_Attributes_Clause]
   [STORAGE Storage_Clause]
   [NOSORT | REVERSE]
   [UNRECOVERABLE | LOGGING | NOLOGGING]
   [ONLINE]
   [COMPUTE STATISTICS]
   [COMPRESS integer | NOCOMPRESS]
   [NOSORT | REVERSE]
   [PARALLEL integer | NOPARALLEL] ] |
[LOCAL {STORE IN (tablespace[,tablespace ...] | DEFAULT) |
       (PARTITION [partition]
          [Physical_Attributes_Clause]
```

```
              [TABLESPACE tablespace]
              {STORE IN {tablespace[,tablespace ...]|DEFAULT) |
                      (SUBPARTITION subpartition [TABLESPACE tablespace]
                      [,SUBPARTITION subpartition [TABLESPACE tablespace] ...]))
                      }
        }
   [TABLESPACE {tablespace | DEFAULT}
   [Physical_Attributes_Clause]
   [STORAGE Storage_Clause]
   [NOSORT | REVERSE]
   [UNRECOVERABLE | LOGGING | NOLOGGING]
   [ONLINE]
   [COMPUTE STATISTICS]
   [COMPRESS integer | NOCOMPRESS]
   [PARALLEL integer | NOPARALLEL]
}]
```

Creates an index on one or more columns of a table or cluster.

```
ALTER INDEX [schema.]indexname
[DEALLOCATE UNUSED [KEEP integer[K | M]]
[ALLOCATE EXTENT (
   [SIZE integer[K | M]]
   [DATAFILE 'filename']
   [INSTANCE integer])]
[PARALLEL integer | NOPARALLEL]
[Physical_Attributes_Clause]
[STORAGE Storage_Clause]
[UNRECOVERABLE | LOGGING | NOLOGGING]
[{REBUILD [{PARTITION partition | SUBPARTITION subpartition}]
    [PARALLEL integer | NOPARALLEL]
    [TABLESPACE tablespace]
    [ONLINE]
    [Physical_Attributes_Clause]
    [COMPRESS integer | NOCOMPRESS]
    [LOGGING | NOLOGGING] ] |
  REBUILD {REVERSE | NOREVERSE} |
  REBUILD PARAMETERS ('rebuild_parameters')
 }]
[PARAMETERS ('alter_parameters')]
[ENABLE | DISABLE]
[UNUSABLE]
[RENAME TO new_index_name]
[COALESCE]
[Partition_Clause]
```

Changes the characteristics of an index.

```
DROP INDEX [schema.]indexname
```

Removes an index from the database.

Keywords

UNIQUE

> Specifies that the value of the column(s) upon which the index is based must be unique.

BITMAP

> Specifies that the index be created as a bitmap rather than using the normal B-tree structure.

ON CLUSTER

> Specifies that the index be built on a cluster (which cannot be a hash cluster) and specifies the cluster name.

ON TABLE

> Specifies that the index be built on a table and specifies the table name.

alias

> Specifies an alias name for the table on which the index is being built. This option is required if the index references any object type attributes or object type methods.

ASC

> Specifies that the index should be created in ascending order, based on the database character set's character values.

DESC

> Specifies that the index should be created in descending order, based on the database character set's character values.

Physical_Attributes_Clause

> Specifies the physical attributes of this index. See Chapter 4 for detailed information.

STORAGE

> Specifies the physical storage characteristics. See Chapter 4 for detailed information.

TABLESPACE

> Specifies the name of the tablespace where this index will be stored. If omitted, the default tablespace for the schema owner will be used.

UNRECOVERABLE

> Specifies that redo log records will not be written during index creation. This option speeds the creation of indexes, but in the case of a database failure, the records cannot be recovered by applying log files. Instead, the index must be recreated. This keyword is Oracle7 syntax, and is equivalent to specifying NOLOGGING in Oracle8 or Oracle8*i*.

LOGGING

Specifies that redo log records will be written during index creation. This option is the default.

NOLOGGING

Specifies that redo log records will not be written during index creation. In case of a database failure, the index cannot be recovered by applying log files. Instead, it must be recreated. This option speeds the creation of indexes.

ONLINE

Specifies that DML operations may be performed on the table being indexed during the index creation.

COMPUTE STATISTICS

Specifies that statistics be computed and inserted into the data dictionary during index creation.

COMPRESS

Specifies that key compression be enabled.

NOCOMPRESS

Specifies that key compression be disabled. This option is the default.

NOSORT

Specifies that the rows being indexed were loaded in ascending order and do not have to be sorted during index creation.

REVERSE

Specifies that (except for ROWID) bytes of the index block will be stored in reverse order. This keyword cannot be used with NOSORT.

PARALLEL

Specifies that Oracle will create the index in parallel, selecting a degree of parallelism equal to the number of CPUs available on all participating instances multiplied by the value of the PARALLEL_THREADS_PER_CPU initialization parameter. If *integer* is specified, this specifies the degree of parallelism.

NOPARALLEL

Specifies that the index be created serially. This option is the default.

GLOBAL PARTITION BY RANGE

Specifies that the global index be partitioned on the range of values from the specified columns.

column_list

Specifies the name(s) of the column(s) on which the index is partitioned.

Global_Partition_Clause

Specifies characteristics of the individual partitions. See Chapter 4 for detailed information.

LOCAL

Specifies that the index is partitioned on the same columns, the same number of partitions, and the same partition bounds as the table on which the index is built.

PARTITION

Specifies the name of individual partitions, which must be equal to the number of table partitions and provided in the same order.

LOCAL STORE IN

Specifies how index hash partitions or index subpartitions will be distributed across tablespaces.

DEFAULT

Specifies that for a local index on a hash or composite-partitioned table, the tablespace specified at the index level will be overridden, and the same partition or subpartition that the table resides in will be used.

SUBPARTITION

Specifies the name of a subpartition.

DEALLOCATE UNUSED

Specifies that unused space at the end of the index be freed and made available for other uses in the database.

KEEP

Specifies a number of bytes above the high water mark that should remain as part of the index after dealloaction.

ALLOCATE EXTENT

Specifies that a new extent be allocated for this index.

SIZE

Specifies the size of the extent to be allocated.

DATAFILE

Specifies the name of the datafile to contain the new extent. If omitted, Oracle chooses a datafile from those available for this index.

INSTANCE

Specifies that the new extent be made available to this instance only. If omitted, the extent will be made available to all instances.

REBUILD PARTITION

Specifies a partition of the index to be rebuilt.

REBUILD SUBPARTITION

Specifies a subpartition of the index to be rebuilt.

REBUILD REVERSE

Specifies that the bytes of the index block be stored in reverse order (without ROWID) when the index is rebuilt.

REBUILD NOREVERSE

Specifies that the bytes of the index block be stored without reversing when the index is rebuilt.

rebuild_ parameters

Specifies the parameter string to be passed to the indextype routine for rebuilding a global index.

alter_ parameters

Specifies the parameter string to be passed to the indextype routine when altering a global index.

ENABLE

Specifies that a disabled function-based index be enabled.

DISABLE

Specifies that a function-based index be disabled.

UNUSABLE

Specifies that the index be marked unusable.

RENAME TO

Specifies that the index be renamed.

COALESCE

Specifies that the contents of index blocks be merged to free blocks for reuse.

If storage options are omitted, Oracle allocates storage for the index as follows:

- If the indexed table has no rows, the default storage values for the tablespace are used.

- If the indexed table has rows and the resulting index can be contained in no more than 25 data blocks, a single extent is allocated for this index.

- If the indexed table has rows and the resulting index is more than 25 data blocks, five equal-sized extents are allocated for this index.

Examples

Create an index on the empno and ename columns of scott's emp table, with the indicated storage parameters:

```
CREATE INDEX emp_ndx ON scott.emp(empno,ename)
    STORAGE (INITIAL 50K NEXT 10K PCTINCREASE 0 MAXEXTENTS 10)
    TABLESPACE users
    PCTFREE 20;
```

Alter the index emp_ndx owned by scott so new extents added for this index will be 4K each and will not grow. Also specify that each data block added to this index will contain five initial transaction entries:

```
ALTER INDEX scott.emp_ndx
          INITTRANS 5
          STORAGE (NEXT 4096 PCTINCREASE 0);
```

Remove the index emp_ndx from scott's schema in the database. When an index is dropped, all space it previously occupied is returned to the free space pool:

```
DROP INDEX scott.emp_ndx;
```

CREATE/ALTER/DROP MATERIALIZED VIEW

```
CREATE MATERIALIZED VIEW [schema.]materialized_view_name
  [Physical_Attributes_Clause]
  [TABLESPACE tablespace]
  [STORAGE Storage_Clause]
  [REFRESH
     [FAST | COMPLETE | FORCE]
     [START WITH date]
     [NEXTREF date]
AS materialized_view_query
```

Creates a materialized view (also called a snapshot), which is the result of a query run against one or more tables or views.

```
ALTER MATERIALIZED VIEW [schema.]materialized_view_name
  [Physical_Attributes_Clause]
  [STORAGE Storage_Clause]
  [REFRESH
     [FAST | COMPLETE | FORCE]
     [START WITH date]
     [NEXTREF date]
```

Changes the storage or automatic refresh characteristics of a materialized view (or snapshot).

```
DROP MATERIALIZED VIEW [schema.]materialized_view_name
```

Removes a materialized view (or snapshot) from the database.

Keywords

TABLESPACE

Specifies the name of the tablespace in which this materialized view will be created. The default tablespace for the schema owner is the default.

STORAGE

Specifies the physical storage characteristics. See Chapter 4 for detailed information.

REFRESH

Specifies the mode and times for automatic refreshes. FAST means use the materialized view log associated with the master table; COMPLETE means refresh by re-executing the materialized view's query; FORCE is the default, and means that Oracle will decide if a FAST refresh is possible and, if not, will do a COMPLETE refresh.

START WITH

Specifies a date for the next automatic refresh time using a standard Oracle date expression.

NEXTREF

Specifies a new date expression for calculating the interval between automatic refreshes.

AS materialized_view_query

Provides the actual SQL query that is used to populate the materialized view and is subject to the same restrictions as a view.

The script *dbmssnap.sql* must be run by SYS before you attempt to create a materialized view.

Because Oracle appends 7-character identifiers to the snapshot name when creating materialized view objects in the schema, you should limit the materialized view name to 27 characters or less.

Examples

Create a materialized view of scott's emp table, which is located on a server called uk. The materialized view will be populated tomorrow. It will then be refreshed seven days from today, and every seven days after that:

```
CREATE MATERIALIZED VIEW uk_emp
    REFRESH COMPLETE
    START WITH SYSDATE + 1
    NEXT SYSDATE + 7
    AS SELECT * FROM scott.emp@UK;
```

Schedule the scott user's materialized view dept_snap to be refreshed at midnight tomorrow, and then every week:

```
ALTER MATERIALIZED VIEW scott.dept_snap
    REFRESH COMPLETE
```

```
      START WITH TRUNC(SYSDATE + 1)
      NEXT TRUNC(SYSDATE + 7);
```

Remove the materialized view uk_emp from the database:

```
DROP MATERIALIZED VIEW uk_emp;
```

CREATE/ALTER/DROP MATERIALIZED VIEW LOG

```
CREATE MATERIALIZED VIEW LOG ON [schema.]tablename
  [Physical_Attributes_Clause]
  [TABLESPACE tablespace]
  [STORAGE Storage_Clause]
```

Creates a materialized view log, which is a table associated with the master table of a materialized view used to control materialized view refreshes.

```
ALTER MATERIALIZED VIEW LOG ON [schema.]tablename
  [Physical_Attributes_Clause]
  [STORAGE Storage_Clause]
```

Changes the materialized view log's storage characteristics.

```
DROP MATERIALIZED VIEW LOG ON [schema.]table_name
```

Removes a materialized view log from the database.

Keywords

tablename

> Specifies the name of the table for which the materialized view log will be maintained.

Physical_Attributes_Clause

> Specifies the physical characteristics of this materialized view log. See Chapter 4 for detailed information.

TABLESPACE

> Specifies the name of the tablespace in which this materialized view log will be created. The default tablespace for the schema owner is the default.

STORAGE

> Specifies the physical storage characteristics. See Chapter 4 for detailed information.

Examples

Create a materialized view log on scott's emp table:

```
CREATE MATERIALIZED VIEW LOG scott.emp
   STORAGE (INITIAL 50K NEXT 50K PCTINCREASE 0)
   TABLESPACE USERS;
```

Change the next extent size for the materialized view log on scott's emp table to 50K:

```
ALTER MATERIALIZED VIEW LOG scott.emp
    STORAGE (NEXT 50K);
```

Remove the materialized view log associated with scott's emp table from the database:

```
DROP MATERIALIZED VIEW LOG ON scott.emp;
```

CREATE/ALTER/DROP PACKAGE

See Chapter 7 for a complete description of these commands.

CREATE/ALTER/DROP PROCEDURE

See Chapter 7 for a complete description of these commands.

CREATE/ALTER/DROP PROFILE

```
CREATE PROFILE profile_name LIMIT
    [SESSIONS_PER_USER  integer | UNLIMITED | DEFAULT]
    [CPU_PER_SESSION  integer | UNLIMITED | DEFAULT]
    [CPU_PER_CALL  integer | UNLIMITED | DEFAULT]
    [CONNECT_TIME  integer | UNLIMITED | DEFAULT]
    [IDLE_TIME  integer | UNLIMITED | DEFAULT]
    [LOGICAL_READS_PER_SESSION  integer | UNLIMITED | DEFAULT]
    [LOGICAL_READS_PER_CALL  integer | UNLIMITED | DEFAULT]
    [PRIVATE_SGA  {integer [K | M] | UNLIMITED | DEFAULT]}]
    [COMPOSITE_LIMIT  {integer | UNLIMITED | DEFAULT}]
    [FAILED_LOGIN_ATTEMPTS expression | UNLIMITED | DEFAULT]
    [PASSWORD_LIFE_TIME expression | UNLIMITED | DEFAULT]
    [PASSWORD_REUSE_TIME expression | UNLIMITED | DEFAULT]
    [PASSWORD_LOCK_TIME expression | UNLIMITED | DEFAULT]
    [PASSWORD_GRACE_TIME expression | UNLIMITED | DEFAULT]
    [PASSWORD_VERIFY_FUNCTION function | NULL | DEFAULT]
```

Creates a profile to set limits on database resources.

```
ALTER PROFILE profile_name LIMIT
    [SESSIONS_PER_USER  integer | UNLIMITED | DEFAULT]
    [CPU_PER_SESSION  integer | UNLIMITED | DEFAULT]
    [CPU_PER_CALL  integer | UNLIMITED | DEFAULT]
    [CONNECT_TIME  integer | UNLIMITED | DEFAULT]
    [IDLE_TIME  integer | UNLIMITED | DEFAULT]
    [LOGICAL_READS_PER_SESSION  integer | UNLIMITED | DEFAULT]
    [LOGICAL_READS_PER_CALL  integer | UNLIMITED | DEFAULT]
    [PRIVATE_SGA  integer [K | M] | UNLIMITED | DEFAULT]
    [COMPOSITE_LIMIT  integer | UNLIMITED | DEFAULT]
    [FAILED_LOGIN_ATTEMPTS expression | UNLIMITED | DEFAULT]
```

```
[PASSWORD_LIFE_TIME expression | UNLIMITED | DEFAULT]
[PASSWORD_REUSE_TIME expression | UNLIMITED | DEFAULT]
[PASSWORD_LOCK_TIME expression | UNLIMITED | DEFAULT]
[PASSWORD_GRACE_TIME expression | UNLIMITED | DEFAULT]
[PASSWORD_VERIFY_FUNCTION function | NULL | DEFAULT]
```

Adds, changes, or removes a resource limit from an existing profile.

```
DROP PROFILE profile_name [CASCADE]
```

Removes a profile from the database.

Keywords

profile_name

Name of the profile to be created.

SESSIONS_PER_USER

Limits the number of concurrent sessions for a user.

CPU_PER_SESSION

Limits the amount of CPU time that can be used in a session (in hundredths of a second).

CPU_PER_CALL

Limits the amount of CPU time for a call (a parse, execute, or fetch) (in hundredths of a second).

CONNECT_TIME

Limits the total elapsed time for a session (in minutes).

IDLE_TIME

Limits the amount of continuous inactive time during a session (in minutes).

LOGICAL_READS_PER_SESSION

Limits the number of database blocks read in a session, including those read from memory and disk.

LOGICAL_READS_PER_CALL

Limits the number of database blocks read for a call (a parse, execute, or fetch).

PRIVATE_SGA

Limits the amount of memory a session can allocate in the SGA's shared pool (in bytes).

COMPOSITE_LIMIT

Limits the total resource cost for a session (in service units). See ALTER RESOURCE COST earlier in this chapter for additional information.

UNLIMITED

Specifying this value means that no limit will be imposed on this resource.

DEFAULT

Specifying this value means that the limit specified in the DEFAULT profile will be used for this resource.

FAILED_LOGIN_ATTEMPTS

Specifies the number of failed login attempts allowed before the account is locked.

PASSWORD_LIFE_TIME

Specifies the number of days the password may be used before it expires and must be changed.

PASSWORD_REUSE_TIME

Specifies the number of days before which a previously used password may be reused. If set to *integer*, PASSWORD_REUSE_MAX must be set to UNLIMITED.

PASSWORD_REUSE_MAX

Specifies the number of password changes required before the current password can be reused. If set to *integer*, PASSWORD_REUSE_TIME must be set to UNLIMITED.

PASSWORD_LOCK_TIME

Specifies the number of days an account will remain locked after the FAILED_LOGIN_ATTEMPTS limit is exceeded.

PASSWORD_GRACE_TIME

Specifies the number of days after password expiration that a login will be allowed with a warning message.

PASSWORD_VERIFY_FUNCTION

Specifies the name of a PL/SQL function used to verify passwords. Setting this parameter to NULL indicates that no verification will be performed. To apply the limits associated with the profile to a specific user, you must assign the profile to the user with the CREATE USER or ALTER USER command. Resource limits must also be enabled either via the RESOURCE_LIMIT *INIT.ORA* parameter or by using the ALTER SYSTEM command.

Examples

Define a limit of 5 concurrent sessions and 10 minutes of inactivity for the admin profile:

```
CREATE PROFILE admin
    SESSIONS_PER_USER 5
    IDLE_TIME 10;
```

Redefine a limit of 10 concurrent sessions and 15 minutes of inactivity for the admin profile:

```
ALTER PROFILE admin
    SESSIONS_PER_USER 10
    IDLE_TIME 15;
```

Remove the admin profile from the database:

```
DROP PROFILE admin;
```

CREATE/ALTER/DROP ROLE

```
CREATE ROLE rolename
    [NOT IDENTIFIED | IDENTIFIED BY password | IDENTIFIED EXTERNALLY]
```

Creates a role, which is a set of privileges that can be granted to users.

```
ALTER ROLE rolename
    [NOT IDENTIFIED | IDENTIFIED BY password | IDENTIFIED EXTERNALLY]
```

Changes the authorization level required to enable a role.

```
DROP ROLE rolename
```

Removes a role from the database.

Keywords

rolename
> Name of the role to be created.

NOT IDENTIFIED
> Specifies that a user who was granted the role does not need to be verified when enabling it.

IDENTIFIED BY
> Specifies that the *password* must be provided when enabling the role.

IDENTIFIED EXTERNALLY
> Specifies that the operating system verifies the user enabling the role.

 When you create a role, you are automatically granted that role WITH ADMIN OPTION, which allows you to grant or revoke the role or modify it using the ALTER ROLE command.

Examples

Create a role called manager and assign the password 'dilbert' to it:

```
CREATE ROLE manager IDENTIFIED BY dilbert;
```

Change the existing MANAGER role to use operating system authentication:

```
ALTER ROLE manager IDENTIFIED EXTERNALLY;
```

Remove the manager role from the database:

```
DROP ROLE manager;
```

CREATE/ALTER/DROP ROLLBACK SEGMENT

```
CREATE [PUBLIC] ROLLBACK SEGMENT segment_name
  TABLESPACE tablespace
  [STORAGE Storage_Clause]
```

Creates a rollback segment, which Oracle uses to store data necessary to roll back changes made by transactions.

```
ALTER ROLLBACK SEGMENT segment_name
  [STORAGE Storage_Clause]
  [ONLINE | OFFLINE]
  [SHRINK]
```

Changes the online status of a rollback segment or modifies storage characteristics.

```
DROP ROLLBACK SEGMENT segment_name
```

Removes a rollback segment from the database.

Keywords

PUBLIC

Specifies that this rollback segment is available to any instance. If omitted, it is only available to the instance naming it in the ROLLBACK_SEGMENTS parameter in the *INIT.ORA* file.

segment_name

Name of the rollback segment to be created.

TABLESPACE

Specifies the name of the tablespace where this rollback segment will be created.

STORAGE

Specifies the physical storage characteristics. See Chapter 4 for detailed information.

ONLINE

Specifies that the named rollback segment be brought online.

OFFLINE

Specifies that the named rollback segment be taken offline.

SHRINK

Specifies that the named rollback segment should be reduced to the size specified, or to the OPTIMAL size if no size is specified.

When it is created, a rollback segment will be offline. It must be brought online by using the ALTER ROLLBACK SEGMENT statement or by restarting the database with the rollback segment named in the *INIT.ORA* file.

Examples

Create a rollback segment rbs02:

```
CREATE ROLLBACK SEGMENT rbs02
   TABLESPACE rollback
   STORAGE (INITIAL 40K NEXT 40K OPTIMAL 80K );
```

Take the rollback segment rbs02 offline:

```
ALTER ROLLBACK SEGMENT rbs02 OFFLINE;
```

Change the storage allocation for rbs02 so each extent will be 30K, its optimal size will be 60K, and a maximum of 10 extents will be permitted:

```
ALTER ROLLBACK SEGMENT rbs02
STORAGE (NEXT 30K MAXEXTENTS 10 OPTIMAL 60K);
```

Remove the rollback segment rbs02 from the database:

```
DROP ROLLBACK SEGMENT rbs02;
```

CREATE SCHEMA

```
CREATE SCHEMA AUTHORIZATION schema
   [CREATE TABLE statement]
   [CREATE VIEW statement]
   [GRANT statement]
```

Creates multiple tables and/or views, and issues grants in a single statement.

Keywords

schema

> Specifies the name of the schema to be created, which must be the same as your username.

CREATE TABLE

> This is a CREATE TABLE statement, as shown later in this chapter.

CREATE VIEW

> This is a CREATE VIEW statement, as shown later in this chapter.

GRANT

> This is a GRANT statement, as shown later in this chapter.

You must have the same privileges required for the CREATE TABLE, CREATE VIEW, and GRANT statements to issue this statement. Individual commands within the CREATE SCHEMA statement must not be terminated with the SQL termination character.

Example

Create a schema for scott consisting of two tables and a view, and grant privileges on the view to a role:

```
CREATE SCHEMA AUTHORIZATION scott
CREATE TABLE dept (
        deptno      NUMBER NOT NULL,
        dname       VARCHAR2(20),
        location    VARCHAR2(15),
        avg_salary  NUMBER (9,2))
CREATE TABLE emp (
        ename       VARCHAR2(20),
        deptno      NUMBER,
        sal         NUMBER (7,2),
        comm        NUMBER (7,2))
CREATE VIEW deptview AS SELECT deptno,dname,location FROM dept
GRANT SELECT ON deptview TO non_admin;
```

CREATE/ALTER/DROP SEQUENCE

```
CREATE SEQUENCE [schema.]sequence_name
  [INCREMENT BY integer]
  [START WITH integer]
  [MAXVALUE integer | NOMAXVALUE]
  [MINVALUE integer | NOMINVALUE]
  [CYCLE | NOCYCLE]
  [CACHE integer | NOCACHE]
  [ORDER | NOORDER]
```

Creates an Oracle sequence that can be used to automatically generate sequential numbers during database operations.

```
ALTER SEQUENCE [schema.]sequence_name
  [INCREMENT BY integer]
  [MAXVALUE integer | NOMAXVALUE]
  [MINVALUE integer | NOMINVALUE]
  [CYCLE | NOCYCLE]
  [CACHE integer | NOCACHE]
  [ORDER | NOORDER]
```

Changes the characteristics of an Oracle sequence, including range, number of sequence numbers cached in memory, and whether sequential order is preserved.

```
DROP SEQUENCE [schema.]sequence_name
```

Removes a sequence from the database.

The DROP SEQUENCE and CREATE SEQUENCE commands can be issued sequentially to restart a sequence at a lower number. However, all GRANTs to the sequence will also have to be recreated.

Keywords

INCREMENT BY

Specifies the increment between sequence numbers and can be positive or negative (but not 0). The default is 1.

START WITH

Specifies the first sequence number to be generated. The default is the MINVALUE for ascending sequences and MAXVALUE for descending sequences.

MAXVALUE

Specifies the largest value the sequence number can reach. The default is NOMAXVALUE, which means the maximum value is 10^{27}.

MINVALUE

Specifies the smallest value the sequence number can reach. The default is NOMINVALUE, which means the minimum value is 1.

CYCLE

Specifies that when sequence numbers reach MAXVALUE they will begin again at MINVALUE. The default is NOCYCLE.

NOCYCLE

Specifies that after reaching the maximum value, no additional sequence numbers will be generated.

CACHE

Specifies how many sequence numbers Oracle will pregenerate and keep in memory. Note that when the database is shut down, unused sequence numbers stored in cache will be lost. The default is 20.

NOCACHE

Specifies that no sequence numbers are pregenerated to memory.

ORDER

Specifies that sequence numbers are guaranteed to be issued in the order of request. The default is NOORDER.

NOORDER

Specifies that sequence numbers are not guaranteed to be generated in the order of request.

The generation of a sequence number is not affected by the subsequent rollback of the transaction; once generated, that sequence number will not be available again, so gaps can occur. Sequence numbers are accessed by using the pseudo-columns CURRVAL and NEXTVAL.

Examples

Create a sequence ord_seq so that the next sequence number generated will be 101 and order will be guaranteed. The sequence will reach a maximum value of 9999 and then recycle to 1:

```
ALTER SEQUENCE ord_seq
   START WITH 101
   MINVALUE 1
   MAXVALUE 9999
   CYCLE
   ORDER;
```

Modify the sequence ord_seq in the scott schema so that the next sequence number generated will be 10,001 and the order will be guaranteed:

```
ALTER SEQUENCE scott.ord_seq
   MINVALUE 10001
   ORDER;
```

Remove the sequence ord_seq from the scott schema in the database:

```
DROP SEQUENCE scott.ord_seq;
```

CREATE/ALTER/DROP SNAPSHOT

```
CREATE SNAPSHOT [schema.]snapshot_name
   [Physical_Attributes_Clause]
   [TABLESPACE tablespace]
   [STORAGE Storage_Clause]
   [REFRESH
      [FAST | COMPLETE | FORCE]
      [START WITH date]
      [NEXTREF date]
AS snapshot_query
```

Creates a snapshot, which is the result of a query run against one or more tables or views.

```
ALTER SNAPSHOT [schema.]snapshot_name
   [Physical_Attributes_Clause]
   [STORAGE Storage_Clause]
   [REFRESH
      [FAST | COMPLETE | FORCE]
```

```
[START WITH date]
[NEXTREF date]
```

Changes the storage or automatic refresh characteristics of a snapshot.

```
DROP SNAPSHOT [schema.]snapshot_name
```

Removes a snapshot from the database.

Keywords

Physical_Attributes_Clause

Specifies physical attributes of this snapshot. See Chapter 4 for detailed information.

TABLESPACE

Specifies the name of the tablespace where this snapshot will be stored. If omitted, the default tablespace for the schema owner will be used.

STORAGE

Specifies physical storage characteristics. See Chapter 4 for detailed information.

REFRESH

Specifies the mode and times for automatic refreshes. FAST means use the snapshot log associated with the master table; COMPLETE means refresh by re-executing the snapshot's query; FORCE is the default, and indicates that Oracle will decide if a FAST refresh is possible or a COMPLETE refresh is necessary.

START WITH

Specifies a date for the next automatic refresh time using a standard Oracle date expression.

NEXTREF

Specifies a new date expression for calculating the interval between automatic refreshes.

AS

Provides the actual SQL query used to populate the snapshot and subject to the same restrictions as a view.

The script *dbmssnap.sql* has to be run by SYS to create the built-in DBMS_SNAPSHOT package before attempting to create a snapshot.

Since Oracle appends seven-character identifiers to the snapshot name when creating snapshot objects in the schema, you should limit the snapshot name to 23 characters or less.

Examples

Create a snapshot of scott's emp table, which is located on a server called uk. The snapshot will be populated tomorrow and refreshed seven days from now and every seven days thereafter:

```
CREATE SNAPSHOT uk_emp
    REFRESH COMPLETE
    START WITH SYSDATE+1
    NEXT SYSDATE+7
    AS SELECT * FROM scott.emp@UK;
```

Schedule scott user's snapshot dept_snap to be refreshed at midnight tomorrow and every week thereafter:

```
ALTER SNAPSHOT scott.dept_snap
    REFRESH COMPLETE
    START WITH TRUNC(SYSDATE + 1)
    NEXT TRUNC(SYSDATE + 7);
```

Remove the snapshot emp_UK from the database:

```
DROP SNAPSHOT emp_UK;
```

CREATE/ALTER/DROP SNAPSHOT LOG

```
CREATE SNAPSHOT LOG ON [schema.]tablename
    [Physical_Attributes_Clause]
    [TABLESPACE tablespace]
    [STORAGE Storage_Clause]
```

Creates a snapshot log (a table associated with the master table of a snapshot and used to control refreshes of snapshots).

```
ALTER SNAPSHOT LOG ON [schema.]tablename
    [Physical_Attributes_Clause]
    [STORAGE Storage_Clause]
```

Changes the storage characteristics of a snapshot log.

```
DROP SNAPSHOT LOG ON [schema.]table_name
```

Removes a snapshot log from the database.

Keywords

tablename

Specifies the name of the table for which the snapshot log will be maintained.

Physical_Attributes_Clause

Specifies the physical attributes of this snapshot. See Chapter 4 for detailed information.

TABLESPACE

Specifies the name of the tablespace where this snapshot will be stored. If omitted, the default tablespace for the schema owner will be used.

STORAGE

Specifies the physical storage characteristics. See Chapter 4 for detailed information.

Examples

Create a snapshot log on scott's emp table:

```
CREATE SNAPSHOT LOG ON scott.emp
    STORAGE (INITIAL 50K NEXT 50K PCTINCREASE 0)
    TABLESPACE users;
```

Change the next extent size for the snapshot log on scott's emp table to 500K:

```
ALTER SNAPSHOT LOG scott.emp
    STORAGE (NEXT 500K);
```

Remove the snapshot log associated with scott's emp table from the database:

```
DROP SNAPSHOT LOG ON scott.emp;
```

CREATE/DROP SYNONYM

```
CREATE [PUBLIC] SYNONYM synonym_name
  FOR [schema.]object_name[@dblink]
```

Creates a public or private synonym for a database object.

```
DROP [PUBLIC] SYNONYM [schema.]synonym_name
```

Removes a public or private synonym from the database.

Keywords

PUBLIC

Specifies that this synonym will be available to all users. If omitted, the synonym will be available only to the schema owner.

synonym_name

Specifies the name of the new synonym.

object_name

Specifies the name of the object to which the synonym will refer. It may include a reference to a remote database by appending the *@dblink* syntax.

Oracle resolves object names in the current schema first, so a PUBLIC synonym will only be used if the object name is not prefaced with a schema name, is not followed by a *dblink*, and does not exist in the current schema.

Examples

Create a public synonym for scott's emp table on the UK database:

```
CREATE PUBLIC SYNONYM uk_emps
FOR scott.emp@UK;
```

Remove the public synonym uk_emps from the database:

```
DROP PUBLIC SYNONYM uk_emps;
```

CREATE/ALTER/DROP TABLE

```
CREATE [GLOBAL] [TEMPORARY] TABLE [schema.]tablename
  (column  datatype [DEFAULT expression] [Column_Contraint]
   [,column  datatype [DEFAULT expression] [Column_Contraint]]…)
[Table_Constraint_Clause]
[Physical_Attributes_Clause]
[TABLESPACE tablespace]
[STORAGE Storage_Clause]
[LOGGING | NOLOGGING]
[CLUSTER (column[,column ...])]
[{ORGANIZATION HEAP
   [Physical_Attributes_Clause]
   [TABLESPACE tablespace]
   [STORAGE Storage_Clause]
   [LOGGING | NOLOGGING] |
  ORGANIZATION INDEX
   [PCTTHRESHOLD integer]
   [COMPRESS integer | NOCOMPRESS]
   [Physical_Attributes_Clause]
   [TABLESPACE tablespace]
   [STORAGE Storage_Clause]
   [LOGGING | NOLOGGING]
   [[INCLUDING column] OVERFLOW
     [Physical_Attributes_Clause]
     [TABLESPACE tablespace]
     [STORAGE Storage_Clause]
     [LOGGING | NOLOGGING]
 }]
[LOB {(lob_item[,lob_item ...]) STORE AS
       ([TABLESPACE tablespace]
        [{ENABLE | DISABLE} STORAGE IN ROW]
        [STORAGE Storage_Clause]
        [CHUNK integer]
        [PCTVERSION integer]
        [CACHE | NOCACHE [LOGGING | NOLOGGING]]
       )
     ) |
     (lob_item) STORE AS [(lob_segname)]
      [([TABLESPACE tablespace]
        [{ENABLE | DISABLE} STORAGE IN ROW]
        [STORAGE Storage_Clause]
        [CHUNK integer]
```

```
            [PCTVERSION integer]
            [CACHE | NOCACHE [LOGGING | NOLOGGING]]
          )]
        }
[Partition_Clause]
[ENABLE | DISABLE ROW MOVEMENT]
[CACHE | NOCACHE]
[MONITORING | NOMONITORING]
[PARALLEL integer | NOPARALLEL]
[ENABLE | DISABLE [VALIDATE | NOVALIDATE]]
    {UNIQUE (column[, column ...] | PRIMARY KEY | CONSTRAINT constraint_name}
    [USING INDEX
    [TABLESPACE tablespace]
    [Physical_Attributes_Clause]
    [STORAGE Storage_Clause]
    [NOSORT]
    [LOGGING | NOLOGGING]]
    EXCEPTIONS INTO [schema.]table_name]
    CASCADE] ]
 [AS subquery]
```

Creates a table either by specifying the structure or by referencing an existing table.

```
ALTER TABLE [schema.]tablename
[ADD ([column  datatype [DEFAULT expression] [Column_Constraint_Clause]
      [,column datatype [DEFAULT expression] [Column_Constraint_Clause] ...)]
      [Table_Constraint_Clause]
      [LOB {(lob_item[,lob_item ...]) STORE AS
        ([TABLESPACE tablespace]
        [{ENABLE | DISABLE} STORAGE IN ROW]
        [STORAGE Storage_Clause]
        [CHUNK integer]
        [PCTVERSION integer]
        [{CACHE | NOCACHE [LOGGING | NOLOGGING]}]
        ) |
        (lob_item) STORE AS [(lob_segname)]
        [([TABLESPACE tablespace]
          [{ENABLE | DISABLE} STORAGE IN ROW]
          [STORAGE Storage_Clause]
          [CHUNK integer]
          [PCTVERSION integer]
          [CACHE | NOCACHE [LOGGING | NOLOGGING]]
        )]
[Partition_Clause]
[MODIFY [(column  datatype [DEFAULT expression] [Column_Constraint_Clause]
      [,column  datatype [DEFAULT expression] [Column_Constraint_Clause] ...)]]
      [{NESTED TABLE | VARRAY} collection_item [RETURN AS {LOCATOR | VALUE}]]
[MOVE [ONLINE] [Physical_Attributes_Clause]
 {[TABLESPACE tablespace] [LOGGING | NOLOGGING] |
  [PCTTHRESHOLD integer]
  [COMPRESS integer | NOCOMPRESS]
  [INCLUDING column] OVERFLOW
    [Physical_Attributes_Clause]
```

```
    [TABLESPACE tablespace]
    [STORAGE Storage_Clause]
    [LOGGING | NOLOGGING]
 }
[LOB {(lob_item[,lob_item ...]) STORE AS
       ([TABLESPACE tablespace
        [{ENABLE | DISABLE} STORAGE IN ROW]
        [STORAGE Storage_Clause]
        [CHUNK integer]
        [PCTVERSION integer
        [{CACHE | NOCACHE [LOGGING | NOLOGGING]}]
        ) |
        (lob_item) STORE AS [(lob_segname)]
        [([TABLESPACE tablespace
          [{ENABLE | DISABLE} STORAGE IN ROW]
          [STORAGE Storage_Clause]
          [CHUNK integer]
          [PCTVERSION integer
          [{CACHE | NOCACHE [LOGGING | NOLOGGING]}]
        )]
[Physical_Attributes_Clause] [STORAGE Storage_Clause]
[LOGGING | NOLOGGING]
[MODIFY CONSTRAINT constraint_name Constraint_State_Clause]
[DROP CONSTRAINT constraint_name] [{PRIMARY | UNIQUE (column[,column ...])}] [CASCADE]]
[{DROP COLUMN column | DROP COLUMN (column[,column ...]}
    [CASCADE CONSTRAINTS] [INVALIDATE] [CHECKPOINT integer]
[DROP {UNUSED COLUMNS | COLUMNS CONTINUE} [CHECKPOINT integer]
[{SET UNUSED COLUMN column | SET UNUSED COLUMN (column[,column ...]}
    [CASCADE CONSTRAINTS | INVALIDATE]
[{ALLOCATE EXTENT ([SIZE integer[K | M]]
                  [DATAFILE 'filename']
                  [INSTANCE integer]
                ) |
  DEALLOCATE UNUSED [KEEP integer[K | M]]
 }]
[CACHE | NOCACHE]
[MONITORING | NOMONITORING]
[RENAME TO new_table_name]
[{MINIMIZE | NOMINIMIZE} RECORDS_PER_BLOCK]
[PCTTHRESHOLD integer | INCLUDING column]
[OVERFLOW [Physical_Attributes_Clause]
          [ALLOCATE EXTENT ([SIZE integer [K | M]]
                           [DATAFILE 'filename']
                           [INSTANCE integer]
                         )
          [DEALLOCATE UNUSED [KEEP integer[K | M]]
          [LOGGING | NOLOGGING]
[Partition_Clause [Partition_Clause] ...]
[PARALLEL integer | NOPARALLEL]
  [{ENABLE | DISABLE}] [{TABLE LOCK | ALL TRIGGERS}]
```

Modifies the column or storage characteristics of a table or the integrity constraints associated with a table and/or its columns.

```
DROP TABLE [schema.]table_name
   [CASCADE CONSTRAINTS]
```

Removes a table from the database.

Keywords

GLOBAL TEMPORARY

Specifies that the table to be created will be a temporary table with a structure visible to all sessions, but with data visible only to the creating session. A temporary table must be created in a temporary tablespace.

column

Specifies the name of a column to be created as part of this table.

datatype

Specifies the datatype to be associated with *column*.

DEFAULT

Specifies a default value for the column, which will be used if rows inserted into the table omit values for the column. The expression must match the datatype of the column.

Column_Constraint_Clause

Specifies a column constraint using the syntax found in Chapter 4.

Table_Constraint_Clause

Specifies a table constraint using the syntax found in Chapter 4.

Physical_Attributes_Clause

Specifies the physical attributes of this table. See Chapter 4 for specifics.

TABLESPACE

Specifies the name of the tablespace where this table will be stored. If omitted, the default tablespace for the schema owner will be used.

STORAGE

Specifies physical storage characteristics. See Chapter 4 for specifics.

LOGGING

Specifies that redo log records will be written during object creation. This option is the default.

NOLOGGING

Specifies that redo log records will not be written during object creation. In case of database failure, the operation cannot be recovered by applying log files, and the object must be recreated. This option will speed the creation of database objects.

ORGANIZATION HEAP

Specifies that no order is associated with the storage of rows of data in this table. This option is the default.

ORGANIZATION INDEX

Specifies that the table be created as an index-organized table, meaning that the data rows are actually held in an index that is defined on the primary key of the table.

PCTTHRESHOLD

Specifies the percentage of space in each index block reserved for data rows. Any part of a data row that cannot fit in this space will be placed in the overflow segment.

COMPRESS

Specifies that keys be compressed.

NOCOMPRESS

Specifies that keys not be compressed. This option is the default.

INCLUDING

Specifies the point at which a table row is to be divided between index and overflow portions. All columns following *column* (except primary key columns) will be stored in the overflow segment.

OVERFLOW

Specifies that index-organized table rows that exceed the PCTTHRESHOLD value be placed in a segment described in this clause.

LOB

Specifies storage attributes for LOB (Large OBject) data.

lob_item

Specifies the name of a LOB column.

STORE AS

Specifies the name of the LOB data segment.

ENABLE STORAGE IN ROW

Specifies that the LOB value is stored in the row. If specified for an index-organized table, OVERFLOW must also be specified. This option is the default.

DISABLE STORAGE IN ROW

Specifies that the LOB value be stored outside the row.

CHUNK

Specifies the number of bytes (rounded up to the nearest database block size) allocated for LOB manipulation.

PCTVERSION

Specifies the maximum percentage of the LOB storage space used in creating a new version of the LOB.

ENABLE ROW MOVEMENT

Specifies that a row may be moved to a different partition or subpartition if required due to an update of the key.

DISABLE ROW MOVEMENT

Specifies that rows may not be moved to a different partition or subpartition, and returns an error if an update to a key would require such a move.

MONITORING

Specifies that modification statistics can be collected for this table.

NOMONITORING

Specifies that modification statistics will not be collected for this table. This option is the default.

ENABLE

Specifies that a constraint will be applied to all new data in the table.

DISABLE

Specifies that a constraint will be disabled for the table.

VALIDATE

When specified with ENABLE, this keyword causes Oracle to verify that all existing data in the table comply with the constraint.

NOVALIDATE

When specified with ENABLE, this keyword prevents Oracle from verifying that existing data in the table comply with the constraint, but ensures that new data added to the table does comply with the constraint.

USING INDEX

Specifies the characteristics of an index used to enforce a constraint.

EXCEPTIONS INTO

Specifies the name of a table into which Oracle places information about rows violating the constraint. This table must be explicitly created by running the *UTLEXCPT1.SQL* script before using this keyword.

AS

Specifies a *subquery* used to insert rows into the table upon creation. If column definitions are omitted from the CREATE TABLE statement, the column names and datatypes will be copied from the table referenced in the *subquery*.

DROP

Drops an integrity constraint.

ALLOCATE EXTENT

Explicitly allocates a new extent for the table using the specified parameters.

CASCADE CONSTRAINTS

Specifies that all referential integrity constraints referring to primary and unique keys in the table to be dropped will also be dropped.

Examples

Create a new table named dept in scott's schema:

```
CREATE TABLE scott.dept (
    deptno              NUMBER(2) NOT NULL,
    dname               VARCHAR2(14),
    loc                 VARCHAR(15))
    TABLESPACE USERS
    STORAGE (INITIAL 40K NEXT 4K PCTINCREASE 0)
    PCTFREE 15;
```

Create a copy of scott's emp table:

```
CREATE TABLE test_emp
    AS SELECT * FROM scott.emp;
```

Add a new column to scott's emp table:

```
ALTER TABLE scott.emp
    ADD (bonus NUMBER(7,2));
```

Increase the size of the bonus column to nine digits:

```
ALTER TABLE scott.emp
    MODIFY (bonus NUMBER(9,2));
```

Add a primary key constraint to scott's emp table:

```
ALTER TABLE scott.emp
    MODIFY (empno  CONSTRAINT pk_emp PRIMARY_KEY);
```

Remove scott's emp table from the database:

```
DROP TABLE scott.emp;
```

 When you drop a table, all rows are deleted. Any indexes remaining on the table are also automatically deleted, regardless of what schema created or currently owns them. If the table to be dropped is a base table for a view, or if it is referenced in any stored procedure, the view or procedure will be marked invalid (but not dropped). If the table is the master table for a snapshot, the snapshot is not dropped. Likewise, if the table has a snapshot log, that snapshot log is not dropped.

CREATE/ALTER/DROP TABLESPACE

```
CREATE TABLESPACE tablespace_name
  DATAFILE 'filename' [SIZE integer [K | M] [REUSE]] [Autoextend_Clause]
        [,'filename' [SIZE integer [K | M] [REUSE]] [Autoextend_Clause]]
  DEFAULT STORAGE Storage_Clause
  [ONLINE | OFFLINE]
  [PERMANENT | TEMPORARY]
  [LOGGING | NOLOGGING]
  [MINIMUM EXTENT integer]
```

Creates a new tablespace, optionally specifying default storage characteristics for objects subsequently created in the tablespace.

```
ALTER TABLESPACE tablespace_name
  {
  [ADD DATAFILE filename [SIZE integer [K | M]] [REUSE]]
  [Autoextend_Clause]
  [RENAME 'filename1' TO 'filename2']
  [DEFAULT STORAGE Storage_Clause
  [ONLINE]|OFFLINE]
  [PERMANENT | TEMPORARY]
  [BEGIN BACKUP | END BACKUP]
  [LOGGING | NOLOGGING]
  [MAXIMUM EXTENT integer]
  }
```

Changes an existing tablespace by adding or changing datafiles, changing storage parameters, taking the tablespace offline, putting the tablespace online, placing it in backup mode, or taking it out of backup mode.

```
DROP TABLESPACE tablespace_name
    [INCLUDING CONTENTS] [CASCADE CONSTRAINTS]
```

Removes a tablespace from the database.

Keywords

DATAFILE

Specifies the name of the operating system datafile for this tablespace. SIZE is required unless the file already exists. If the file does already exist, the REUSE keyword must be specified.

DEFAULT STORAGE

Specifies the physical storage characteristics. See Chapter 4 for detailed information.

ONLINE

Brings the tablespace online after creation. This option is the default.

OFFLINE

Leaves the tablespace offline after creation.

PERMANENT

Specifies that the tablespace may contain permanent objects.

TEMPORARY

Specifies that the tablespace will create only temporary objects.

LOGGING

Specifies that redo log records will be written during object creation within this tablespace. This option is the default, but may be overridden by specifying NOLOGGING at the object level.

NOLOGGING

Specifies that redo log records will not be written during object creation in this tablespace. In case of a database failure, such operations cannot be recovered by applying log files and the objects must be recreated. This option speeds the creation of database objects.

MINIMUM EXTENT

Specifies that every used or free extent size in the tablespace is at least as large as, and is a multiple of, *integer*. This parameter controls free space fragmentation.

BEGIN BACKUP

Signals to Oracle that the tablespace is being backed up, thereby changing log file behavior to accumulate all block changes for this tablespace. Note that this statement does not actually perform a backup; it signals to Oracle that the backup is about to begin.

END BACKUP

Signals to Oracle that the tablespace backup is complete, thereby restoring log file behavior to normal.

INCLUDING CONTENTS

Specifies that any objects contained in this tablespace be dropped automatically. If this keyword is not included and any objects exist in the tablespace, the statement will fail.

CASCADE CONSTRAINTS

Specifies that referential integrity constraints from tables outside this tablespace that refer to primary and unique keys in the tables of this tablespace be dropped.

Examples

Create a new 25-megabyte tablespace called users:

```
CREATE TABLESPACE users
    DATAFILE '/disk09/oracle/oradata/users01.dbf' SIZE 25M
    DEFAULT STORAGE (INITIAL 500K NEXT 50K PCTINCREASE 0);
```

Add a new 25-megabyte datafile to the users tablespace:

```
ALTER TABLESPACE users
    ADD DATAFILE '/disk09/oracle/oradata/users02.dbf' SIZE 25M;
```

Signal Oracle that a backup of the users tablespace is about to begin:

```
ALTER TABLESPACE users
    BEGIN BACKUP;
```

Remove the users tablespace and (all objects it contains) from the database:

```
DROP TABLESPACE users INCLUDING CONTENTS;
```

CREATE TEMPORARY TABLESPACE

```
CREATE TEMPORARY TABLESPACE
    TEMPFILE 'filename' [SIZE integer [K | M] [REUSE]]
    [Autoextend_clause]
    [EXTENT MANAGEMENT LOCAL]
    [UNIFORM] [SIZE integer [K | M]]
```

Creates a temporary tablespace, which is used to hold temporary objects (retained only for the duration of a session).

 Like any other tablespace, a temporary tablespace can be dropped with the DROP TABLESPACE command.

Keywords

TEMPFILE

> Specifies the name of the operating system datafile for this temporary tablespace.

SIZE

> Specifies the size of the file in bytes, kilobytes (K), or megabytes (M). SIZE is required unless the file already exists. If the file already exists, the REUSE keyword must be specified.

REUSE

> Specifies that the operating system file must already exist and be reused for this temporary tablespace.

INITIAL

> Specifies the size of the first extent for a new object in bytes, kilobytes (K), or megabytes (M). If not a multiple of the database block size, the size will be rounded up to a multiple of it.

Autoextend_clause

Specifies whether autoextend will be in effect for the datafile. See Chapter 4 for more information.

EXTENT MANAGEMENT LOCAL

Specifies that the temporary tablespace be locally managed, meaning that some portion of this tablespace is set aside for a bitmap.

UNIFORM SIZE

Specifies the size for all extents in this tablespace in bytes, kilobytes (K) or megabytes (M), and indicates that all extents will be equally sized. If omitted, the extent size defaults to 1 megabyte.

 Temporary tablespaces are not affected by media recovery.

Example

Create a temporary tablespace called tempspace that contains 100 megabytes of space allocated in equal-sized extents of 2 megabytes each:

```
CREATE TEMPORARY TABLESPACE tempspace
    TEMPFILE '/disk09/oracle/oradata/tempsp01.dbf' SIZE 100M
    EXTENT MANAGEMENT LOCAL UNIFORM SIZE 2M;
```

CREATE/ALTER/DROP TRIGGER

See Chapter 7 for a complete description of these statements.

CREATE/ALTER/DROP USER

```
CREATE USER username
    [IDENTIFIED [BY password | EXTERNALLY]]
    [DEFAULT TABLESPACE tablespace
    [TEMPORARY TABLESPACE tablespace]
    [QUOTA [INTEGER [K | M] | UNLIMITED] ON tablespace]
    [QUOTA [INTEGER [K | M] | UNLIMITED] ON tablespace]
    ...
    [PROFILE profilename]
```

Creates a new database user and assigns security and storage properties.

```
ALTER USER username
    [IDENTIFIED [BY password | EXTERNALLY]]
    [DEFAULT TABLESPACE tablespace]
    [TEMPORARY TABLESPACE tablespace]
    [QUOTA [INTEGER [K | M] | UNLIMITED] ON tablespace]
```

```
[QUOTA [INTEGER [K | M] | UNLIMITED] ON tablespace]
...
[PROFILE profilename]
[DEFAULT ROLE
  {rolename[,rolename ...] |
  ALL [EXCEPT rolename[,rolename ...]] |
  NONE
  }]
```

Changes the security and storage characteristics of a user.

```
DROP USER username [CASCADE]
```

Removes a user from the database, and optionally removes objects created by that user.

Keywords

IDENTIFIED BY

Specifies the password used for this user account, or if EXTERNALLY is specified, that authentication of this user will be handled by the operating system.

 You can use the ALTER USER command to change your own password, regardless of whether or not you have the ALTER USER system privilege.

DEFAULT TABLESPACE

Specifies the name of the tablespace used by default when this user creates a database object.

TEMPORARY TABLESPACE

Specifies the name of the tablespace used for the creation of temporary segments when operations such as sorts require more memory than is available.

QUOTA

Specifies the amount of space this user is permitted to use for object storage in the specified tablespace. UNLIMITED means that there is no limit to the storage used (subject to the total size of the tablespace).

PROFILE

Sets the user's profile to *profilename*, which subjects the user to the limits specified in that profile.

CASCADE

Specifies that all objects in the user's schema be dropped before removing the user. This keyword must be specified if the user schema contains any objects; otherwise, the command will fail.

If you specify the CASCADE option, referential integrity constraints on tables in other schemas that refer to primary and unique keys on tables in this schema will also be dropped. If tables or other database objects in this schema are referred to by views or synonyms, or stored procedures, functions, or packages in another schema, then those referring objects will be marked invalid, but not dropped.

Examples

Create a new user scott:

```
CREATE USER scott IDENTIFIED BY tiger
    DEFAULT TABLESPACE users
    TEMPORARY TABLESPACE temp
    QUOTA 500K ON users;
```

Create the same user, but ensure that the account be authenticated by the operating system:

```
CREATE USER ops$scott IDENTIFIED EXTERNALLY
    DEFAULT TABLESPACE users
    TEMPORARY TABLESPACE temp
    QUOTA 500K ON users;
```

Assign a new password to scott:

```
ALTER USER scott IDENTIFIED BY lion;
```

Change the default and temporary tablespaces for user scott:

```
ALTER USER scott
    TEMPORARY TABLESPACE temp
    DEFAULT TABLESPACE users;
```

Remove the user scott and the contents of his schema from the database:

```
DROP USER scott CASCADE;
```

CREATE/ALTER/DROP VIEW

```
CREATE [OR REPLACE] [FORCE|NOFORCE] VIEW [schema.]viewname
  [(alias[,alias ...])]
AS viewquery
  [WITH CHECK OPTION [CONSTRAINT constraint]]
```

Creates a view.

```
ALTER VIEW [schema.]viewname COMPILE
```

Recompiles a view.

```
DROP VIEW [schema.]view_name
```

Removes a view from the database.

Keywords

OR REPLACE

Specifies that the view be replaced if it already exists.

FORCE

Specifies that the view be created regardless of whether the view's base tables exist, or whether the owner of the schema has privileges on them.

NOFORCE

Specifies that the view be created only if the base tables exist and the owner of the schema has privileges on them. This option is the default.

viewname

Specifies the name of the view to be created.

alias

One or more aliases that correspond to columns or expressions returned by the view's query.

viewquery

Any SQL SELECT statement. See Chapter 3 for the syntax of the SELECT statement.

WITH CHECK OPTION

Specifies that inserts and updates performed through the view must result in rows that the view query can select.

CONSTRAINT

Specifies a name for the CHECK OPTION constraint. The default is a system-assigned name in the form SYS_Cn, for which n is an integer resulting in a unique name.

COMPILE

This keyword is required when altering a view and causes the view to be recompiled.

The ALTER VIEW statement explicitly recompiles a view, and its use is recommended after changes are made to any of the view's underlying base tables.

Examples

Create a view called emploc:

```
CREATE OR REPLACE VIEW emploc
    (empno,lname,location) AS
SELECT empno,ename,loc
```

```
      FROM scott.emp,scott.dept
      WHERE emp.deptno = dept.deptno;
```

Recompile scott's view emploc:

```
ALTER VIEW scott.emploc RECOMPILE;
```

Remove scott's emploc view from the database:

```
DROP VIEW scott.emploc;
```

DISASSOCIATE STATISTICS

```
DISASSOCIATE STATISTICS FROM
  {COLUMNS [schema.]table.column[, [schema.]table.column ...] |
   FUNCTIONS [schema.]function[,[schema.]function ...] |
   PACKAGES [schema.]package[,[schema.]package ...] |
   INDEXES [schema.]index[,[schema.]index ...]
  }
```

Disassociates a method of statistics computation from database objects.

Keywords

COLUMNS

    Specifies that a list of one or more columns be provided.

schema

    The schema containing the specified table.

table

    The name of the table containing the specified column.

column

    The column name for which an association is defined.

FUNCTIONS

    Specifies that one or more functions will be disassociated.

PACKAGES

    Specifies that one or more packages will be disassociated.

INDEXES

    Specifies that one or more indexes will be disassociated.

Example

Remove a statistics association from function emp_sal:

```
DISASSOCIATE STATISTICS FROM FUNCTIONS emp_sal;
```

EXPLAIN PLAN

See Chapter 3 and Chapter 8, *SQL Statement Tuning*, for a complete explanation of this statement.

GRANT (Object Privileges)

```
GRANT {object_priv[,object_priv ...] | ALL [PRIVILEGES]}
   ON {[schema.]object_name |
       DIRECTORY directory_name |
       JAVA {SOURCE | RESOURCE} [schema.]java_object
       }
   TO {username | role | PUBLIC}
   [WITH GRANT OPTION]
```

Grants privileges on a database object to one or more users or roles.

Keywords

object_priv

> Specifies the name of the object privilege to be granted. Valid privileges are: ALTER, DELETE, EXECUTE, INDEX, INSERT, REFERENCES, SELECT, and UPDATE.

object_name

> Specifies the name of the object on which privileges are to be granted.

DIRECTORY

> Specifies the name of a directory object on which privileges are to be granted.

JAVA SOURCE

> Specifies the name of a Java source object on which privileges are to be granted.

JAVA RESOURCE

> Specifies the name of a Java resource object on which privileges are to be granted.

username

> Specifies the name of the user who will be granted the object privilege.

role

> Specifies the name of a role that will be granted the object privilege.

PUBLIC

> Specifies that the object privilege be granted to all current and future users.

WITH ADMIN OPTION

> Specifies that the grantee of the privilege can grant the privilege to others.

The object must be in your schema, or you must have been granted the object privileges with the GRANT OPTION.

Example

Grant INSERT and UPDATE privileges on scott's emp table to debby:

```
GRANT insert, update ON scott.emp TO debby;
```

GRANT (System Privilege or Role)

```
GRANT {privilege | role}[,{privilege | role} ...]
  TO {username | rolename | PUBLIC}[,{username | rolename | PUBLIC} ...]
  [WITH ADMIN OPTION]
```

Grants a system privilege or role to one or more users and/or roles.

Keywords

privilege

Specifies the name of a system privilege to be granted.

role

Specifies the name of a role to be granted.

username

Specifies the name of a user to be granted a privilege or role.

rolename

Specifies the name of a role to be granted a privilege or role.

PUBLIC

Specifies that the granted privilege or role be granted to all users, including those not yet created.

WITH ADMIN OPTION

Specifies that the grantee of the privilege or role can grant the privilege or role to others, and may alter or drop the role.

Examples

Grant the account_admin role to scott and debby:

```
GRANT account_admin TO scott, debby;
```

Grant the CREATE USER and DROP USER privileges to the dba_assist role:

```
GRANT create user, drop user TO dba_assist;
```

NOAUDIT (Schema Objects)

```
NOAUDIT object_option[,object_option ...]
ON {[schema.]objectname | DIRECTORY directory_name | DEFAULT}
[WHENEVER [NOT] SUCCESSFUL]
```

Stops auditing defined by a prior AUDIT statement for schema objects.

Keywords

object_option

Indicates that auditing on a particular operation will be stopped. The following operations are valid: ALTER, AUDIT, COMMENT, DELETE, EXECUTE, GRANT, INDEX, INSERT, LOCK, RENAME, SELECT, and UPDATE. The keyword ALL is equivalent to specifying all of the operations.

object_name

Specifies the name of the schema object for which auditing will be stopped.

DIRECTORY

Specifies the name of a directory for which auditing will be stopped.

DEFAULT

Specifies that no auditing will be performed as the default for objects that have not yet been created for the specified object option.

WHENEVER SUCCESSFUL

Turns off auditing only for SQL statements that complete successfully.

WHENEVER NOT SUCCESSFUL

Turns off auditing only for SQL statements that fail or result in errors.

Examples

Turn off auditing for any UPDATE statement issued for scott's bonus table:

```
NOAUDIT UPDATE ON scott.bonus;
```

Turn off auditing for any unsuccessful operation on scott's emp table:

```
NOAUDIT ALL ON scott.emp WHENEVER NOT SUCCESSFUL;
```

NOAUDIT (SQL Statements)

```
NOAUDIT {statement_opt | system_priv}[,{statement_opt | system_priv} ...]
  [BY {username[,username ...] | proxy [ON BEHALF OF {ANY | username
     [,username ...]}]}]
  [WHENEVER [NOT] SUCCESSFUL]
```

Stops auditing defined by a prior AUDIT statement for SQL statements.

Keywords

statement_opt
> Specifies a statement option for which auditing will be stopped.

system_priv
> Specifies a system privilege for which auditing will be stopped.

BY username
> Stops auditing only for SQL statements issued by a *username* in this list. The default option is to stop auditing for all users.

BY proxy
> Stops auditing only for SQL statements issued by *proxy* on behalf of a user or a list of specific users.

WHENEVER SUCCESSFUL
> Stops auditing only for SQL statements that complete successfully. If NOT is specified, auditing stops only for SQL statements that result in an error. If this clause is omitted, auditing stops for all SQL statements, successful or not.

Example

Stop auditing of INSERT and DELETE statements issued by scott:

```
NOAUDIT INSERT,DELETE BY scott;
```

RENAME

```
RENAME oldname TO newname
```

Changes the name of an existing table, view, sequence, or private synonym.

 Integrity constraints, indexes, and grants on the old object are automatically transferred to the new object.

Keywords

oldname
> Specifies the name of the existing object for which you want to assign a new name.

newname
> Specifies the new name for the database object.

Objects that depend on the renamed object (e.g., views, synonyms, stored procedures, or functions) will be marked invalid.

Example

Change the name of the emp table to employees:

```
RENAME emp TO employees;
```

REVOKE (Object Privileges)

```
REVOKE {object_priv[,object_priv ...] | ALL [PRIVILEGES]}
  ON [schema.]object_name
  FROM {username | role | PUBLIC}
```

Revokes privileges on a database object from one or more users or roles.

Keywords

object_priv

Specifies the name of the object privilege to be granted. Valid privileges are: ALTER, DELETE, EXECUTE, INDEX, INSERT, REFERENCES, SELECT, and UPDATE.

object_name

Specifies the name of the object on which privileges are granted.

username

Specifies the name of the user who will be granted the object privilege.

role

Specifies the name of a role that will be granted the object privilege.

PUBLIC

Specifies that the object privilege be granted to all current and future users.

Example

Revoke INSERT and UPDATE privileges on scott's emp table from debby:

```
REVOKE insert,update ON scott.emp FROM debby;
```

REVOKE (System Privilege or Role)

```
REVOKE {privilege | role}[,{privilege | role} ...]
  FROM {username | rolename | PUBLIC}[,{username | rolename | PUBLIC} ...]
```

Removes a system privilege or role from one or more users and/or roles.

Keywords

privilege
> Specifies the name of a system privilege to be revoked.

role
> Specifies the name of a role to be revoked.

username
> Specifies the name of a user from whom a privilege or role is to be revoked.

rolename
> Specifies the name of a role from which a privilege or role is to be revoked.

PUBLIC
> Specifies that the granted privilege or role no longer be available to all users by default.

Examples

Revoke the account_admin role from scott and debby:

```
REVOKE account_admin FROM scott,debby;
```

Revoke the CREATE USER and DROP USER privileges from the dba_assist role:

```
REVOKE create user, drop user FROM dba_assist;
```

3

Data Manipulation and Control Statements

Data Manipulation Language (DML) statements access and manipulate data stored in the Oracle database. You can use them to insert, update, delete, and read data. Control statements are related, since they are used to control how Oracle operates when accessing data in the database. There are not as many DML and control statements as there are DDL (Data Definition Language) statements, but many do have a wide range of options and syntax choices. This chapter provides a quick reference to the functionality of these SQL commands and a guide to the syntax of each.

SQL DML and Control Statements by Task

Table 3-1 lists the most common data manipulation tasks, along with the appropriate SQL statements used to accomplish each task. The detailed syntax of each statement is listed later in this chapter.

Table 3-1. Common DML Tasks, Control Tasks, and SQL Statements

If you want to	Use this command
Change data in rows of a table, view, or snapshot	UPDATE
Change the characteristics of your session	ALTER SESSION
Check constraints after each DML statement	SET CONSTRAINT
Collect statistics about an object in the database	ANALYZE
Create an explanation of the execution plan for a SQL statement	EXPLAIN PLAN
Defer checking of constraints until the end of the transaction	SET CONSTRAINT
Delete rows from a table, view, or snapshot	DELETE
Delete statistics about an object in the database	ANALYZE

Table 3-1. Common DML Tasks, Control Tasks, and SQL Statements (continued)

If you want to	Use this command
Disable roles for the current session	SET ROLE
Enable roles for the current session	SET ROLE
Establish the current transaction as read-write	SET TRANSACTION
Establish the current transaction as read-only	SET TRANSACTION
Identify migrated and chained rows in a table or cluster	ANALYZE
Insert a row of data into a table or view	INSERT
Mark a point in a transaction to which you can roll back	SAVEPOINT
Remove all rows from a table or cluster	TRUNCATE
Retrieve data from tables, views, or snapshots	SELECT
Specify the rollback segment to be used by the transaction	SET TRANSACTION
Validate the structure of an object	ANALYZE

SQL Statement Syntax

This section provides a detailed reference to each of the SQL statements likely to be used when working with data in an Oracle database. Each statement is listed in one or more of its forms, with a short explanation of the statement's purpose, its exact syntax and associated parameters, an example, and usage notes when applicable.

ALTER SESSION

```
ALTER SESSION
  {{SET
    [CONSTRAINT[S] = IMMEDIATE | DEFERRED | DEFAULT] |
    [CREATE_STORED_OUTLINES = TRUE | FALSE | category_name] |
    [CURRENT_SCHEMA = schema] |
    [CURSOR_SHARING = FORCE | EXACT] |
    [DB_BLOCK_CHECKING = TRUE | FALSE] |
    [DB_FILE_MULTIBLOCK_READ_COUNT = integer] |
    [FAST_START_IO_TARGET = integer] |
    [FLAGGER = ENTRY | INTERMEDIATE | FULL | OFF] |
    [GLOBAL_NAMES = [TRUE | FALSE] |
    [HASH_AREA_SIZE = integer] |
    [HASH_JOIN_ENABLED = TRUE | FALSE] |
    [HASH_MULTIBLOCK_IO_COUNT = integer] |
    [INSTANCE = integer] |
    [ISOLATION_LEVEL = SERIALIZABLE | READ COMMITTED] |
    [LABEL = 'text' | DBHIGH | DBLOW | OSLABEL] |
    [LOG_ARCHIVE_DEST_integer =
       {'' | LOCATION=pathname | SERVICE=tnsnames_service}
       [MANDATORY | OPTIONAL] [REOPEN[=integer]]] |
    [LOG_ARCHIVE_DEST_STATE_integer = ENABLE | DEFER] |
    [LOG_ARCHIVE_MINIMUM_SUCCEED_DEST = integer] |
```

```
            [MAX_DUMP_FILE_SIZE = integer | UNLIMITED]
            [NLS_CALENDAR = 'text'] |
            [NLS_COMP = 'text'] |
            [NLS_CURRENCY = 'text'] |
            [NLS_DATE_FORMAT = 'date_format'] |
            [NLS_DATE_LANGUAGE = language] |
            [NLS_DUAL_CURRENCY = 'text'] |
            [OPTIMIZER_GOAL = ALL_ROWS | FIRST_ROWS | RULE | CHOOSE] |
            [NLS_ISO_CURRENCY = territory] |
            [NLS_LABEL_FORMAT = label_format] |
            [NLS_NUMERIC_CHARACTERS = 'text'] |
            [NLS_LANGUAGE = language] |
            [NLS_SORT = sort | BINARY] |
            [NLS_TERRITORY = territory] |
            [OBJECT_CACHE_MAX_SIZE_PERCENT = integer] |
            [OBJECT_CACHE_OPTIMAL_SIZE = integer] |
            [OPTIMIZER_INDEX_CACHING = integer] |
            [OPTIMIZER_INDEX_COST_ADJ = integer] |
            [OPTIMIZER_MAX_PERMUTATIONS = integer] |
            [OPTIMIZER_MODE = ALL_ROWS | FIRST_ROWS | RULE | CHOOSE] |
            [OPTIMIZER_PERCENT_PARALLEL = integer] |
            [PARALLEL_BROADCAST_ENABLED = TRUE | FALSE] |
            [PARALLEL_INSTANCE_GROUP = 'text'] |
            [PARTITION_VIEW_ENABLED = TRUE | FALSE] |
            [PLSQL_V2_COMPATIBILITY = TRUE | FALSE] |
            [QUERY_REWRITE_ENABLED = TRUE | FALSE] |
            [QUERY_REWRITE_INTEGRITY = ENFORCED | TRUSTED | STALE_TOLERATED] |
            [REMOTE_DEPENDENCIES_MODE = TIMESTAMP | SIGNATURE] |
            [SESSION_CACHED_CURSORS = integer] |
            [SKIP_UNUSABLE_INDEXES = TRUE | FALSE] |
            [SORT_AREA_RETAINED_SIZE = integer] |
            [SORT_AREA_SIZE = integer] |
            [SORT_MULTIBLOCK_READ_COUNT = integer] |
            [SQL_TRACE = TRUE | FALSE] |
            [STAR_TRANSFORMATION_ENABLED = TRUE | FALSE] |
            [TIMED_STATISTICS = TRUE | FALSE] |
            [USE_STORED_OUTLINES = TRUE | FALSE | 'category_name'] |
        } |
        [CLOSE DATABASE LINK dblink] |
        [ADVISE COMMIT | ROLLBACK | NOTHING] |
        [{ENABLE|DISABLE} COMMIT IN PROCEDURE] |
        [{ENABLE|DISABLE|FORCE} PARALLEL {DML | DDL} [PARALLEL integer]
    }
```

Changes the current database session's functional characteristics, including several National Language Support (NLS) characteristics.

Keywords

CONSTRAINT[S]

> Specifies when conditions defined by a deferrable constraint are enforced. IMMEDIATE means that conditions are checked immediately after each DML statement. DEFERRED indicates that the conditions are checked when the

transaction is committed. DEFAULT restores all constraints to their initial state, as defined when they were created.

CREATE_STORED_OUTLINES

Specifies whether Oracle will store an outline for each query. If *category_name* is provided, then outlines will be created and stored in the *category_name* category.

CURRENT_SCHEMA

Changes the current schema to the specified *schema*. Although the schema is changed, the user is not, and no additional privileges are available.

CURSOR_SHARING

Specifies the kind of SQL statements that can share a cursor. If FORCE is specified, statements may share a cursor if they are identical except for some literals and if the differences do not affect the meaning of the statement. EXACT means that only identical SQL statements may share a cursor.

DB_BLOCK_CHECKING

Specifies whether data block checking is performed.

DB_FILE_MULTIBLOCK_READ_COUNT

Specifies the number of blocks read during a single I/O operation when performing a sequential scan. The default is 8.

FAST_START_IO_TARGET

Specifies the target number of reads and writes to and from cache that should be performed during crash or instance recovery.

FLAGGER

Specifies a FIPS flagging level, which causes an error message to be generated whenever a SQL statement does not conform to ANSI SQL-92 standards. Note that there is currently no difference between ENTRY, INTERMEDIATE, and FULL.

GLOBAL_NAMES

Controls whether global name resolution will be enforced for this session.

HASH_AREA_SIZE

Specifies the amount of memory (in bytes) used for hash joins.

HASH_JOIN_ENABLED

Specifies whether hash joins will be performed in queries.

HASH_MULTIBLOCK_IO_COUNT

Specifies the number of data blocks to be read or written during a hash join.

INSTANCE

Specifies that in a Parallel Server environment, database files should be accessed as though the session were connected to the specified instance.

ISOLATION_LEVEL

Specifies how database modifications are to be handled. SERIALIZABLE means if an attempt is made to update a row that has been updated and not yet committed by another session, the statement will fail; this option is consistent with the serializable transaction isolation mode specified in the SQL-92 standard. READ COMMITTED means that Oracle's default behavior will be in effect, and if a row is locked by another uncommitted transaction, the statement will wait until the row locks are released.

LABEL

Changes the DBMS session label to the label specified by *text*, the label equivalent of DBHIGH or DBLOW, or the operating system label (OSLABEL).

LOG_ARCHIVE_DEST_integer

Specifies a location for archived redo log file groups. Up to five locations may be defined, as specified by *integer*, and the archiving process will attempt to archive redo log files to each.

"

Specifies that no destination is defined for this archive log destination. However, at least one archive log destination (1–5) must have a location defined.

LOCATION

Specifies the operating system location for archived redo log files.

SERVICE

Specifies the name of a Net8 service running a standby database associated with the *tnsnames_service* entry in the *tnsnames.ora* file.

MANDATORY

Specifies that archiving to the destination must succeed before the redo log file is made available for reuse.

OPTIONAL

Specifies that archiving to the destination does not have to succeed before the redo log file is made available for reuse.

REOPEN

Specifies the number of seconds that must pass after an error is encountered during archiving to the destination before future archives to the destination can be attempted.

LOG_ARCHIVE_DEST_STATE_integer

Specifies the state to be associated with the corresponding LOG_ARCHIVE_ DEST_*integer*. ENABLE means that any valid LOG_ARCHIVE_DEST can be used. DEFER indicates that the LOG_ARCHIVE_DEST_*integer* with the same value of *integer* will not be used.

LOG_ARCHIVE_MINIMUM_SUCCEED_DEST

Specifies the minimum number of destinations that must be written to successfully before a redo log file can be reused.

MAX_DUMP_FILE_SIZE

Specifies the maximum size for a trace dump file in blocks. If UNLIMITED is specified, there is no size limit.

NLS_CALENDAR

Specifies a new calendar type.

NLS_COMP

Specifies the linguistic comparison to be performed using the rules associated with the NLS_SORT parameter supplied as *text*.

NLS_CURRENCY

Specifies the local currency symbol returned by the number format element L. This parameter overrides the defaults set by NLS_TERRITORY.

NLS_DATE_FORMAT

Specifies the default date format. The *date_format* must be a valid Oracle date format mask. This parameter overrides the defaults set by NLS_TERRITORY.

NLS_DATE_LANGUAGE

Specifies the language to use for day and month names, as well as for other specified date values. This parameter overrides the defaults set by NLS_LANGUAGE.

NLS_DUAL_CURRENCY

Specifies the value to be returned by the number format element U (normally used for the Euro).

NLS_ISO_CURRENCY

Specifies the territory whose ISO currency symbol should be used. This parameter may override the defaults set by NLS_TERRITORY.

NLS_LABEL_FORMAT

For Trusted Oracle only; changes the default label format for the session.

NLS_LANGUAGE

Specifies the language for Oracle messages, day and month names, and *sort* sequences.

NLS_NUMERIC_CHARACTERS

Specifies the decimal character and group separator. The value of '*text*' must be in the form '*dg*', where *d* is the decimal character, and *g* is the group character. This parameter may override the defaults set by NLS_TERRITORY.

NLS_SORT

Specifies the collating sequence for character sorts. BINARY specifies a binary sort, while *sort* specifies the name of a specific sort sequence.

NLS_TERRITORY

Specifies the values of the default date format, numeric decimal, and group separator, and the local and ISO currency symbols. This parameter may override the defaults set by NLS_LANGUAGE.

OBJECT_CACHE_MAX_SIZE_PERCENT

Specifies the percentage by which the object cache can grow beyond the optimal size. The default is 10.

OBJECT_CACHE_OPTIMAL_SIZE

Specifies the optimal size (in kilobytes) for the object cache. The default is 100.

OPTIMIZER_GOAL

For Oracle7, specifies the optimization goal for this session. The following goals are valid:

ALL_ROWS

Optimize for best overall throughput.

FIRST_ROWS

Optimize for best response time.

RULE

Use rule-based optimization.

CHOOSE

Use cost-based optimization if possible; otherwise, use rule-based optimization.

OPTIMIZER_INDEX_CACHING

Specifies the percentage of index blocks assumed to be in the cache.

OPTIMIZER_INDEX_COST_ADJ

Specifies a percentage indicating the importance that the optimizer attaches to the availability of an index path instead of a full table scan.

OPTIMIZER_MAX_PERMUTATIONS

Specifies the number of table permutations the optimizer will consider for large join operations.

OPTIMIZER_MODE

For Oracle8, specifies the optimization goal for this session. The following goals are valid:

ALL_ROWS

Optimize for best overall throughput.

FIRST_ROWS

Optimize for best response time.

RULE

Use rule-based optimization.

CHOOSE

Use cost-based optimization if possible; otherwise, use rule-based optimization.

OPTIMIZER_PERCENT_PARALLEL

Specifies the amount of parallelism the optimizer uses when computing costs. The default is 0, which indicates no parallelism.

PARALLEL_BROADCAST_ENABLED

Specifies that parallel processing can be used to enhance performance during hash and merge joins.

PARALLEL_INSTANCE_GROUP

Specifies the parallel instance group used when spawning parallel query slave processes. This option is valid only when running Parallel Server in parallel mode.

PARTITION_VIEW_ENABLED

Specifies that unnecessary table access can be eliminated during operations on partitioned views.

PLSQL_V2_COMPATIBILITY

Specifies whether or not PL/SQL constructs that were legal in Oracle7 (under PL/SQL 2.0), but are now illegal in Oracle8, are allowed. A value of TRUE allows the old constructs. A value of FALSE disallows them.

QUERY_REWRITE_ENABLED

Specifies whether query rewrite will be in effect for materialized views. Query rewrite is disabled if OPTIMIZER_MODE is set to RULE.

QUERY_REWRITE_INTEGRITY

Specifies consistency levels for query rewrites. ENFORCED indicates that system-enforced relationships are relied on so that data integrity can be guaranteed. TRUSTED means that materialized views created with the ON PREBUILD TABLE clause are supported and unenforced join relationships are accepted. STALE_TOLERATED means that any stale but usable materialized view may be used.

REMOTE_DEPENDENCIES_MODE

Specifies how dependencies of remote stored procedures are handled.

SESSION_CACHED_CURSORS

Specifies the number of cursors for this session that may be retained in cache.

SKIP_UNUSABLE_INDEXES

Specifies whether operations will be permitted on tables with unusable indexes or index partitions. TRUE means all such operations will be allowed, while FALSE causes such operations to return an error.

SORT_AREA_RETAINED_SIZE

Specifies the maximum amount of memory in bytes that will be retained by each sort operation after the first fetch.

SORT_AREA_SIZE

Specifies the maximum amount of memory in bytes that each sort operation will use.

SORT_MULTIBLOCK_READ_COUNT

Specifies the number of blocks to read each time the sort performs a read from temporary segments. The default is 2.

SQL_TRACE

Controls whether performance statistics are generated. The initial value is set in the *INIT.ORA* file.

STAR_TRANSFORMATION_ENABLED

Specifies whether cost-based optimization will be applied to star queries.

TIMED_STATISTICS

Specifies whether (TRUE) or not (FALSE) Oracle requests time information from the operating system when generating time-based statistics.

USE_STORED_OUTLINES

Specifies whether the optimizer will use stored outlines when generating execution plans. If *category_name* is provided, only outlines stored under that category will be used.

CLOSE DATABASE LINK

Closes a connection to a remote database using the database link *dblink*. This command succeeds only if the database link is not in use and there is no pending commit across the link.

ADVISE

Sends advice for forcing a distributed transaction to a remote database by placing the value 'C' (COMMIT), 'R' (ROLLBACK), or '' (NOTHING) in DBA_2PC_PENDING_ADVICE on the remote database.

ENABLE COMMIT IN PROCEDURE

Specifies that procedures and stored functions can issue COMMIT and ROLLBACK statements.

DISABLE COMMIT IN PROCEDURE

Specifies that procedures and stored functions may not issue COMMIT and ROLLBACK statements.

ENABLE PARALLEL

Specifies that the DML or DDL statements following in the session be executed in parallel, if possible. This option is the default for DDL statements.

DISABLE PARALLEL

Specifies that the DML or DDL statements following in the session be executed serially. This option is the default for DML statements.

FORCE PARALLEL

Specifies that subsequent statements in the session be executed in parallel.

DML

Specifies that the ENABLE, DISABLE, or FORCE PARALLEL keyword applies to DML (Data Manipulation Language) statements.

DDL

Specifies that the ENABLE, DISABLE, or FORCE PARALLEL keyword applies to DDL (Data Definition Language) statements.

PARALLEL

Specifies the degree of parallelism. The integer will override a parallel clause specified in a DDL statement, but will not override a parallel hint specified in a subsequent DML statement.

 Many of the parameters that may be set using this command are defined on an instance-wide basis by parameters in the initialization file (*INIT.ORA*). Although defaults are indicated here when appropriate, the values of the initialization parameters will override those defaults and be the *de facto* default values. Be sure that you understand the use of each parameter before attempting to set it for a session.

Examples

Enable the SQL Trace facility for your session:

```
ALTER SESSION
    SET SQL_TRACE = TRUE;
```

SQL_TRACE should be set to FALSE except when performance statistics are desired, since this option degrades overall database performance. If SQL_TRACE is set to TRUE, a trace file will be created in the *udump* directory. If a large number of SQL statements are executed, this directory may become filled.

Set the language to French and then override the date format with an American-style date format using a four-digit year:

```
ALTER SESSION
  SET NLS_LANGUAGE = French;
ALTER SESSION
  SET NLS_DATE_FORMAT = 'mm/dd/yyyy';
```

ANALYZE

```
ANALYZE {TABLE [schema.]tablename |
        INDEX [schema.]indexname |
        CLUSTER [schema.]clustername
        }
       {COMPUTE STATISTICS |
        ESTIMATE [SAMPLE integer {ROWS | PERCENT}] STATISTICS
        DELETE STATISTICS
        VALIDATE STRUCTURE [CASCADE]
        LIST CHAINED ROWS [INTO [schema.]tablename]
        }
```

Collects or deletes statistics about an object in the database, validates the structure of an object, or identifies migrated and chained rows in a table or cluster.

Keywords

COMPUTE STATISTICS

Computes the exact statistics for the entire named object and stores them in the data dictionary.

ESTIMATE STATISTICS

Estimates statistics for the named object and stores them in the data dictionary. The optional SAMPLE clause may be used to specify the sample size to use. The SAMPLE clause contains the following keywords:

ROWS

Causes *integer* rows of a table or cluster, or *integer* entries from an index, to be sampled.

PERCENT

Causes *integer* percent of the rows of a table or cluster, or *integer* percent of the entries in an index, to be sampled. The valid range for PERCENT is

1–99. If SAMPLE is not specified, a default value of 1050 rows will be used as the sample size.

DELETE STATISTICS

Causes all statistics stored in the data dictionary for the named object to be deleted.

VALIDATE STRUCTURE

Causes the structure of the named object to be validated. The CASCADE keyword will also cause indexes associated with the named object to be validated.

LIST CHAINED ROWS

Generates a list of chained and migrated rows for the named table or cluster (this operation is not permitted on an index). Entries are made in a table named CHAINED_ROWS, which is assumed to exist in the user's schema. The INTO clause may be used to specify a different name for the target table.

You must own the object to be analyzed or have the ANALYZE ANY privilege. If you want to use the LIST CHAINED ROWS operation to list into a table, that table must be in your schema or you must have the INSERT privilege on it. COMPUTE STATISTICS results in more accurate statistics, but is likely to take longer. ESTIMATE STATISTICS is normally much faster and almost as accurate. The object being analyzed will be locked while statistics are being collected, so the faster ESTIMATE STATISTICS may be preferable in a heavy transaction environment. Statistics are accessible in the ALL_TABLES, USER_TABLES, and DBA_TABLES views. Some column statistics are accessible in the ALL_TAB_COLUMNS, USER_TAB_COLUMNS, and DBA_TAB_COLUMNS views. Cluster statistics also appear in USER_CLUSTERS and DBA_CLUSTERS.

Example

Analyze scott's emp table using a 50 percent sample size:

```
ANALYZE TABLE scott.emp ESTIMATE SAMPLE 50 PERCENT STATISTICS;
```

DELETE

```
DELETE [FROM] {[schema.]table[@dblink] |
               [schema.]table PARTITION (partition) |
               [schema.]table SUBPARTITION (subpartition) |
               [schema.]view[@dblink] |
               [schema.]snapshot[@dblink] |
               (subquery[WITH {READ ONLY]] |
               CHECK OPTION [CONSTRAINT constraint_name])
                 }]
             }
```

```
[table_alias]
[WHERE condition]
[RETURNING expression[,expression ...] INTO data_item[,data_item ...]]
```

Deletes rows from a table, view, or snapshot.

Keywords

FROM

Optional keyword to aid readability.

schema

The name of the schema containing the table or view from which rows are deleted. If omitted, the current userid is assumed.

table

The name of a table from which rows are to be deleted.

dblink

The name of a database link used to access the table or view from which rows are to be deleted.

PARTITION

Specifies that rows are to be deleted from a partition (named *partition*) of the specified table.

SUBPARTITION

Specifies that rows are to be deleted from a subpartition (named *subpartition*) of the specified table.

subquery

Specifies a subquery, which determines the rows that are candidates for deletion. See SELECT later in this chapter for more information on subqueries.

WITH READ ONLY

Specifies that the subquery cannot be updated.

WITH CHECK OPTION

Specifies that no changes can be made to the table underlying the subquery that would result in rows that are not included in the subquery.

CONSTRAINT

Specifies a constraint name to associate with the CHECK OPTION.

`table_alias`

Specifies an alias (or alternate name) for the table, view, or subquery.

WHERE

Specifies the *condition* that will be used to identify the rows to be deleted. The specified *condition* may be any valid WHERE condition.

RETURNING

Specifies that the value(s) of the specified *expression(s)* are to be returned for rows deleted by this command. This keyword is valid only from within a PL/SQL program.

INTO

Specifies the PL/SQL variables into which the values returned for rows deleted by this command are to be stored.

 If a *table_alias* is specified, any columns referenced in the DELETE statement with a specific table reference must be qualified using the *table_alias* and not the table name.

Examples

Delete all rows from scott's emp table for employees who have salaries above 2000:

```
DELETE FROM scott.emp
WHERE sal>2000;
```

Delete all rows from scott's emp table for employees who have salaries greater than the average salary:

```
DELETE FROM scott.emp
WHERE sal>(SELECT AVG(sal) FROM scott.emp);
```

EXPLAIN PLAN

```
EXPLAIN PLAN
    SET STATEMENT_ID = 'text'
    [INTO [schema.]tablename[@dblink]]
    FOR SQL_statement
```

Creates an explanation of the execution plan for a SQL statement.

Keywords

SET STATEMENT_ID

Specifies a text string used to identify the result of this EXPLAIN PLAN statement. The default is NULL.

INTO

Specifies the name and location of the plan table. The default is to use a table named PLAN_TABLE in your current schema.

FOR

Specifies the SQL statement for which the plan is to be generated.

You must have the INSERT privilege on the destination table (specified by INTO) before issuing this command. The destination table is usually called PLAN_TABLE, and can be created by running the script *utlxplan.sql.* The value specified in the SET clause appears in the STATEMENT_ID column of the destination table.

Example

The following example generates an execution plan for a SQL statement. The output will be placed in the plan_table table in the current schema:

```
EXPLAIN PLAN
    SET STATEMENT_ID = 'Plan1'
    FOR
    SELECT ename, sal, comm, loc
    FROM emp,dept
    WHERE emp.deptno = dept.deptno;
```

See Chapter 8, *SQL Statement Tuning,* for a discussion of the plan table.

INSERT

```
INSERT INTO {schema.{table[{@dblink] |
                    table PARTITION (partition) |
                    table SUBPARTITION (subpartition) |
                    view[@dblink] |
            }[table_alias]
[(column[,column..])
{VALUES (expr[,expr..]) |
 subquery
}
[RETURNING expression[,expression...] INTO data_item[,data_item..]]
```

Inserts a row of data into a table or view.

If a *table_alias* is specified, any columns referenced in the INSERT statement with a specific table reference must be qualified using the *table_alias* and not the table name.

Keywords

schema

The name of the schema containing the table or view into which rows are to be inserted. If omitted, the current userid is assumed.

table

The name of a table into which rows are to be inserted.

dblink

The name of a database link used to access the table or view into which rows are to be inserted.

PARTITION

Specifies that rows are to be inserted into a partition (named *partition*) of the specified table.

SUBPARTITION

Specifies that rows are to be inserted into a subpartition (named *subpartition*) of the specified table.

view

The name of a view into which rows are to be inserted.

`table_alias`

Specifies an alias (or alternate name) for the table or view.

`column`

Specifies the name(s) of one or more columns in the table or view into which values will be stored. If the VALUES keyword is specified, then for each column specified, a corresponding *expr* must be specified in the VALUES clause. If the list of column names is omitted, the list is considered to contain all columns of the table or view.

VALUES

Specifies the value(s) to be stored in each column of the row to be inserted. *expr* can be any valid SQL expression, and there must be exactly as many *expr*s listed as there are columns specified for the table or view. If no column list is supplied, there must be the same number of expressions as columns in the table or view.

subquery

Specifies a subquery, which returns values to be stored in the row to be inserted. If a list of columns is specified for the table or view into which rows are to be inserted, *subquery* must return exactly the same number of columns, in the same sequence. If no column list is specified, *subquery* must return the same number of columns as *table* or *view*. See SELECT later in the chapter for more information on subqueries.

RETURNING

Specifies that the value(s) of *expression* for rows inserted by this command are to be returned. This keyword is valid only from within a PL/SQL program.

INTO

> Specifies that value(s) returned for rows inserted by this command are to be stored in the PL/SQL variable(s) *data_item*.

Examples

Insert new rows into scott's emp table. Only the five specified columns will have values:

```
INSERT INTO emp (empno, ename, hiredate, mgr, sal)
VALUES (7999, 'KREINES', '01-JUN-00', 7839, 500)
```

Insert new rows into a table called newemp using a subquery to populate the rows. All columns receive values from the subquery:

```
INSERT INTO newemp
    SELECT * FROM scott.emp WHERE comm > 0;
```

SAVEPOINT

```
SAVEPOINT savepoint
```

Identifies a point in a transaction to which you can roll back using the ROLLBACK command.

savepoint

> Specifies a name for the *savepoint* being created.

Example

Set a savepoint, update the *sal* column of the emp table, and then issue a ROLL-BACK command to return the state of the table to the condition at the time the savepoint was established:

```
UPDATE emp
    SET comm = comm * 1.1;

SAVEPOINT updtsal;

UPDATE emp
    SET sal = sal * 1.1;

ROLLBACK TO updtsal;
```

SELECT

```
SELECT [DISTINCT | UNIQUE | ALL]
{[schema.]{table. | view. | snapshot.}* |
 expr [[AS] alias][,expr [[AS] alias] ...] |
 *
FROM {schema.{table[@dblink] |
          table PARTITION (partition) |
```

```
            table SUBPARTITION (subpartition) |
            table SAMPLE [BLOCK] sample_percent |
            view[@dblink] |
            snapshot[@dblink] |
            (subquery)
      } [table_alias]
      [,{schema.{table[@dblink] |
                 table PARTITION (partition) |
                 table SUBPARTITION (subpartition) |
                 table SAMPLE [BLOCK] sample_percent |
                 view[@dblink] |
                 snapshot[@dblink] |
                 (subquery)
      } |
        }[table_alias]
      ...]
[WHERE condition]
[GROUP BY {expr[,expr ...] |
          CUBE (expr[,expr ...]) |
          ROLLUP (expr[,expr ...])
          }
          [HAVING condition]
[[START WITH condition] CONNECT BY condition]
[{UNION [ALL] | INTERSECT | MINUS} {subquery)
 [,{UNION [ALL] | INTERSECT | MINUS} {subquery) ...]]
[ORDER BY {expr | position | alias} [ASC | DESC]
 [, {expr | position | alias} [ASC | DESC] ...]
[FOR UPDATE [OF schema.{table | view}.column[,schema.{table | view}.column ...]
    [NOWAIT]
```

Retrieves data from tables, views, or snapshots.

Keywords

DISTINCT

Specifies that only one copy of a row should be returned, even if there are duplicate rows. A duplicate row is one that returns the same values for all columns listed in the SELECT list.

ALL

Specifies that all rows should be returned, including duplicates. This option is the default.

schema

The name of the schema containing the table or view. If omitted, the current userid is assumed.

table

Specifies the name of a table.

view

Specifies the name of a view.

snapshot
> Specifies the name of a snapshot.

* Specifies that all columns are to be returned, and is the equivalent of listing each column of the table, view, or snapshot.

expr
> Any valid Oracle expression, usually involving one or more columns from the table, view, or snapshot.

AS Specifies an *alias* (or alternate name) for a column or expression. The keyword AS is optional.

FROM
> Specifies the name(s) of one or more tables, views, or snapshots from which data is to be retrieved.

PARTITION
> Specifies that data be retrieved from the partition of *table* identified by *partition.*

SUBPARTITION
> Specifies that data be retrieved from the subpartition of *table* identified by *subpartition.*

SAMPLE [BLOCK]
> Specifies that a random sample of the rows in the table is to be selected. Replace *sample_percent* in the syntax with the percentage that you want to use. If the optional keyword BLOCK is specified, block sampling instead of row sampling will be performed.

subquery
> Any valid SELECT statement. Note that a subquery may not contain a FOR UPDATE clause.

table_alias
> Specifies an alias (or alternate name) for a table, view, or snapshot.

WHERE
> Specifies that only rows meeting *condition* will be retrieved. *condition* will be evaluated, and only rows that evaluate to TRUE will be returned. If this clause is omitted, all rows will be returned.

GROUP BY
> Specifies that rows are to be grouped according to the provided expression(s) (*expr*), and a single row of summary information be returned for each group.

CUBE
> Specifies that rows are to be grouped based on all possible combinations of values from the provided list of expressions.

ROLLUP

Specifies that rows are to be grouped based on values from the provided list of expressions, and summary rows be returned for each *expr,* along with an additional superaggregate row.

HAVING

Specifies that data be returned only for groupings meeting *condition,* which is evaluated for TRUE in the same manner as a WHERE condition.

START WITH

Specifies the row(s) used as the root of a hierarchical query. If omitted, all rows of the table will be considered root rows.

CONNECT BY

Specifies the relationship between parent and child rows in the hierarchy.

UNION [ALL]

Specifies that the results of the SELECT statement that precedes this keyword are to be combined with the results of the SELECT statement that follows.

INTERSECT

Specifies that the results of the SELECT statement that precedes this keyword are to be combined with the results of the SELECT statement that follows, and only the rows that appear in both are to be returned.

MINUS

Specifies that the results of the SELECT statement that precedes this keyword are to be combined with the results of the SELECT statement that follows. Any row appearing in the following SELECT will be removed from the set of rows to be returned by the first.

ORDER BY

Specifies that rows are to be sorted before being returned. The sort may be performed on expression(s), alias(es), or position(s). In the syntax, *position* is an integer referring to the expression's position in the SELECT list. The first item in the SELECT list is considered to be in position 1.

ASC

Specifies that values are to be sorted in ascending sequence—from lowest to highest. This is the default.

DESC

Specifies that values are to be sorted in descending sequence—from highest to lowest.

FOR UPDATE

Specifies that the selected rows are to be locked. If the keyword OF is specified, only rows in the table specified will be locked.

NOWAIT

> Specifies that if a table is already locked, Oracle should not wait for the lock to be released. If NOWAIT is not specified, Oracle will wait for the lock to be released.

 If a *table_alias* is specified, any ambiguously defined columns referenced in the SELECT statement must be qualified using the *table_alias*, and not the table name.

Examples

Retrieve all columns for all rows of scott's emp table:

```
SELECT *
FROM scott.emp;
```

Retrieve a specified set of columns from the emp and dept tables in scott's schema:

```
SELECT ename, dname, hiredate, sal, comm
FROM scott.emp, scott.dept
WHERE emp.deptno = dept.deptno;
```

Retrieve a specified set of columns from the emp and dept tables in scott's schema. Use a table alias for the emp table. Use a subquery to limit the rows selected to those with a salary higher than the average salary. Then return the rows in order from the lowest salary to the highest salary:

```
SELECT ename, dname, hiredate, sal, comm
FROM scott.emp a, scott.dept
WHERE a.deptno = dept.deptno
AND sal > (SELECT AVG(sal)
           FROM scott.emp)
ORDER BY sal;
```

Retrieve the highest and lowest salaries for each department. Column aliases are used:

```
SELECT dname Department, MAX(sal) Maximum, MIN(sal) Minimum
FROM scott.emp, scott.dept
WHERE emp.deptno = dept.deptno
GROUP BY dname;
```

SET CONSTRAINT

```
SET {CONSTRAINT | CONSTRAINTS} {ALL | constraint[,constraint...]}
{IMMEDIATE | DEFERRED}
```

Specifies at the transaction level whether specific constraints are checked after each DML statement or deferred until the end of a transaction.

 This statement applies only to deferrable constraints.

Keywords

ALL

Specifies that all deferrable constraints for the transaction are affected by this statement.

constraint

Specifies the name of a deferrable constraint.

IMMEDIATE

Specifies that the conditions enforced by the constraints are to be checked after each DML statement is completed.

DEFERRED

Specifies that the conditions enforced by the constraints are to be checked after the entire transaction is complete and committed.

 The success of deferrable constraints can be tested by issuing the statement SET CONSTRAINTS ALL IMMEDIATE before the COMMIT statement is issued.

Example

Defer two constraints until the transaction is complete:

```
SET CONSTRAINTS chk_sal,chk_comm DEFERRED;
```

SET ROLE

```
SET ROLE
    {role [IDENTIFIED BY password][,role [IDENTIFIED BY password ...]] |
    ALL EXCEPT role[,role ...] |
    NONE
    }
```

Enables or disables roles for the current session.

Keywords

role

Specifies the name of the role to be enabled.

IDENTIFIED BY

Specifies the password for the role. This option is required if the role is password protected.

ALL

Specifies that all roles granted to you are to be enabled. If the EXCEPT clause is included, the specified roles will not be enabled, but all other roles granted to you will be.

NONE

Specifies that all roles granted to you are to be disabled for this session.

Example

Enable the developer role for the current session:

```
SET ROLE developer IDENTIFIED BY manager;
```

SET TRANSACTION

```
SET TRANSACTION {READ ONLY |
                 READ WRITE |
                 ISOLATION LEVEL {SERIALIZABLE | READ COMMITTED} |
                 USE ROLLBACK SEGMENT seg_name
                 }
```

Establishes the current transaction as read-only or read-write or specifies the rollback segment to be used by the transaction.

Keywords

READ ONLY

Specifies that the current transaction is read-only.

READ WRITE

Specifies that the current transaction is read-write.

ISOLATION_LEVEL

Specifies how database modifications are to be handled. SERIALIZABLE means that if an attempt is made to update a row that has been updated and not yet committed by another session, the statement will fail; this situation is consistent with the serializable transaction isolation mode specified in the ANSI SQL-92 standard. READ COMMITTED means that Oracle's default behavior will be in effect, and if a row is locked by another uncommitted transaction, the statement will wait until the row locks are released.

USE ROLLBACK SEGMENT

Assigns this transaction to the rollback segment specified by *seg_name*. This clause implies READ WRITE and cannot be specified with READ ONLY.

If used, this statement must be the first in your transaction. A transaction is ended with a COMMIT or COMMIT WORK statement.

Example

Specify a rollback segment and perform an update transaction:

```
SET TRANSACTION
    USE ROLLBACK SEGMENT rbs99;

UPDATE emp
SET SAL = SAL*1.1;

COMMIT;
```

TRUNCATE

```
TRUNCATE {TABLE [schema.]table [{PRESERVE | PURGE} SNAPSHOT LOG] |
        CLUSTER [schema.]cluster
        }
    [{DROP | REUSE} STORAGE]
```

Removes all rows from a table or cluster.

To execute a TRUNCATE command, you must either be the owner of the table to be truncated, or have the DROP ANY TABLE system privilege. Merely being granted privileges on the table will not be sufficient.

Keywords

table

Specifies the name of the table from which rows are to be removed.

cluster

Specifies the name of the cluster from which rows are to be removed.

PRESERVE SNAPSHOT LOG

Specifies that existing snapshot logs on this table should be preserved when the table is truncated. This option is useful when a table is being reloaded during an EXPort/TRUNCATE/IMPort operation, since a fast refresh will not be triggered.

PURGE SNAPSHOT LOG

Specifies that existing snapshot logs on this table should be purged when the table is truncated.

DROP STORAGE

Deallocates storage used by the rows and returns the space to the free space pool. This option is the default.

REUSE STORAGE

Retains the space used by the deleted rows. This option is useful if the table or cluster will be reloaded with data.

 The TRUNCATE statement does not create rollback records, so it cannot be rolled back. This characteristic makes TRUNCATE extremely fast, and it is preferable to DELETE FROM, unless the roll-back capability is required. When a table is truncated and the DROP STORAGE clause is specified, only the initial extent of the table is retained; all other storage is deallocated.

Example

Remove all rows from scott's emp table, and deallocate the space used:

```
TRUNCATE TABLE scott.emp;
```

UPDATE

```
UPDATE {[schema.]table[{@dblink] |
        [schema.]table PARTITION (partition) |
        [schema.]table SUBPARTITION (subpartition) |
        [schema.]table SAMPLE [BLOCK] sample_percent |
        [schema.]view[@dblink] |
        [schema.]snapshot[@dblink]
      }
      [table_alias]
SET {column={expr | (subquery)}[,column={expr | (subquery)} ... |
    (column[,column ...])=subquery
    }
[WHERE condition]
[RETURNING expression[,expression ...] INTO data_item[,data_item ...]]
```

Changes the value stored in one or more columns of data in one or more tables, views, or snapshots.

Keywords

schema

The name of the schema containing the table or view that is to be updated. If omitted, the current userid is assumed.

table

Specifies the name of a table to be updated.

view

Specifies the name of a view to be updated.

snapshot

Specifies the name of a snapshot to be updated.

PARTITION

Specifies that data be updated in the partition of *table* identified by *partition*.

SUBPARTITION

Specifies that data be updated in the subpartition of *table* identified by *subpartition*.

SAMPLE

Specifies that a random sample of the rows in the table be updated. The sample size is specified by *sample_percent*. If the optional keyword BLOCK is specified, block sampling rather than row sampling will be performed.

subquery

Any valid SELECT statement. Note that a subquery may not contain a FOR UPDATE clause.

table_alias

Specifies an alias (or alternate name) for a table, view, or snapshot.

column

The name of a column in the table, view, or snapshot that will be updated.

expr

Any valid Oracle expression.

WHERE

Specifies that only rows meeting *condition* will be updated. The *condition* will be evaluated, and only rows that evaluate to TRUE will be updated. If this clause is omitted, all rows will be updated.

RETURNING

Specifies that the value(s) of *expression* for rows updated by this statement are to be returned. This keyword is valid only from within a PL/SQL program.

INTO

Specifies that value(s) returned for rows updated by this statement are to be stored in the PL/SQL variable(s) *data_item*.

Examples

Update all employees in scott's emp table who have a current salary of less than 2000. Increase their salary by 10 percent:

```
UPDATE scott.emp
SET sal = sal * 1.1
WHERE sal < 2000;
```

Update all employees in scott's emp table who have a current salary less than 2000. Increase both their salary and commission by 10 percent:

```
UPDATE scott.emp
SET sal = sal * 1.1,
    comm=comm*1.1
WHERE sal < 2000;
```

Update a random 15 percent sample of employees in scott's emp table. Increase both salary and commission by 10 percent for employees whose current salary is less than 2000:

```
UPDATE scott.emp SAMPLE 15
SET sal = sal * 1.1,
    comm = comm * 1.1
WHERE sal < 2000;
```

4

Common SQL Elements

Many components of SQL syntax are used in multiple SQL statements. These components, often referred to as *SQL clauses*, can be somewhat complex themselves. To simplify the presentation of SQL syntax in Chapter 2, *Data Definition Statements*, and Chapter 3, *Data Manipulation and Control Statements*, I have collected these common elements here. In the earlier chapters, I simply referenced their names and syntactical positions in the individual SQL syntax descriptions.

Autoextend_Clause

```
AUTOEXTEND {OFF |
            ON [NEXT integer[K | M]]
               [MAXSIZE {integer[K | M] | UNLIMITED}]
```

Specifies whether or not files will be permitted to grow in size. When files are allowed to grow in size, this clause also specifies the growth parameters.

Keywords

OFF

> Specifies that the autoextend feature should not be enabled, and that the file will not be permitted to grow in size.

ON

> Specifies that when the file becomes full and additional space is requested, the file will be extended in size by the amount specified by the NEXT parameter, up to the limit specified by the MAXSIZE parameter.

NEXT

> Specifies the amount of space in bytes, kilobytes (K), or megabytes (M) that will be added to the file when growth occurs.

MAXSIZE

Specifies the maximum size in bytes, kilobytes (K), or megabytes (M) for the file. The autoextend feature does not extend the file beyond this size.

UNLIMITED

Specifies that the file is permitted to grow up to the capacity of the physical disk, or the maximum size permitted by the operating system, whichever is less.

Column_Constraint_Clause

```
[CONSTRAINT constraint_name]
{[NULL | NOT NULL] |
 [UNIQUE | PRIMARY KEY (column[,column ...])] |
 [REFERENCES [schema.]table [(column[,column ...])]] [ON DELETE {CASCADE | SET NULL}] |
 [CHECK (condition)]
}
[Constraint_State_Clause]
```

Defines column constraints.

Keywords

CONSTRAINT

Specifies the name for the constraint. If omitted, Oracle will assign a name in the form SYS_C*nnn*, where *nnn* is an integer number.

NULL

Specifies that the column may contain a value of NULL.

NOT NULL

Specifies that the column may not contain a value of NULL.

UNIQUE

Specifies that the value in this column must not duplicate a value for the same column in any other row of the table; that is, the value of this column must be unique for all rows of the table. Note, however, that more than one row may contain NULL in this column.

PRIMARY KEY

Specifies that the column or combination of columns, serves as the primary key for the table in which it is defined. A primary key column may not contain NULL, and no value of the primary key may appear in the same column of any other row in the table (i.e., the key value must be unique).

REFERENCES

Specifies the *table* and *column*(s) which are referenced by a foreign key. The combination of referenced columns must represent either a PRIMARY KEY constraint or a UNIQUE constraint on the target table.

ON DELETE CASCADE

Specifies that when a row containing a primary or unique key is deleted, rows containing dependent foreign keys will also be automatically deleted.

ON DELETE SET NULL

Specifies that when a row containing a primary or unique key is deleted, dependent foreign keys will be automatically changed to NULL.

CHECK

Specifies a *condition* that must evaluate to TRUE or NULL for the constraint to be satisfied.

Constraint_State_Clause

Specifies how the constraint will be applied to data in the column.

Constraint_State_Clause

```
[{DEFERRABLE [INITIALLY {IMMEDIATE | DEFERRED} |
   NOT DEFERRABLE [INITIALLY IMMEDIATE ] |
   INITIALLY IMMEDIATE  [[NOT] DEFERRABLE] |
   INITIALLY  DEFERRED
 }]
[RELY | NORELY]
[USING INDEX
  [INITRANS integer]
  [MAXTRANS integer]
  [PCTFREE  integer]
  [TABLESPACE tablespace_name]
  [NOSORT]
  [LOGGING | NOLOGGING]
  [Storage_Clause]
[ENABLE | DISABLE]
[VALIDATE | NOVALIDATE]
[EXCEPTIONS INTO [schema.]table]]
```

Allows a constraint to be selectively enabled or disabled.

DEFERRABLE

Specifies that the constraint may be deferred. A deferred constraint will not be checked until the transaction is committed.

INITIALLY IMMEDIATE

Specifies that the constraint should initially be evaluated immediately after the execution of each DML statement. The SET CONSTRAINTS statement may be used within a transaction to alter this behavior.

INITIALLY DEFERRED

Specifies that the constraint should initially be checked only when a transaction is committed. The SET CONSTRAINTS statement may be used within a transaction to alter this behavior.

NOT DEFERRABLE

Specifies that constraint checking may not be deferred for this constraint.

RELY

Specifies that a materialized view (or snapshot) will be eligible for query rewrite even if an associated constraint is not validated. This keyword is valid only for materialized views.

NORELY

Specifies that a materialized view (or snapshot) will be not be eligible for query rewrite if an associated constraint is not validated. This keyword is valid only for materialized views.

USING INDEX

Specifies that an index will be used to validate a unique or primary key constraint.

INITRANS

Specifies the initial number of transaction entries allocated in each data block of an index. One transaction entry is required for each concurrent transaction that updates the block.

MAXTRANS

Specifies the largest number of transaction entries that may be allocated in each data block for this index. This keyword limits the number of concurrent transactions that can update the block. The default is based on the block size.

PCTFREE

Specifies the percentage of space in each index block reserved for updates of index values.

TABLESPACE

Specifies the name of the tablespace where the index for a constraint will be stored.

NOSORT

Specifies that the data rows are stored in the database in ascending order, so no sort is required when creating the index.

LOGGING

Specifies that redo log records will be written during index creation. This option is the default behavior.

NOLOGGING

Specifies that redo log records will not be written during index creation. In the case of a database failure, the index creation operation cannot be recovered by applying log files. Instead, the index must be recreated. This option speeds the creation of constraints using indexes.

Storage_Clause

Specifies the storage characteristics for the index used to enforce the constraint. See the "Storage_Clause" section later in this chapter.

ENABLE

Specifies that the constraint be applied immediately to all new data in the table or view.

DISABLE

Specifies that the constraint be disabled and not applied to data in the table or view.

VALIDATE

Specifies that any existing data in the table or view must comply with the constraint.

NOVALIDATE

Specifies that any existing data in the table or view should not be checked for compliance with the constraint.

EXCEPTIONS INTO

Specifies a table into which Oracle will place the rowids of rows violating this constraint. The table must already exist and can be created with the script *UTLEXCPT1.SQL*. Note that VALIDATE must be specified to use this keyword.

LOB_Storage_Clause

```
{LOB {(lob_item[,lob_item..]) STORE AS
   ([TABLESPACE tablespace]
      [{ENABLE | DISABLE} STORAGE IN ROW]
      [STORAGE Storage_Clause]
      [CHUNK integer]
      [PCTVERSION integer
      [CACHE | NOCACHE [LOGGING | NOLOGGING]]
      ) |
  LOB (lob_item) STORE AS [(lob_segname)]
   [((TABLESPACE tablespace]
      [{ENABLE | DISABLE} STORAGE IN ROW]
      [STORAGE Storage_Clause]
      [CHUNK integer]
      [PCTVERSION integer
      [CACHE | NOCACHE [LOGGING | NOLOGGING]]
   ]
```

Specifies storage parameters to be applied to LOB (Large OBject) data segments in a table, partition, or subpartition.

Keywords

LOB

Specifies that LOB storage parameters be provided for the listed LOB items. Any unlisted LOB item will use the same storage parameters as the table, partition, or subpartition. Note that Oracle automatically creates a system-managed index for each LOB item listed with this keyword.

STORE AS

The storage parameters to be applied immediately follow this keyword.

TABLESPACE

Specifies the name of the tablespace in which the LOB will be stored.

ENABLE STORAGE IN ROW

Specifies that the LOB data may be stored in the data row if its size is less than approximately 4000 bytes. This option is the default behavior.

DISABLE STORAGE IN ROW

Specifies that the LOB data is always stored outside the data row.

STORAGE

Specifies the storage parameters for the LOB segment. See the "Storage_ Clause" section later in this chapter for details.

CHUNK

Specifies that *integer* bytes should be allocated for LOB manipulation. Note that *integer* will be rounded up to a multiple of the Oracle block size.

PCTVERSION

Specifies the maximum percentage of LOB storage space to be used for creating new versions of the LOB. The default is 10 percent.

CACHE

Specifies that LOB data will be retained in memory for faster access.

NOCACHE

Specifies that LOB data will not be retained in memory. This option is the default behavior.

LOGGING

Specifies that redo log records will be written during creation of LOB storage. This option is the default behavior.

NOLOGGING

Specifies that redo log records will not be written during creation of LOB storage. In case of a database failure, the operation cannot be recovered by applying log files and the object must be recreated. This option speeds creation of database objects. Note that this option cannot be specified if CACHE is specified.

STORE AS

Specifies the name of a LOB segment, which can only be used when listing a single LOB item.

Partition_Clause

```
{PARTITION BY RANGE (column[,column...])
   PARTITION [partition_name] VALUES LESS THAN (value_list)
      [LOB_Storage_Clause]
      [Physical_Attributes_Clause]
      [TABLESPACE tablespace_name] [LOGGING | NOLOGGING]
      [{SUBPARTITIONS integer [STORE IN (tablespace_name[,tablespace_name ...]) |
          (SUBPARTITION [subpartition_name] [TABLESPACE tablespace_name]
             [LOB_Storage_Clause]
       [, SUBPARTITION [subpartition_name] [TABLESPACE tablespace_name]
             [LOB_Storage_Clause] ...]
      }]
 [, PARTITION [partition_name] VALUES LESS THAN (value_list)
      [LOB_Storage_Clause]
      [Physical_Attributes_Clause]
      [TABLESPACE tablespace_name] [LOGGING | NOLOGGING]
      [{SUBPARTITIONS integer [STORE IN (tablespace_name[,tablespace_name ...]) |
          (SUBPARTITION [subpartition_name] [TABLESPACE tablespace_name]
             [LOB_Storage_Clause]
       [, SUBPARTITION [subpartition_name] [TABLESPACE tablespace_name]
             [LOB_Storage_Clause] ...]
      }] ...]  |

PARTITION BY RANGE (column[,column ...])
   [SUBPARTITION BY HASH (column[,column]
      [SUBPARTITIONS integer [STORE IN (tablespace_name[,tablespace_name ...]]]]
   {PARTITION [partition_name] VALUES LESS THAN (value_list)
      [LOB_Storage_Clause]
      [Physical_Attributes_Clause]
      [TABLESPACE tablespace_name] [LOGGING | NOLOGGING]
      [{SUBPARTITIONS integer [STORE IN (tablespace_name[,tablespace_name ...]) |
          (SUBPARTITION [subpartition_name] [TABLESPACE tablespace_name]
             [LOB_Storage_Clause [, LOB_storage_clause ...]
          [, SUBPARTITION [subpartition_name] [TABLESPACE tablespace_name]
             [LOB_Storage_Clause [, LOB_storage_clause ...]
      }]
   [, PARTITION [partition_name] VALUES LESS THAN (value_list)
      [LOB_Storage_Clause]
      [Physical_Attributes_Clause]
      [TABLESPACE tablespace_name] [LOGGING | NOLOGGING]
      [{SUBPARTITIONS integer [STORE IN (tablespace_name[,tablespace_name ...]) |
          (SUBPARTITION [subpartition_name] [TABLESPACE tablespace_name]
             [LOB_Storage_Clause]
          [, SUBPARTITION [subpartition_name] [TABLESPACE tablespace_name]
             [LOB_Storage_Clause] ...]
      }] ...]  |
```

```
PARTITION BY HASH (column[,column ...])
  [{PARTITIONS integer [STORE IN (tablespace_name[,tablespace_name ...]) |
    (PARTITION [partition_name] [TABLESPACE tablespace_name] [LOB_Storage_Clause]
      [, PARTITION [partition_name] [TABLESPACE tablespace_name] [LOB_Storage_Clause]
        ...]
}
```

Specifies partitioning parameters and is also used to define range partitioning, composite partitioning, or hash partitioning.

Keywords

PARTITION BY RANGE

Specifies that the table is to be partitioned by ranges of values in the listed columns.

PARTITION... VALUES LESS THAN

Specifies a name for the partition and one or more values (corresponding 1 to 1 with the column list of the PARTITION BY RANGE keyword) serving as maximum values for inclusion in the partition. The value list may contain the keyword MAXVALUE, which represents the highest possible value for a given column.

LOB_Storage_Clause

Specifies the LOB storage parameters for this partition. See the "LOB_Storage_ Clause" section earlier in this chapter for details.

Physical_Attributes_Clause

Specifies the physical attributes for this partition; see the "Physical_Attributes_ Clause" section later in this chapter.

TABLESPACE

Specifies the name of the tablespace where this partition or subpartition will be stored.

LOGGING

Specifies that redo log records will be written during object creation. This option is the default.

NOLOGGING

Specifies that redo log records will not be written during object creation. In case of a database failure, the operation cannot be recovered by applying log files and the object must be recreated. This option speeds creation of database objects.

SUBPARTITIONS

Specifies that *integer* subpartitions are to be created for this partition.

STORE IN

Specifies the name or names of one or more tablespaces in which subpartitions are to be created.

SUBPARTITION

Specifies subpartitions by name.

PARTITION BY HASH

Specifies that hash subpartitions are to be created based on the column list supplied.

PARTITIONS

Specifies that *integer* partitions are to be created.

PARTITION

Specifies the name for a partition in *partition_name.* If *partition_name* is omitted, Oracle assigns a name using the format SYS_P*nnn.*

 Partitioning is an extra-cost option and is only available in the Oracle Enterprise Server products.

Physical_Attributes_Clause

```
[INITRANS integer]
[MAXTRANS integer]
[PCTFREE integer]
[PCTUSED integer]
```

Specifies schema object characteristics affecting the utilization of space in an Oracle block.

Keywords

INITTRANS

Specifies the number of transaction entries allocated to each block of the object. The allowed range of values is 1 to 255, and should not normally be changed from the default of 2.

MAXTRANS

Specifies the maximum number of concurrent transactions that can update a block of the object. Values are 1 to 255, and should not normally be changed from the default. The default is a function of the Oracle block size.

PCTFREE

Specifies the percentage of space in each data block kept free for future updates to the object. The permissible range of values is 0 to 99. The default value is 10.

PCTUSED

Specifies the percentage of space in each data block that Oracle attempts to keep filled. The permissible range of values is 0 to 99, and the default is 40.

Storage_Clause

```
STORAGE (
  [INITIAL integer [K | M]]
  [NEXT integer [K | M]]
  [MINEXTENTS integer]
  [MAXEXTENTS [integer | UNLIMITED] ]
  [PCTINCREASE integer ]
  [FREELISTS integer ]
  [FREELIST GROUPS integer ]
  [OPTIMAL [integer [K | M]]]
  [BUFFER_POOL {KEEP | RECYCLE | DEFAULT}]
  )
```

Specifies how storage within an Oracle tablespace is allocated to an individual object.

Keywords

STORAGE

Specifies the database object's physical storage characteristics.

INITIAL

Specifies the size of the first extent for the database object in bytes, kilobytes (K), or megabytes (M). If not a multiple of the database block size, this size will be rounded up to a multiple of the database block size.

NEXT

Specifies the size of the next extent for the database object in bytes, kilobytes (K) or megabytes (M). If not a multiple of the database blocksize, this size will be rounded up to a multiple of database blocksize.

MINEXTENTS

Specifies the number of extents to be allocated when the database object is created. The minimum and default value is 1, except for rollback segments, which have a minimum and default of 2.

MAXEXTENTS

Specifies the maximum number of extents that may be allocated for the database object. The default varies according to the database block size. If the keyword UNLIMITED is specified, there is no upper limit to the number of extents allowed.

PCTINCREASE

Specifies the percentage by which each extent grows over the previous extent. The default is 50, which means that each extent will be one and one-half times larger than the previous extent.

FREELISTS

Specifies the number of free lists contained in each freelist group for this database object. The default is 1, and the maximum depends on the database block size.

FREELIST GROUPS

Specifies the number of groups of free lists for this database object. The default is 1. This parameter should be used only with the Parallel Server option.

OPTIMAL

For rollback segments only, *integer* specifies the optimal size Oracle attempts to maintain by deallocating unused rollback segment extents. If no size is specified, the rollback segment will never be reduced in size. The default behavior, which you get when you omit the OPTIMAL clause, is to never shrink rollback segments at all.

BUFFER_POOL

Specifies how schema objects are to be assigned to buffer pools. KEEP means the object will be assigned to the KEEP buffer pool and retained in memory permanently, if possible. RECYCLE means that the object will be assigned to the RECYCLE buffer pool and removed from memory as soon as it is not needed. DEFAULT means the object will be assigned to the DEFAULT buffer pool, which will utilize the standard least-recently-used (LRU) algorithm for buffer reuse. Note that the KEEP and RECYCLE pools must be configured by the DBA prior to use.

Table_Constraint_Clause

```
[CONSTRAINT constraint_name]
{[UNIQUE | PRIMARY KEY] (column[,column ...])] |
 [CHECK (condition) ] |
 [FOREIGN KEY (column[,column ...])
    REFERENCES [schema.]table [(column[,column ...])]
    [ON DELETE {CASCADE | SET NULL}]]
}
 [Constraint_State_Clause]
```

Defines constraints on a table.

Keywords

CONSTRAINT

Specifies a name for the constraint. If omitted, Oracle assigns a name in the form SYS_C*nnn*, where *nnn* is an integer number.

UNIQUE

Specifies that the value in the column(s) must not duplicate a value for the same column(s) in any other row of the table. The value of the column or columns in the constraint must be unique for each row in the table. Note, however, that more than one column may contain the value NULL.

PRIMARY KEY

Specifies that the column(s) identified by *column* will serve as the primary key for the table in which it is defined. A primary key column may not contain NULL, and no value of the primary key may appear in the same column(s) of any other row in the table.

CHECK

Specifies a *condition* that must evaluate to TRUE or NULL for the constraint to be satisfied.

FOREIGN KEY

Specifies that one or more columns in this table participate in a foreign key referential integrity relationship.

REFERENCES

Specifies the table and column(s) that are referenced by this foreign key constraint.

ON DELETE CASCADE

Specifies that when a row containing a primary or unique key is deleted, dependent foreign keys will be deleted automatically.

ON DELETE SET NULL

Specifies that when a row containing a primary or unique key is deleted, dependent foreign keys will be changed to NULL automatically.

Constraint_State_Clause

Specifies how the constraint will be applied to data in the table. See the "Constraint_State_Clause" section earlier in this chapter.

5

SQL Functions

Oracle implements a large number of built-in functions you can invoke from SQL or PL/SQL. If you're going to be working in either of these languages, you must have a good knowledge of these functions. If you're working with SQL, you'll also have a number of aggregate functions at your disposal. All are documented in this chapter, along with examples. Many of these examples show how to invoke the functions via SQL*Plus; for more information, see Chapter 6, *SQL*Plus*.

This chapter describes SQL functions within the following categories:

- Aggregate functions
- Numeric functions
- Character functions
- Date functions
- Conversion functions
- Other (miscellaneous) functions

A note about function parameters is in order. Each function description contains a syntax block showing the parameters that may be passed to a function. In many cases, the parameter descriptions are obvious, and I've chosen not to specifically describe them. The ABS function is an example of this type of description. If you read the function description and look at the examples, it will be obvious how the function can be used. When necessary, I've included detailed parameter descriptions for other functions.

Aggregate Functions

Aggregate functions are SQL functions designed to allow you to summarize data from multiple rows of a table or view. These aggregate functions, many of which are useful for data warehouse applications, are only valid for use in SQL statements. Unlike the other built-in functions, they cannot be directly invoked from a PL/SQL expression (see Chapter 7, *PL/SQL*, for more information about PL/SQL programming). Table 5-1 lists the available aggregate functions.

Table 5-1. Oracle's Aggregate Functions

Function	Description
AVG	Returns the average value of a column over a set of rows
COUNT	Returns the number of non-NULL values in a column over a set of rows
GROUPING	Allows you to insert subtotal (superaggregate) rows into a query that uses Oracle's ROLLUP and CUBE extensions
MAX	Returns the maximum value of a column over a set of rows
MIN	Returns the minimum value of a column over a set of rows
STDDEV	Returns the standard deviation of all values in a column for a set of rows
SUM	Sums the values in a column for a set of rows
VARIANCE	Returns the variance of values in a column for a set of rows

GROUP BY

When used with an aggregate function, the GROUP BY clause causes Oracle to report the result for each distinct value of a column. The following example uses GROUP BY to break out the count of objects by database user:

```
SQL> SELECT owner, COUNT(object_name)
  2  FROM dba_objects
  3  GROUP BY owner;

OWNER                              COUNT(OBJECT_NAME)
------------------------------     ------------------
CTXSYS                                            164
DBSNMP                                              4
GNIS                                                2
MDSYS                                             137
OEMREP                                            230
...
```

The GROUP BY clause causes results to be sorted into different buckets—one for each distinct value in the GROUP BY column. The COUNT function then reports the count of OBJECT_NAME columns in each of those buckets.

If you want to count rows, not values, in a specific column, you can use the asterisk (*) as the COUNT parameter. For example:

```
SELECT COUNT(*) FROM dba_objects
```

When you count column values, whether a column contains NULL values makes a difference. NULLs are generally ignored. In the case of COUNT, NULL values won't be counted. Using the asterisk causes all rows to be counted, including those with NULL values.

DISTINCT and ALL

Most aggregate functions optionally accept the DISTINCT and ALL keywords in their parameter list. These keywords allow you to control the manner in which duplicate column values are handled. The keywords have the following meanings:

DISTINCT
> Causes the aggregate function to look only at distinct values, ignores duplicates.

ALL
> Causes the aggregate function to look at all values, including duplicates.

Consider a table with the values shown in the following query:

```
SQL> SELECT * FROM agg_demo;

         X
----------
         1
         2
         2
```

The agg_demo table contains three rows, with two distinct values stored in column x. Two rows have a value of 2, and one has a 1. Note the effect of the DISTINCT and ALL keywords in the following example:

```
SQL> SELECT COUNT(x), COUNT(DISTINCT x), COUNT(ALL x)
  2  FROM agg_demo;

  COUNT(X) COUNT(DISTINCTX) COUNT(ALLX)
---------- ---------------- -----------
         3                2           3
```

Counting all values is the default behavior. The DISTINCT keyword causes only the distinct values to be counted. In this example, there are two distinct values: 1 and 2. The ALL keyword explicitly asks for the default behavior.

Aggregate Functions and NULL Values

In most cases, aggregate functions ignore NULL values. Consider the following extension of the previous section's example. This time, the agg_demo table contains a NULL value:

```
SQL> SELECT * FROM agg_demo;

         X
----------
         1
         2
         2
*null*
```

This version of the agg_demo table is used in most aggregate function examples given in this chapter.

Using the COUNT function to count the number of values in column X yields the following results:

```
SQL> SELECT COUNT(x), COUNT(DISTINCT x), COUNT(ALL x)
  2  FROM agg_demo;

  COUNT(X)  COUNT(DISTINCTX)  COUNT(ALLX)
---------- ----------------- -----------
         3                 2           3
```

Notice that in no case was the NULL value counted; instead, the NULL values were totally ignored.

There are two cases when aggregate functions do not ignore NULLS. One is the special case when COUNT(*) is used, causing Oracle to count rows, not column values. The GROUPING function represents the other case. GROUPING summarizes the data for a group of rows containing a NULL value in a GROUP BY column.

AVG

AVG([DISTINCT | ALL] *expr*)

Computes the average value of a column or expression over the set of rows returned by a query, or the set of rows specified by a GROUP BY clause.

Example

```
SQL> SELECT AVG(x), AVG(DISTINCT x), AVG(ALL x)
  2  FROM agg_demo;

   AVG(X) AVG(DISTINCTX)  AVG(ALLX)
---------- -------------- ----------
1.66666667            1.5 1.66666667
```

COUNT

COUNT({*|[DISTINCT | ALL] *expr*})

Counts the number of values in a column or expression over the set of rows returned by a query, or the set of rows specified by a GROUP BY clause.

Example

```
SQL> SELECT owner, object_type, COUNT(*)
  2  FROM dba_objects
  3  GROUP BY owner, object_type;
```

OWNER	OBJECT_TYPE	COUNT(*)
CTXSYS	INDEX	35
CTXSYS	INDEXTYPE	1
CTXSYS	LIBRARY	2
CTXSYS	OPERATOR	2
CTXSYS	PACKAGE	29
CTXSYS	PACKAGE BODY	24

GROUPING

GROUPING (*expr*)

Determines whether a NULL value for a specified column or expression represents an added row or a legitimate group of values.

The GROUPING function was introduced in Oracle8*i*, and is designed for use in SELECT statements that use the CUBE and ROLLUP operators that were also introduced in Oracle8*i*. CUBE and ROLLUP both cause extra rows to be inserted into a query to summarize a group of records. These extra rows contain NULL values in the GROUP BY columns. GROUPING returns a 1 if the NULL value results from an additional row returned from using CUBE or ROLLUP; otherwise, it returns a 0.

Example

The query in this example returns a count of database objects by owner and type. The ROLLUP keyword causes Oracle to insert an extra row for each owner that gives the total count for that owner. This row has a NULL value in the OBJECT_ TYPE column. An additional row is inserted at the end of the rowset that gives the total number of objects for all owners. This row has NULL values for both the OWNER and the OBJECT_TYPE columns.

In this particular query, the OWNER and OBJECT_TYPE columns would never normally be NULL, so you can safely take the presence of a NULL value as an indicator that the row was inserted as a subtotal row. However, that won't be the case for all queries. A mechanism is thus needed to reliably determine whether a row returned by a query represents an additional rollup row as opposed to database information. Enter the GROUPING function. In this example, the GROUPING function was applied to the OBJECT_TYPE column, and it will return a 1 to indicate rows that contain a NULL object type because that row was added as a result of using the ROLLUP keyword:

```
SQL> SELECT owner, object_type, COUNT(*), GROUPING(object_type)
  2  FROM dba_objects
  3  GROUP BY ROLLUP (owner, object_type);

OWNER         OBJECT_TYPE          COUNT(*) GROUPING(OBJECT_TYPE)
------------- -------------------- -------- ---------------------
CTXSYS        INDEX                      35                     0
CTXSYS        INDEXTYPE                   1                     0
CTXSYS        LIBRARY                     2                     0
CTXSYS        OPERATOR                    2                     0
CTXSYS        PACKAGE                    29                     0
CTXSYS        PACKAGE BODY               24                     0
CTXSYS        PROCEDURE                   1                     0
CTXSYS        SEQUENCE                    3                     0
CTXSYS        TABLE                      26                     0
CTXSYS        TYPE                        4                     0
CTXSYS        TYPE BODY                   3                     0

OWNER         OBJECT_TYPE          COUNT(*) GROUPING(OBJECT_TYPE)
------------- -------------------- -------- ---------------------
CTXSYS        UNDEFINED                   1                     0
CTXSYS        VIEW                       33                     0
CTXSYS        *null*                    164                     1
DBSNMP        SYNONYM                     4                     0
DBSNMP        *null*                      4                     1
GNIS          INDEX                       1                     0
GNIS          TABLE                       1                     0
GNIS          *null*                      2                     1
*null*        *null*                  12185                     1
```

MAX

```
MAX([DISTINCT | ALL] expr)
```

Computes the maximum value of a column or expression over the set of rows returned by a query or specified by a GROUP BY clause.

Example

This example uses the MAX function in several ways to find the largest value of
the X column in the agg_demo table:

```
SQL> SELECT MAX(x), MAX(DISTINCT x), MAX(ALL X)
  2  FROM agg_demo;

    MAX(X) MAX(DISTINCTX)  MAX(ALLX)
---------- -------------- ----------
         2              2          2
```

Notice that using ALL or DISTINCT does not affect the value
returned by the MAX function. It doesn't matter whether MAX looks
at one or many occurrences of each value. In either case, the maximum value will be the same.

MIN

MIN([DISTINCT | ALL] *expr*)

Computes the minimum value of a column or expression over the set of rows
returned by a query or the set of rows specified by a GROUP BY clause.

Examples

This example uses the MIN function in several ways to find the smallest value of
the X column of the agg_demo table:

```
SQL> SELECT MIN(x), MIN(DISTINCT x), MIN(ALL X)
  2  FROM agg_demo;

    MIN(X) MIN(DISTINCTX)  MIN(ALLX)
---------- -------------- ----------
         1              1          1
```

Using ALL or DISTINCT does not affect the value returned by the
MIN function. It doesn't matter whether MIN looks at one or many
occurrences of each value. In either case, the minimum value will be
the same.

STDDEV

STDDEV([DISTINCT | ALL] *expr*)

Computes the standard deviation of the values of a column or expression over the set of rows returned by a query or the set of rows specified by a GROUP BY clause.

Example

This example uses the STDDEV function to find several standard deviations of values in the x column of the agg_demo table:

```
SQL> SELECT STDDEV(x), STDDEV(DISTINCT x), STDDEV(ALL X)
  2  FROM agg_demo;

 STDDEV(X)  STDDEV(DISTINCTX)  STDDEV(ALLX)
---------- ----------------- ------------
.577350269        .707106781    .577350269
```

 The standard deviation of distinct values is different from the other two methods; a standard deviation depends on the number of observations and DISTINCT returns fewer values than the other two methods.

SUM

SUM([DISTINCT | ALL] *expr*)

Computes the sum of the values of a column or expression over the set of rows returned by a query or specified by a GROUP BY clause.

Example

```
SQL> SELECT SUM(x), SUM(DISTINCT x), SUM(ALL x)
  2  FROM agg_demo;

    SUM(X) SUM(DISTINCTX)  SUM(ALLX)
---------- -------------- ----------
         5              3          5
```

VARIANCE

VARIANCE([DISTINCT | ALL] *expr*)

Computes the variance of the values of a column or expression over the set of rows returned by a query or the set of rows specified by a GROUP BY clause.

Example

```
SQL> SELECT VARIANCE(x), VARIANCE(DISTINCT x), VARIANCE(ALL x)
  2  FROM agg_demo;

VARIANCE(X)  VARIANCE(DISTINCTX)  VARIANCE(ALLX)
-----------  -------------------  --------------
 .333333333                  .5      .333333333
```

 Like the standard deviation, a variance depends on the number of observations, so DISTINCT returns fewer rows and therefore results in a different variance.

Numeric Functions

Numeric functions include those that take numbers as arguments and return numeric values. Many of these functions are related to trigonometry. There are also logarithmic functions and several general-purpose functions.

ABS

ABS(*n*)

Returns the absolute value of a number: the value with any negative sign removed.

Example

```
SQL> SELECT ABS(-1), ABS(1)
  2  FROM dual;

  ABS(-1)     ABS(1)
---------- ----------
         1          1
```

ACOS

ACOS(*n*)

Returns the arc cosine of a value between -1 and 1. This function reverses the output of the COS function. The result is an angle expressed in radians, which will fall between inclusively in the range 0 to π.

Example

```
SQL> SELECT ACOS(-1), ACOS(0), ACOS(1)
  2  FROM dual;

  ACOS(-1)    ACOS(0)    ACOS(1)
---------- ---------- ----------
3.14159265 1.57079633          0
```

ASIN

ASIN(*n*)

Returns the arc sine of a value between -1 and 1. This function reverses the output of the SIN function. The result is an angle expressed in radians, which will fall inclusively in the range -$\pi/2$ and $\pi/2$.

Example

```
SQL> SELECT ASIN(-1), ASIN(0), ASIN(1)
  2  FROM dual;

  ASIN(-1)    ASIN(0)    ASIN(1)
---------- ---------- ----------
-1.5707963          0 1.57079633
```

ATAN

ATAN(*n*)

Returns the arc tangent of a value. This function reverses the TAN function output. The result is an angle expressed in radians, which will fall inclusively in the range -$\pi/2$ and $\pi/2$.

Example

```
SQL> SELECT ATAN(.781285627), TAN(.663225116)
  2  FROM dual;

ATAN(.781285627) TAN(.663225116)
---------------- ---------------
     .663225116      .781285627
```

ATAN2

ATAN2(*n*, *m*)

Returns the arc tangent of the value n/m. In other words ATAN2(n, m) is the same as ATAN(n/m). The result is an angle expressed in radians, which will fall inclusively in the range -$\pi/2$ and $\pi/2$.

Example

```
SQL> SELECT ATAN2(.4,2), ATAN(.2)
  2  FROM dual;

ATAN2(.4,2)   ATAN(.2)
----------- ----------
  .19739556  .19739556
```

CEIL

CEIL(*n*)

Returns the lowest valued integer that is greater than or equal to the input. If *n* is already an integer, *n* will be returned.

Example

```
SQL> SELECT CEIL(10), CEIL(10.5), CEIL(-10.5)
  2  FROM dual;

  CEIL(10) CEIL(10.5) CEIL(-10.5)
---------- ---------- -----------
        10         11         -10
```

Notice that for negative numbers, the sign is relevant: -10 is greater than -10.5.

COS

COS(*n*)

Returns the cosine of an angle, where the angle is expressed in radians.

Example

```
SQL> SELECT COS(0)
  2  FROM dual;

    COS(0)
----------
         1
```

COSH

COSH(*n*)

Returns the hyperbolic cosine of an angle, where that angle is expressed in radians.

Example

```
SQL> SELECT COSH(0)
  2  FROM dual;

   COSH(0)
----------
         1
```

EXP

EXP(*n*)

Returns the value of *e* raised to the power *n*.

Example

The constant *e* is approximately equal to 2.71828183. The following example shows two ways of computing *e* raised to the third power. The results are slightly different because the EXP function uses a closer approximation of *e* than was used in the other expression.

```
SQL> SELECT EXP(3), 2.71828183*2.71828183*2.71828183
  2  FROM dual;

   EXP(3) 2.71828183*2.71828183*2.71828183
---------- --------------------------------
20.0855369                        20.085537
```

FLOOR

FLOOR(*n*)

Returns the largest integer value that is less than or equal to the input value.

Example

```
SQL> SELECT FLOOR(9.9), FLOOR(-9.9)
  2  FROM dual;

FLOOR(9.9) FLOOR(-9.9)
---------- -----------
         9         -10
```

As with CEIL, the sign is relevant; -10 is less than -9.9.

GREATEST

GREATEST(*expr* [,*expr*...])

Returns the highest value from the list of arguments supplied. The GREATEST function can be used with character strings and dates, as well as with numbers.

Examples

Return the largest value from a list of numbers:

```
SQL> SELECT GREATEST(1,2,3) FROM dual;

GREATEST(1,2,3)
---------------
              3
```

Return the largest value from a list of character strings:

```
SQL> SELECT GREATEST('One','Two') FROM dual;

GRE
---
Two
```

Return the largest (most recent) value from a list of dates:

```
SQL> SELECT GREATEST(TO_DATE('11/15/1961','MM/DD/YYYY'),
  2                  TO_DATE('12/29/1988','MM/DD/YYYY'))
  3  FROM dual;

GREATEST(
---------
29-DEC-88
```

If you mix datatypes, Oracle uses the datatype of the first argument as a base and converts (if possible) all other arguments to that type before choosing the greatest value.

LEAST

LEAST(*expr* [,*expr*...])

Returns the lowest value from the list of arguments supplied. The LEAST function can be used with character strings and dates, as well as with numbers.

Example

```
SQL> SELECT LEAST(1,2,3) FROM dual;

LEAST(1,2,3)
------------
           1
```

LN

LN(*n*)

Returns the natural logarithm of a number. The LN and EXP functions are complementary.

Example

```
SQL> SELECT LN(100), EXP(4.60517019) FROM dual;

   LN(100) EXP(4.60517019)
---------- ---------------
4.60517019             100
```

LOG

LOG(m, n)

Returns the base m logarithm of the number n.

Parameters

m Specifies a positive number other than 0 or 1 that represents the logarithm base.

n Specifies a number, which must be positive, for which you want the base m logarithm.

Example

```
SQL> SELECT LOG(10,10000) FROM dual;

LOG(10,10000)
-------------
            4
```

MOD

MOD (m, n)

Returns the remainder left over when m is divided by n.

Example

```
SQL> SELECT MOD(18,12), MOD(30,12), MOD(30,30)
  2  FROM dual;

MOD(18,12) MOD(30,12) MOD(30,30)
---------- ---------- ----------
         6          6          0
```

In the first case, 12 goes into 18 once with 6 left over. In the second case, 12 goes into 30 twice, but still with 6 left over. In the final case, 30 goes into 30 evenly, and nothing is left over.

POWER

POWER(*m, n*)

Raises *m* to the power of *n*. In other words, this function returns m^n.

Parameters

m   Specifies a nonzero number.

n   Specifies a power. If *m* is positive, *n* may be any positive or negative number. If *m* is negative, *n* must be an integer.

Example

```
SQL> SELECT POWER(10,3), POWER(-10,-3), POWER(-10,3)
  2  FROM dual;

POWER(10,3) POWER(-10,-3) POWER(-10,3)
----------- ------------- ------------
       1000         -.001        -1000
```

   m^{-n} is equivalent to $1/m^n$.

ROUND

ROUND(*n, m*)

Rounds a value to a specified number of decimal places.

Parameters

n   Specifies a value to be rounded.

m   Specifies the number of decimal places to preserve in the result. This number must be an integer. A negative value for *m* results in the value being rounded to the left of the decimal point.

Example

```
SQL> SELECT ROUND(123.45), ROUND(123.45,1), ROUND(123.45,-1)
  2  FROM dual;

ROUND(123.45) ROUND(123.45,1) ROUND(123.45,-1)
------------- --------------- ----------------
          123           123.5              120
```

SIGN

SIGN(*n*)

Returns a value indicating the sign of *n*. The number returned by the SIGN function will be one of the following:

-1   The number is negative

0   The number is zero

1   The number is positive

Example

```
SQL> SELECT SIGN(76), SIGN(0), SIGN(-76.17)
  2  FROM dual;

  SIGN(76)    SIGN(0)  SIGN(-76)
---------- ---------- ----------
         1          0         -1
```

SIN

SIN(*n*)

Returns the sine of the angle *n*, which must be expressed in radians.

Example

```
SQL> SELECT SIN(3.14), SIN(0)
  2  FROM dual;

 SIN(3.14)     SIN(0)
---------- ----------
.001592653          0
```

SQRT

SQRT(*n*)

Returns the square root of *n*, which must be a positive number.

Examples

```
SQL> SELECT SQRT(100), 10*10, SQRT(81), 9*9 FROM dual;

 SQRT(100)      10*10   SQRT(81)        9*9
---------- ---------- ---------- ----------
        10        100          9         81
```

TAN

TAN(*n*)

Returns the tangent of the angle *n*, which must be expressed in radians.

Example

```
SQL> SELECT TAN(.291456794), ATAN(.3) FROM dual;

TAN(.291456794)    ATAN(.3)
--------------- ----------
     .299999999 .291456794
```

TANH

TANH(*n*)

Returns the hyperbolic tangent of the angle *n*, which must be expressed in radians.

Example

```
SQL> SELECT TANH(0), TANH(3.14) FROM dual;

  TANH(0) TANH(3.14)
---------- ----------
        0 .996260205
```

TRUNC

TRUNC (*n* [,*m*])

Truncates a number to a specific number of decimal places.

Parameters

n   Specifies a number to be truncated.

m   Specifies the number of decimal places to preserve in the result. Truncating all decimal places is the default. Negative values for *m* result in digits being truncated to the left of the decimal point.

Example

```
SQL> SELECT TRUNC(99.99), TRUNC(99.99,1), TRUNC(99.99,-1)
  2  FROM dual;

TRUNC(99.99) TRUNC(99.99,1) TRUNC(99.99,-1)
------------ -------------- ---------------
          99           99.9              90
```

This function truncates at the specified number of decimal places and does not perform rounding.

Character Functions

In its manuals, Oracle divides character functions into two classes—those that return character values and those that return numeric values. The SUBSTR function, which returns a substring of a larger string, is an example of the former. The LENGTH function, which returns the length of a string, is an example of the latter. This book combines the two types into one section for ease of reference.

ASCII

ASCII(*char*)

Returns the decimal representation of a character, based on the character set in effect for the database. A true ASCII value will be returned only if a 7-bit ASCII character set is in use for the database. Notice that the parameter to the ASCII function may be a string as well as a single character. However, if a string is provided, the ASCII function returns a value based on the first character of that string.

Example

```
SQL> SELECT ASCII('D'), ASCII('Dave') FROM dual;

ASCII('D') ASCII('DAVE')
---------- -------------
        68            68
```

CHR

CHR(*n* [USING NCHAR_CS])

Returns the character from the database character set associated with the specified numeric value. If USING NCHAR_CS is specified, the database's national character set is used.

Example

```
SQL> SELECT CHR(68), CHR(68 USING NCHAR_CS) FROM dual;

C C
- -
D D
```

This example was generated using an ASCII character set.

CONCAT

CONCAT(*string1, string2*)

Concatenates two input strings and returns the result. The CONCAT function is equivalent to using the concatenation operator (||); see Chapter 1, *Elements of SQL,* for more information about this operator.

Example

```
SQL> SELECT CONCAT('Good ','Morning'), 'Good ' || 'Morning'
  2  FROM dual;

CONCAT('GOOD 'GOOD'||'MOR
------------ ------------
Good Morning Good Morning
```

GREATEST

See the definition for GREATEST in the section describing numeric functions.

INITCAP

INITCAP(*string*)

Changes the first letter of each word in a string to uppercase and all other letters to lowercase.

Example

```
SQL> SELECT INITCAP('good MORNING, dave') FROM dual;

INITCAP('GOODMORNI
------------------
Good Morning, Dave
```

INSTR

INSTR(*string1, string2*[, *n*[, *m*]])

Searches *string1* to find *string2* and returns the character position in *string1* where *string2* begins.

Parameter

string1

Specifies the string you want to search.

string2

Specifies the string you want to find.

n   Specifies the character position from which the search should begin. The default is to begin searching from the first character, which is position 1. Use negative values to specify the starting position relative to the right end of *string1,* rather than the left.

m   Specifies which occurrence of *string2* you want to find (if it occurs more than once). The default is to find the first occurrence.

Examples

```
SQL> SELECT INSTR('easy come, easy go','easy') FROM dual;

INSTR('EASYCOME,EASYGO','EASY')
-------------------------------
                              1

SQL> SELECT INSTR('easy come, easy go','easy',1,2) FROM dual;

INSTR('EASYCOME,EASYGO','EASY',1,2)
-----------------------------------
                                 12
```

INSTRB

```
INSTRB(string1, string2[, n[, m]])
```

Searches *string1* to find *string2* and returns the byte position in *string1* where *string2* begins.

INSTRB is similar to INSTR, except that the return value represents a byte index into *stringr1*, not a character index. When a single-byte character set is used, INSTR and INSTRB return the same result; a difference only occurs when using a multibyte character set.

LEAST

See the definition for LEAST in the section describing numeric functions.

LENGTH

LENGTH(*string*)

Returns the number of characters in a string.

Example

```
SQL> SELECT LENGTH('Dave'), LENGTH('Brighten the corner where you are.')
  2  FROM dual;

LENGTH('DAVE') LENGTH('BRIGHTENTHECORNERWHEREYOUARE.')
-------------- -------------------------------------
            4                                      34
```

LENGTHB

LENGTHB(*string*)

Returns the length of a string in bytes. LENGTHB returns the same result as LENGTH, except when a multibyte character set is used.

LOWER

LOWER(*string*)

Converts all characters in a string to lowercase.

Example

```
SQL> SELECT LOWER('LIFE IS a Wonderful tHINg.') FROM dual;

LOWER('LIFEISAWONDERFULTHI
--------------------------
life is a wonderful thing.
```

LPAD

LPAD(*string1*, *n*[, *string2*])

Pads the left side of *string1* with spaces, or with copies of the character string specified by *string2*, until the size of the resulting string reaches *n* characters.

Parameters

string1

    Specifies the string that you want padded.

n   Specifies the number of characters that you want in the result.

string2

Specifies the character sequence used to pad the input string to reach the desired length. This parameter defaults to a single space.

Example

```
SQL> SELECT LPAD('X',3), LPAD('X',3,'Y'), LPAD('RIGHT',12,'LEFT')
  2  FROM dual;

LPA LPA LPAD('RIGHT'
--- --- ------------
  X YYX LEFTLEFTRIGHT
```

LTRIM

LTRIM(*string1* [,*string2*])

Removes specific characters from the left side of a string.

Parameters

string1

Specifies the string from which you want leading characters removed.

string2

Specifies a string containing the set of characters to remove. This parameter defaults to a single space. Trimming stops when the function encounters a character not present in this string.

Examples

```
SQL> SELECT LTRIM('   The default is to trim leading spaces.')
  2  FROM dual;

LTRIM('THEDEFAULTISTOTRIMLEADINGSPACES
--------------------------------------
The default is to trim leading spaces.

SQL> SELECT LTRIM('***You can trim other characters as well.','*')
  2  FROM dual;

LTRIM('***YOUCANTRIMOTHERCHARACTERSASW
--------------------------------------
You can trim other characters as well.

SQL> SELECT LTRIM('**@@*@You can even trim multiple characters.','*@')
  2  FROM dual;

LTRIM('**@@*@YOUCANEVENTRIMMULTIPLECHA
--------------------------------------
You can even trim multiple characters.
```

NLS_INITCAP

NLS_INITCAP(*string*[, 'NLS_SORT=*sort*'])

Performs like INITCAP, but uses the national character set.

Parameters

string

Specifies the input character string.

sort

Specifies the name of the linguistic sort sequence specifying capitalization rules for the language being used.

Example

```
SQL> SELECT NLS_INITCAP('money','NLS_SORT=XFRENCH')
  2  FROM dual;

NLS_I
-----
Money
```

NLS_LOWER

NLS_LOWER(*string*[, 'NLS_SORT=*sort*'])

Performs like LOWER, but uses the national character set.

Parameters

sting

Specifies the input character string.

sort

Specifies the name of the linguistic sort sequence specifying capitalization rules for the language being used.

Example

```
SQL> SELECT NLS_LOWER('MONEY','NLS_SORT=XFRENCH')
  2  FROM dual;

NLS_L
-----
money
```

NLS_UPPER

NLS_UPPER(*string*[, 'NLS_SORT=*sort*'])

Performs like UPPER, but uses the national character set.

Parameters

string

Specifies the input character string.

sort

Specifies the name of the linguistic sort sequence specifying capitalization rules for the language being used.

Example

```
SQL> SELECT NLS_UPPER('money','NLS_SORT=XFRENCH')
  2  FROM dual;

NLS_L
-----
MONEY
```

NLSSORT

```
NLSSORT(string[, 'NLS_SORT=sort'])
```

Returns the byte string used to represent a value that is being sorted using a linguistic sort sequence.

Parameters

string

Specifies a character string.

sort

Specifies the name of a linguistic sort sequence or the keyword BINARY. If BINARY is used, NLSSORT returns the exact byte values of the input string.

Example

```
SQL> SELECT NLSSORT('MONEY','NLS_SORT=XFRENCH') FROM dual;

NLSSORT('MONEY','NLS_SORT=XFRENCH')
-------------------------------------------
505A55288200010101010100

SQL> SELECT NLSSORT('money','NLS_SORT=XFRENCH') FROM dual;

NLSSORT('MONEY','NLS_SORT=XFRENCH')
-------------------------------------------
505A55288200020202020200
```

REPLACE

REPLACE(*string, search_string* [,*replacement_string*])

Searches a string and replaces one substring with another. This function also may be used to delete occurrences of a substring.

Parameters

string

Specifies the input string and the string to search.

search_string

Specifies the substring to search for.

replacement_string

Specifies the string you want to use in place of the *search_string*. If you omit this optional argument, all occurrences of *search_string* will be deleted.

Examples

```
SQL> SELECT REPLACE('The sky is blue.','blue','red') FROM dual;

REPLACE('THESKY
---------------
The sky is red.

SQL> SELECT REPLACE('The sky is blue red.',' red') FROM dual;

REPLACE('THESKYI
----------------
The sky is blue.
```

RPAD

RPAD(*string1, n*[, *string2*])

Pads the right side of *string1* with spaces or copies of the character string specified by *string2* until the size of the resulting string reaches *n* characters.

Parameters

string1

Specifies the string that you want padded.

n   Specifies the number of characters you want in the result.

string2

Specifies the character sequence used to pad the input string to reach the desired length. This parameter defaults to a single space.

Example

```
SQL> SELECT RPAD('X',3), RPAD('X',3,'Y'), RPAD('RIGHT',12,'LEFT')
  2  FROM dual;

RPA RPA RPAD('RIGHT'
--- --- ------------
X   XYY RIGHTLEFTLEF
```

RTRIM

RTRIM(*string1* [,*string2*])

Removes specific characters from the right side of a string.

Parameters

string1

Specifies the string from which you want trailing characters removed.

string2

Specifies a string containing the set of characters to remove. This defaults to a single space. Trimming is performed from right to left and stops when the function encounters a character not in this set.

Examples

```
SQL> SELECT RTRIM('The default is to trim trailing spaces.   ')
  2  FROM dual;

RTRIM('THEDEFAULTISTOTRIMLEADINGSPACES
--------------------------------------
The default is to trim trailing spaces.

SQL> SELECT RTRIM('You can trim other characters as well.***','*')
  2  FROM dual;

RTRIM('***YOUCANTRIMOTHERCHARACTERSASW
--------------------------------------
You can trim other characters as well.

SQL> SELECT RTRIM('You can even trim multiple characters. **@@*@','*@')
  2  FROM dual;

RTRIM('**@@*@YOUCANEVENTRIMMULTIPLECHA
--------------------------------------
You can even trim multiple characters.
```

SOUNDEX

SOUNDEX(*string*)

Returns a string of digits representing phonetic pronunciation of the input string. The following steps are used to derive the output string:

1. The first letter of the string is retained.

2. All occurrences of the following letters are removed: a, e, h, i, o, u, w, and y.

3. Any remaining letters are replaced with digits as shown in Table 5-2.

4. The resulting string is truncated to four characters in length.

Using SOUNDEX can make it easier to search for a given string, because you don't need to spell it in exactly the correct way to get a match.

Table 5-2. SOUNDEX Letter-to-Digit Correspondence

Letters	SOUNDEX Digit
b, f, p, v	1
c, g, j, k, q, s, x, z	2
d, t	3
l	4
m, n	5
r	6

Example

```
SQL> SELECT SOUNDEX('O''Reilly'), SOUNDEX('ORiley'), SOUNDEX('OH Riley')
  2  FROM dual;

SOUN SOUN SOUN
---- ---- ----
0640 0640 0640
```

SUBSTR

SUBSTR(*string*, *m* [,*n*])

Returns a portion of a string.

Parameters

string
    Specifies the input string.

m Specifies the index of the first character to extract from *char*. Indexing begins with 1 and is an offset from the left end of the string. You can use a negative value to specify an offset from the right end of the string.

n   Specifies the number of characters to extract. This parameter is optional. By default, you get all characters from position *m* to the end of the string.

Examples

```
SQL> SELECT SUBSTR('OneTwoThree',7) FROM dual;

SUBST
-----
Three

SQL> SELECT SUBSTR('OneTwoThree',4,3) FROM dual;

SUB
---
Two

SQL> SELECT SUBSTR('OneTwoThree',-5) FROM dual;

SUBST
-----
Three
```

SUBSTRB

```
SUBSTRB(string, m [,n])
```

Returns a portion of a string. SUBSTRB is identical to SUBSTR, except that *m* and *n* refer to bytes, not to characters. This is only an issue when the string is based on a multibyte character set.

TRANSLATE

```
TRANSLATE(string, from_string, to_string)
```

Modifies a string by translating one set of characters into another.

string
    The input character string.

from_string
    The set of characters you want to translate.

to_string
    The set of new characters that will replace *from_string*. Each character of *from_string* in the input string is replaced by the corresponding character from the *to_string*. Characters in *from_string* with no corresponding elements in *to_string* are deleted.

Examples

The following two examples translate the digits 0 through 9 into the letters a through j. In the second example, the *from_string* contains a period and the *to_string* does not. This situation causes the period to be deleted:

```
SQL> SELECT TRANSLATE('123.45','0123456789','abcdefghij') FROM dual;

TRANSL
------
bcd.ef

SQL> SELECT TRANSLATE('123.45','0123456789.','abcdefghij') FROM dual;

TRANS
-----
bcdef
```

TRIM

```
TRIM([LEADING | TRAILING | BOTH]
    [trim_character FROM] string)
```

Removes both leading and trailing spaces (or other character) from a string.

Parameters

LEADING

Specifies that only leading spaces be trimmed.

TRAILING

Specifies that only trailing spaces be trimmed.

BOTH

Specifies that both leading and trailing spaces be trimmed.

trim_character

Specifies some other character to trim instead of a space.

string

Specifies the input string.

Examples

```
SQL> SELECT TRIM('   TEENA   ') FROM dual;

TRIM(
-----
TEENA

SQL> SELECT TRIM(LEADING '$' FROM '$123.45') FROM dual;

TRIM(L
------
123.45
```

UPPER

UPPER(*string*)

Converts all the characters in a string to uppercase.

Example

```
SQL> SELECT UPPER('LIFE IS a Wonderful tHINg.') FROM dual;

UPPER('LIFEISAWONDERFULTHI
--------------------------
LIFE IS A WONDERFUL THING.
```

Date Functions

Date functions operate on dates or return date values. Some of the functions return the current date and time, truncate a date/time value to a specific unit, or compute the number of months between two dates.

Many examples in the section use the TO_CHAR and TO_DATE functions. These date conversion functions accept date format strings as arguments. To keep the examples as simple to read as possible, I've assumed that the default date format is 'dd-Mon-yyyy'. In some examples in which a different format is used (to include time, for example), the example begins with an ALTER SESSION command.

ADD_MONTHS

ADD_MONTHS(*d*, *n*)

Adds *n* months to the date *d*. Negative values of *n* may be used to subtract months from *d*. The following rules control whether or not the day of the month is affected:

- If the original date represents the last day of its month, the resulting date will be adjusted so that it is also the last day of the month.

- If keeping the same day of the month results in an invalid date, because the new month has fewer days than the original (e.g., January has 31, but February has 28), the day will be adjusted downward to fit the new month.

If neither of the rules listed here applies, the day of the month will not be changed.

Examples

```
SQL> SELECT ADD_MONTHS(TO_DATE('1-Jan-2000'), 3) FROM dual;

ADD_MONTHS(
-----------
01-Apr-2000
```

```
SQL> SELECT ADD_MONTHS(TO_DATE('31-Jan-2000'), 1) FROM dual;

ADD_MONTHS(
-----------
29-Feb-2000

SQL> SELECT ADD_MONTHS(TO_DATE('29-Feb-2000'), -1) FROM dual;

ADD_MONTHS(
-----------
31-Jan-2000
```

GREATEST

See the definition for GREATEST in the section describing numeric functions.

LAST_DAY

LAST_DAY(*d*)

Returns the date corresponding to the last day of the month in which the date *d* falls.

Example

```
SQL> SELECT LAST_DAY(TO_DATE('13-FEB-2000')) FROM dual;

LAST_DAY(TO
-----------
29-Feb-2000
```

LEAST

See the definition for LEAST in the section describing numeric functions.

MONTHS_BETWEEN

MONTHS_BETWEEN(*d1,d2*)

Returns the number of months between the two dates *d1* and *d2*.

If both dates represent the same day of the month or represent the last day of their respective months, an integer value will be returned. Otherwise, MONTHS_ BETWEEN will return a fractional value.

Examples

```
SQL> SELECT MONTHS_BETWEEN(TO_DATE('29-Dec-1999'), TO_DATE('29-Dec-1988'))
  2  FROM dual;

MONTHS_BETWEEN(TO_DATE('29-DEC-1999'),TO_DATE('29-DEC-1988'))
------------------------------------------------------------
```

```
SQL> SELECT MONTHS_BETWEEN(TO_DATE('12-May-2000'), TO_DATE('29-Dec-1988'))
  2  FROM dual;

MONTHS_BETWEEN(TO_DATE('12-MAY-2000'),TO_DATE('29-DEC-1988'))
-------------------------------------------------------------
                                                    136.451613
```

 The fractional value returned by MONTHS_BETWEEN is based on a 31-day month. This value gets a bit weird when you cross a month boundary. In the second example, you can see that 136 months gets you from 29-Dec-1988 to 29-Apr-2000. Multiply the fractional portion of 0.451613 by 31, and you get 14 days. This seems rather strange since there are only 13 days between April 29 and May 12, but for purposes of calculating the fractional result, the MONTHS_BETWEEN function uses 31 for the number of days in April.

NEW_TIME

NEW_TIME(*d*, *z1*, *z2*)

Converts a date/time value from one time zone to another.

Parameters

d   Specifies the date/time value to convert.

z1   Specifies the source time zone. This parameter must be one of the time zone identifiers shown in Table 5-3.

z2   Specifies the destination time zone. This parameter must be one of the time zone identifiers shown in Table 5-3.

Table 5-3. Time Zone Identifiers

Time Zone Identifier	Time Zone
AST	Atlantic Standard Time
ADT	Atlantic Daylight Time
BST	Bering Standard Time
BDT	Bering Daylight Time
CST	Central Standard Time
CDT	Central Daylight Time
EST	Eastern Standard Time
EDT	Eastern Daylight Time
GMT	Greenwich Mean Time

Table 5-3. Time Zone Identifiers (continued)

Time Zone Identifier	Time Zone
HST	Alaska-Hawaii Standard Time
HDT	Alaska-Hawaii Daylight Time
MST	Mountain Standard Time
MDT	Mountain Daylight Time
NST	Newfoundland Standard Time
PST	Pacific Standard Time
PDT	Pacific Daylight Time
YST	Yukon Standard Time
YDT	Yukon Daylight Time

Example

The following example demonstrates that 8:00 A.M. Pacific Standard Time is equivalent to 11:00 A.M. Eastern Standard Time. The ALTER SESSION command alters the default date format to cause the time of day to be displayed along with the date:

```
SQL> ALTER SESSION SET NLS_DATE_FORMAT = 'dd-Mon-yyyy hh:mi am';

Session altered.

SQL> SELECT NEW_TIME(TO_DATE('8-May-2000 8:00 am','dd-mon-yyyy hh:mi am'),
  2                  'PST','EST')
  3  FROM dual;

NEW_TIME(TO_DATE('8-
--------------------
08-May-2000 11:00 am
```

NEXT_DAY

NEXT_DAY(*d*, *string*)

Computes the next occurrence of a specific weekday.

Parameters

d   Specifies a date value. Any time component in the date is preserved and is returned in the result.

string

Specifies the name of a weekday. This parameter may be a full name, such as **Wednesday**, or an abbreviation, such as **Wed**. Day names must be valid for your current NLS_DATE_LANGUAGE setting.

Example

```
SQL> SELECT NEXT_DAY('20-May-2000', 'SATURDAY'),
  2         NEXT_DAY('20-May-2000', 'Sun')
  3  FROM dual;

NEXT_DAY('2 NEXT_DAY('2
----------- -----------
27-May-2000 21-May-2000
```

NEXT_DAY always looks forward. If the date you pass in as a parameter happens to fall on the day you are searching for, NEXT_DAY returns the subsequent occurrence of that day. In the example, 20-May-2000 happens to fall on a Saturday, yet the function returns 27-May-2000 as a result because that is the "next" Saturday. If you want NEXT_DAY to return your input date as a result, you should subtract 1 from it first. For example:

```
SQL> SELECT NEXT_DAY(TO_DATE('20-May-2000')-1, 'SATURDAY')
  2  FROM dual;

NEXT_DAY(TO
-----------
20-May-2000
```

The TO_DATE function was used in this second example because Oracle won't allow you to subtract 1 from a character string. Subtracting 1 from the date caused NEXT_DAY to return 20-May-2000, which happens to fall on a Saturday.

ROUND

ROUND(*d* [,*fmt*])

Rounds a date/time value to the nearest date/time unit specified.

Parameters

d   Specifies a date/time value.

fmt

Specifies a date format element. See Table 5-4 for a complete list. The input value will be rounded to the unit specified by this format element. Rounding a date/time value to the nearest day is the default.

Rounding is not the same as truncating. Rounding a date may result in a new date that is greater than the date you started with. If you don't want to round up, use the TRUNC function instead.

Example

```
SQL> ALTER SESSION SET NLS_DATE_FORMAT = 'DD-Mon-YYYY hh24:mi';

Session altered.

SQL> SELECT ROUND(TO_DATE('21-Jul-2000 15:20')) day,
  2         ROUND(TO_DATE('21-Jul-2000 15:20'),'HH') hour,
  3         ROUND(TO_DATE('21-Jul-2000 15:20'),'YYYY') year
  4  FROM dual;

DAY               HOUR               YEAR
----------------- ------------------ -----------------
22-Jul-2000 00:00 21-Jul-2000 15:00 01-Jan-2001 00:00
```

Table 5-4. Date Format Elements

Format Element	Function
- / , . ; :	Punctuation may be included anywhere in the date format string, and will be included in the output.
'text'	Quoted text may also be included in the date format string, and will be reproduced in the output.
AD or A.D. BC or B.C.	Includes an A.D. or B.C. indicator with the date.
AM or A.M. PM or P.M.	Prints AM or PM, whichever applies to the time.
CC	The century number. This number is 20 for years 1900 through 1999.
SCC	Same as CC, but B.C. dates are negative.
D	The number of the day of the week (1 through 7).
DAY	The name of the day (Saturday, Sunday, Monday, etc.).
DD	The day of the month.
DDD	The day of the year.
DY	The abbreviated name of the day (Sat, Sun, Mon, etc.).
HH	The hour of the day. This hour will be 1 through 12.
HH12	The hour of the day. This hour will be 1 through 12, the same as HH.
HH24	The hour of the day on a 24-hour clock (0 through 23).
IW	The week of the year (1 through 53).
IYYY	The four-digit year.
IYY	The last three digits of the year.
IY	The last two digits of the year.
I	The last digit of the year.
J	The Julian day. Day 1 is equivalent to Jan 1, 4712 B.C.
MI	The minute.
MM	The month number.
MON	The three-letter month abbreviation.

Table 5-4. Date Format Elements (continued)

Format Element	Function
MONTH	The month name, fully spelled out.
Q	The quarter of the year. Quarter 1 is Jan–Mar, quarter 2 is Apr–Jun, etc.
RM	The month's number in Roman numerals.
RR	When used with TO_CHAR, returns the last two digits of the year.
RRRR	When used with TO_CHAR, returns the four-digit year.
SS	The second.
SSSSS	The number of seconds since midnight.
WW	The week of the year.
W	The week of the month. Week 1 starts on the first of the month, Week 2 starts on the eighth of the month, etc.
Y,YYY	The four-digit year with a comma after the first digit.
YEAR	The year spelled out in words.
SYEAR	The year spelled out in words, with a leading negative sign when the year is B.C.
YYYY	The four-digit year.
SYYYY	The four-digit year, with a leading negative sign when the year is B.C.
YYY	The last three digits of the year number.
YY	The last two digits of the year number.
Y	The last digit of the year number.

SYSDATE

SYSDATE

Returns the current date and time. The time component of the result includes hours, minutes, and seconds. SYSDATE is also known as a pseudo-column. See Chapter 1 for more information.

Examples

```
SQL> SELECT SYSDATE FROM dual;

SYSDATE
-----------
21-May-2000

SQL> ALTER SESSION SET NLS_DATE_FORMAT = 'DD-Mon-YYYY hh24:mi';

Session altered.

SQL> SELECT SYSDATE FROM dual;

SYSDATE
--------------------
21-May-2000 15:16:40
```

TRUNC

TRUNC(*d* [,*fmt*])

Returns a date/time value truncated to the unit specified. TRUNC is similar to ROUND, but it always rounds down, never up.

 Use TRUNC when you want to be sure that you are working with only a date, and not a date combined with a time component.

Parameters

d   Specifies a date/time value.

fmt

Specifies a date format element. See Table 5-4 for a list of these elements. The input value will be truncated (rounded down) to the unit specified by this format element. Truncating a date/time value to the day is the default.

Examples

```
SQL> ALTER SESSION SET NLS_DATE_FORMAT = 'DD-Mon-YYYY hh24:mi';

Session altered.

SQL> SELECT TRUNC(TO_DATE('21-Jul-2000 15:20')) day,
  2         TRUNC(TO_DATE('21-Jul-2000 15:20'),'HH') hour,
  3         TRUNC(TO_DATE('21-Jul-2000 15:20'),'YYYY') year
  4  FROM dual;

DAY               HOUR               YEAR
----------------- ------------------ -----------------
21-Jul-2000 00:00 21-Jul-2000 15:00 01-Jan-2000 00:00
```

Conversion Functions

Conversion functions allow the conversion of values from one datatype to another. The most commonly used conversion functions are:

TO_CHAR

Converts a date or a numeric value to a character string.

TO_NUMBER

Converts a character string to a numeric value.

TO_DATE

Converts a character string to a date value.

There are a number of other conversion functions available; all are included in this section.

CHARTOROWID

CHARTOROWID(*char*)

Converts a CHAR or VARCHAR2 value to a ROWID value. The ROWID type in this case is the Oracle7 type.

Example

```
SQL> SELECT *
  2 FROM dual
  3 WHERE ROWID = CHARTOROWID('AAAADCAABAAAAVUAAA');

D
-
X
```

CONVERT

CONVERT (*string, dest_char_set*[, *source_char_set*])

Converts a character string from one character set to another.

Parameters

string

Specifies a character string to convert.

dest_char_set

Specifies the name of the destination character set.

source_char_set

Specifies the name of the source character set. This parameter defaults to the database character set.

Example

```
SQL> SELECT CONVERT(CHR(194) || CHR(133) || CHR(64) || CHR(213)
  2                 || CHR(137) || CHR(131) || CHR(133),
  3                 'US7ASCII','WE8EBCDIC37C')
  4 FROM dual;

CONVERT
-------
Be Nice
```

HEXTORAW

HEXTORAW(*string*)

Converts hexadecimal digits contained in a character string to a RAW value composed of bytes corresponding to those digits.

Example

```
SQL> SELECT DUMP(HEXTORAW('C28540D5898385'))
  2  FROM dual;

DUMP(HEXTORAW('C28540D5898385'))
----------------------------------------
Typ=23 Len=7: 194,133,64,213,137,131,133
```

RAWTOHEX

RAWTOHEX(*raw*)

Converts a RAW value to a character string of hexadecimal digits in which each 2-character hex digit corresponds to one byte of the raw value.

Example

```
SQL> SELECT RAWTOHEX(HEXTORAW('C28540D5898385'))
  2  FROM dual;

RAWTOHEX(HEXTO
--------------
C28540D5898385
```

ROWIDTOCHAR

ROWIDTOCHAR(*rowid*)

Converts a ROWID value to a character string.

Example

The following example uses the ROWIDTOCHAR function to explicitly convert a ROWID value to a character string:

```
SQL> SELECT ROWID, ROWIDTOCHAR(ROWID) FROM dual;

ROWID              ROWIDTOCHAR(ROWID)
------------------ ------------------
AAAADCAABAAAAVUAAA AAAADCAABAAAAVUAAA
```

As this example shows, ROWID values are implicitly converted to character strings whenever you select them from a table using SQL*Plus. For this reason, you often see SELECT statements that retrieve ROWIDs, but that do not explicitly convert them.

TO_CHAR (Converting Dates to Character Strings)

TO_CHAR(d [, fmt [, 'nlsparams']])

Converts a date/time value into a character-based representation of that value.

Parameters

d   Specifies a date/time value (of type DATE).

fmt
     Specifies a date format string made up of the elements shown in Table 5-4.

nlsparams
     Specifies a string in the form NLS_DATE_LANGUAGE=langname, where langname represents a valid NLS language name. The NLS language name affects the spelling used for day and month names.

Examples

```
SQL> SELECT TO_CHAR(SYSDATE),TO_CHAR(SYSDATE, 'dd-Mon-yyyy hh:mi:ss PM')
  2  FROM dual;

TO_CHAR(SYSDATE)   TO_CHAR(SYSDATE, 'DD-MON
----------------   ----------------------
21-May-2000 17:40 21-May-2000 05:40:43 PM

SQL> SELECT TO_CHAR(SYSDATE, 'dd-Mon-yyyy', 'NLS_DATE_LANGUAGE=FRENCH')
  2  FROM dual;

TO_CHAR(SYS
-----------
21-Mai-2000
```

TO_CHAR (Converting Numbers to Character Strings)

TO_CHAR(n [, fmt [, 'nlsparams']])

Converts a numeric value into a character-based representation of that value.

Parameters

n   Specifies a numeric value to convert.

fmt
     Specifies a number format specification made up of the elements shown in Table 5-5.

nlsparams

Specifies a character string made up of one or more of the following elements, allowing you to specify various NLS characteristics for the result.

NLS_NUMERIC_CHARACTERS=''*dg*''

Allows you to specify the characters to use for decimal points and group separators. The *d* character becomes the decimal point and the *g* character becomes the group separator. For this parameter to take effect, you must use D and G in your format specification to mark the location of the decimal point and group separator, respectively.

NLS_CURRENCY=''*text*''

Allows you to specify the currency symbol (up to 10 characters long) to use in place of any L characters contained in the format specification.

NLS_ISO_CURRENCY=''*territory*''

Allows you to specify the NLS territory whose currency symbol you want to use in place of any C characters contained in the format specification.

The *nlsparams* settings are strings embedded within a string. The quotes you see around the values are doubled single quotes, not double quotes.

Example

```
SQL> SELECT TO_CHAR(75917.63,'$99,999.99') a,
  2        TO_CHAR(75917.63,'L99G999D99',
  3               'NLS_NUMERIC_CHARACTERS='',*'' NLS_CURRENCY=''$$$''') b,
  4        TO_CHAR(75917.63,'C99G999D99',
  5               'NLS_ISO_CURRENCY=''JAPAN''') c
  6  FROM dual;

A           B                    C
----------- -------------------- -------------
 $75,917.63          $$$759*18   JPY759,18
```

Table 5-5. Numeric Format Elements

Format Element	Function
9	Used to control the number of significant digits to be displayed.
0	Used to mark the spot in the result where you want to begin displaying leading 0s. It replaces one of the 9s. The extreme left of the format string is the most common location for a 0, but you can place it elsewhere.
$	Causes a number to be displayed with a leading dollar sign.

Table 5-5. Numeric Format Elements (continued)

Format Element	Function
,	Places a comma in the output.
.	Marks the location of the decimal point.
B	Forces 0 values to be displayed as blanks.
MI	Used at the end of a format string to cause a trailing negative sign to be displayed for negative values.
S	May be used at the beginning or end of a format string and causes a sign to be displayed. The "+" sign is used to mark positive numbers, and the "-" negative sign marks negative numbers. When you use S, a sign will always be displayed.
PR	Causes negative values to be displayed within angle brackets. For example: -123.99 will be displayed as "<123.99>". Positive values will be displayed with one leading and one trailing space in place of the angle brackets.
D	Marks the location of the decimal point.
G	Places a group separator (usually a comma) in the output.
C	Marks the place where you want the ISO currency indicator to appear. For U.S. dollars, this will be USD.
L	Marks the place where you want the local currency indicator to appear. For U.S. dollars, this will be the "$" (dollar sign) character. You cannot use L and C in the same format specification.
V	Used to display scaled values. The number of digits to the right of the V indicates how many places to the right the decimal point is shifted before the number is displayed.
EEEE	Causes SQL*Plus to use scientific notation to display a value. You must use exactly four Es and they must appear at the right end of the format string.
RN	Allows you to display a number using Roman numerals. This is the only format element for which case makes a difference. An uppercase "RN" yields uppercase Roman numerals, while a lowercase "rn" yields Roman numerals in lowercase. Numbers displayed as Roman numerals must be integers and must be from 1 to 3,999.
DATE	Causes SQL*Plus to assume that the number represents a Julian date and display it in mm/dd/yy format.

TO_DATE

`TO_DATE(string [, fmt [, 'nlsparams']])`

Converts the character-string representation of a date/time value into a value of type DATE.

Parameters

string

Specifies a character-string representation of the date/time value to be converted.

fmt

Specifies a date format string made up of the elements shown in Table 5-4.

nlsparams

Specifies a string in the form NLS_DATE_LANGUAGE=*langname*, where *langname* represents a valid NLS language name. The NLS language name affects the spelling used for day and month names.

Example

```
DECLARE
  x DATE;
BEGIN
  x := TO_DATE('21-May-2000','dd-Mon-yyyy');

  x := TO_DATE('5/21/2000 7:15 PM','mm/dd/yyyy hh:mi pm');
END;
```

TO_LOB

TO_LOB(*long_column*)

Converts a LONG or LONG RAW value into a CLOB, BLOB, or NCLOB. This function can be used only in the subquery of an INSERT . . . SELECT FROM statement when using that statement to populate a LOB column. LONG values are converted to either CLOB or NCLOB values, depending on the destination column's datatype. LONG RAW values are converted to BLOB values.

Example

```
SQL> CREATE TABLE lob_table(x CLOB);

Table created.

SQL> CREATE TABLE long_table(x LONG);

Table created.

SQL> INSERT INTO long_table (x) VALUES ('test');

1 row created.

SQL> INSERT INTO lob_table (x)
  2      SELECT TO_LOB(x)
  3      FROM long_table;

1 row created.
```

TO_MULTI_BYTE

TO_MULTI_BYTE(*char*)

Converts single-byte characters to their multibyte equivalents. If a single-byte character does not have a multibyte equivalent, it is left unchanged. This function is designed for use with strings based on a multibyte character set.

Example

```
SQL> SELECT TO_MULTI_BYTE('Be Nice') FROM dual;

TO_MULT
--------
Be Nice
```

TO_NUMBER

TO_NUMBER(*string* [,*fmt*[, '*nlsparams*']])

Converts a character-based representation of a numeric value to a NUMBER value.

Parameters

string

Specifies a character string containing the character-based representation that you want to convert.

fmt

Specifies a number format specification made up of the elements shown in Table 5-5.

nlsparams

Specifies a character string made up of one or more of the following elements, allowing you to specify various NLS characteristics for the result:

NLS_NUMERIC_CHARACTERS=''*dg*''

Allows you to specify the characters to use for decimal points and group separators. The *d* character becomes the decimal point and the *g* character becomes the group separator. For this to take effect, you must use D and G in your format specification to mark the location of decimal point and group separator, respectively.

NLS_CURRENCY=''*text*''

Allows you to specify the currency symbol (up to 10 characters long) to use in place of any L characters contained in the format specification.

NLS_ISO_CURRENCY=''*territory*''

Allows you to specify the NLS territory whose currency symbol you want to use in place of any C characters contained in the format specification.

Examples

```
SQL> VARIABLE x NUMBER
SQL> SELECT TO_NUMBER('123.45') INTO :x FROM dual;

TO_NUMBER('123.45')
-------------------
             123.45

SQL> SELECT TO_NUMBER('$123,456.78','$999,999.99') INTO :x FROM dual;

TO_NUMBER('$123,456.78','$999,999.99')
--------------------------------------
                            123456.78
```

TO_SINGLE_BYTE

TO_SINGLE_BYTE(*char*)

Converts multibyte characters to their single-byte equivalents. If a multibyte character does not have a multibyte equivalent, it is left unchanged. This function is designed for use with strings based on a multibyte character set.

Example

```
SQL> SELECT TO_SINGLE_BYTE('Be Nice') FROM dual;

TO_SING
-------
Be Nice
```

TRANSLATE USING

TRANSLATE(*text* USING {CHAR_CS | NCHAR_CS})

Converts text into the database character set or the national character set.

Parameters

text

Specifies a string that you want to translate.

CHAR_CS

Causes the string to be converted from the national character set into the database character set. The result is returned as a VARCHAR2 value.

NCHAR_CS

Causes the string to be converted from the database character set into the national character set. The result is returned as an NVARCHAR2 value.

Example

```
SQL> SELECT TRANSLATE('Be Nice' USING NCHAR_CS)
  2  FROM dual;
```

```
TRANSLA
-------
Be Nice
```

Other Functions

Several functions don't fall neatly into any of the other categories, so they are listed here. The DECODE, NVL, and USER functions are three of the most important in this category. Others to be aware of include SYS_CONTEXT, DUMP, and VSIZE.

BFILENAME

BFILENAME(*directory*, *filename*)

Returns a BFILE locator that points to a file that you specify.

Parameters

directory

  Specifies a directory, previously created using the CREATE DIRECTORY statement that contains the file.

filename

  Specifies a name of the file to which you want the locator to point. Note that you can create locators to files that do not exist.

Example

```
DECLARE
    admin_photo BFILE;
BEGIN
    admin_photo := BFILENAME('/home/oracle','administrator_photo.jpg');
    ...
END;
```

DECODE

DECODE(*expr*,   *search*,*result* [,*search*,*result*...] [,*default*])

Provides the capabilities of an inline IF statement. DECODE is arguably one of the most useful of Oracle's built-in functions. You pass DECODE an input value and a list of value/result pairs. DECODE then looks for the pair in which the value matches the input. When that pair is found, DECODE returns the result from that pair as the result of the function. If no matching value is found, DECODE returns the default result.

DECODE is one of the few functions that can correctly operate on a NULL value.

DECODE cannot be invoked from a PL/SQL expression; it can only be invoked from an SQL statement.

Parameters

expr

Specifies an input value. DECODE compares this value with subsequent *search* values to find the matching value/result pair.

search

Specifies the value portion of a value/result pair.

result

Specifies the result portion of a value/result pair.

default

Specifies an optional default result that DECODE returns if none of the *search* values match the input expression.

DECODE is limited to a maximum of 255 parameters.

Datatypes are controlled by the first *search,result* pair. The input expression and all *search* values are converted to the datatype of the first *search* value. The return value is converted to the datatype of the first *result* value.

Examples

DECODE can be used for many creative purposes. Three common uses are to expand coded values into more readable forms, to convert rows into columns, and to return one of several columns based on the value of another. The following example shows DECODE being used to interpret a coded field in the V$DATA-FILE view. The default return value, Invalid plugged_in "/value", should never be returned.

```
SQL> COLUMN name FORMAT A50
SQL> SELECT name,
  2         DECODE(plugged_in,
  3                0,'Not Plugged In',
  4                1,'Plugged In',
  5                'Invalid pugged_in value') plugged_in
  6  FROM v$datafile;
```

```
NAME                                                       PLUGGED_IN
-------------------------------------------------------    --------------------
/s01/app/oracle/oradata/donna/system01.dbf                 Not Plugged In
/s01/app/oracle/oradata/donna/oemrep01.dbf                 Not Plugged In
/s01/app/oracle/oradata/donna/rbs01.dbf                    Not Plugged In
/s01/app/oracle/oradata/donna/temp01.dbf                   Not Plugged In
/s01/app/oracle/oradata/donna/users01.dbf                  Not Plugged In
/s01/app/oracle/oradata/donna/indx01.dbf                   Not Plugged In
/s01/app/oracle/oradata/donna/drsys01.dbf                  Not Plugged In
/s01/app/oracle/oradata/donna/oemrep02.dbf                 Not Plugged In
/s01/app/oracle/oradata/donna/gnis_data_01.dbf             Plugged In
/s01/app/oracle/oradata/donna/gnis_index_01.dbf            Plugged In
```

Another creative use of DECODE is to convert query results that would normally be returned as several rows into one row consisting of several columns. Consider the query in the following example that counts the number of objects owned by SYS and SYSTEM:

```
SQL> SELECT owner, COUNT(*)
  2  FROM dba_objects
  3  WHERE OWNER IN ('SYS','SYSTEM')
  4  GROUP BY owner;

OWNER                              COUNT(*)
------------------------------    ----------
SYS                                    6174
SYSTEM                                  161
```

What if you wanted to get just one row back with a value for each of those users? You can do that using DECODE. The trick is to write two DECODE expressions that each checks for a different username. For example:

```
SQL> SELECT SUM(DECODE(owner,'SYS',1,0)), SUM(DECODE(owner,'SYSTEM',1,0))
  2  FROM dba_objects;

SUM(DECODE(OWNER,'SYS',1,0)) SUM(DECODE(OWNER,'SYSTEM',1,0))
---------------------------- -------------------------------
                        6174                             161
```

Here, the first DECODE returns a value of 1 for all objects owned by SYS, and 0 for everything else. The second DECODE does the same thing, but for SYSTEM. Summing on the two columns allows you to get one total for each user, with only one row returned by the query. This technique works only when you have a fixed number of results that you are looking for. There is no way to extend the technique to list a variable number of users horizontally.

The third use for DECODE mentioned earlier is to return one of several different columns (or expressions) based on the value of a column. The following query against DBA_TAB_COLUMNS uses DECODE to return the appropriate datatype declaration based on the DATA_TYPE column:

```
SELECT owner, table_name, column_name,
       DECODE(data_type,
              'VARCHAR2','VARCHAR2 (' || TO_CHAR(data_length) || ')',
              'NUMBER', DECODE(data_precision,
                               NULL, 'NUMBER',
                               'NUMBER (' ||
                               TO_CHAR(data_precision) || ',' ||
                               TO_CHAR(data_scale) || ')'))
FROM dba_tab_columns
WHERE data_type IN ('VARCHAR2','NUMBER');
```

For simplicity, this example handles only VARCHAR2 and NUMBER datatypes, but you can readily see how the logic could be extended to properly display other datatypes. Note the use of a nested DECODE function to handle NUMBER types. Floating-point numbers are declared without a precision and scale. The nested DECODE causes NUMBER declarations to include a precision and scale only when one was originally specified.

DUMP

DUMP(*expr* [,*return_format* [,*start_position* [,*length*]]])

Returns a VARCHAR2 string showing the datatype and the internal representation of data stored within a column or of the data returned by an expression.

Parameters

expr

Specifies the data to be dumped. This parameter can be a column name or a valid SQL expression.

return_format

Specifies a format that controls the manner in which the dumped data is formatted:

8 Use octal notation.

10 Use decimal notation. This is the default.

16 Use hexadecimal notation.

17 Display the result using characters.

If you add 1000 to the format specifier, the name of the character set will be returned as well. This is useful only when you dump a character column or the result of a character expression.

start_position

Specifies a starting byte for the data to be dumped. The default is to start with the first byte of data.

length

Specifies a number of bytes to dump. The default is to dump all the data.

Examples

```
SQL> SELECT DUMP(SYSDATE) FROM dual;

DUMP(SYSDATE)
-------------------------------------
Typ=13 Len=8: 208,7,5,21,16,59,57,0

SQL> SELECT DUMP('Hi There',16) FROM dual;

DUMP('HITHERE',16)
-------------------------------------
Typ=96 Len=8: 48,69,20,54,68,65,72,65

SQL> SELECT DUMP('Hi There',1016) FROM dual;

DUMP('HITHERE',1016)
-----------------------------------------------------------
Typ=96 Len=8 CharacterSet=US7ASCII: 48,69,20,54,68,65,72,65
```

EMPTY_BLOB

EMPTY_BLOB()

Returns an empty BLOB locator, which can be used to initialize a BLOB column.

Example

```
SQL> CREATE TABLE x(b blob);

Table created.

SQL> INSERT INTO x (b) VALUES (EMPTY_BLOB());

1 row created.
```

 Unlike other functions, EMPTY_BLOB must be followed with parentheses even though no parameters are passed.

EMPTY_CLOB

EMPTY_CLOB()

Returns an empty CLOB locator, which can be used to initialize a CLOB column.

Example

```
SQL> CREATE TABLE x(c clob);

Table created.

SQL> INSERT INTO x (c) VALUES (EMPTY_CLOB());

1 row created.
```

 Unlike other functions, EMPTY_CLOB must be followed with parentheses even though no parameters are passed.

NLS_CHARSET_DECL_LEN

NLS_CHARSET_DECL_LEN(*bytecnt, csid*)

Returns the declaration width of an NCHAR column (in terms of the number of characters), based on the byte count provided.

Parameters

bytecnt
　　Specifies the size, in bytes, of the NCHAR column.

csid
　　Specifies a number identifying the NLS character set you use for the column. You can use the NLS_CHARSET_ID function to get the character set number to correspond to a character set name.

Example

```
SQL> SELECT NLS_CHARSET_DECL_LEN(100,NLS_CHARSET_ID('US7ASCII'))
  2  FROM dual;

NLS_CHARSET_DECL_LEN(100,NLS_CHARSET_ID('US7ASCII'))
----------------------------------------------------
                                                 100
```

NLS_CHARSET_ID

NLS_CHARSET_ID(*text*)

Returns the ID number corresponding to a given NLS character set name.

Example

```
SQL> SELECT NLS_CHARSET_ID('US7ASCII'), NLS_CHARSET_ID('WE8EBCDIC37C')
  2  FROM dual;

NLS_CHARSET_ID('US7ASCII') NLS_CHARSET_ID('WE8EBCDIC37C')
-------------------------- -----------------------------
                         1                            90
```

NLS_CHARSET_NAME

NLS_CHARSET_NAME(*n*)

Returns the name corresponding to a given NLS character set ID number.

Example

```
SQL> SELECT NLS_CHARSET_NAME(1), NLS_CHARSET_NAME(90)
  2  FROM dual;

NLS_CHAR NLS_CHARSET_
-------- ------------
US7ASCII WE8EBCDIC37C
```

NVL

NVL(*expr1*, *expr2*)

Returns an alternative value to use if a given input value is NULL. NVL returns *expr2* if *expr1* is NULL; otherwise, it simply returns *expr1*.

Parameters

expr1

Specifies a value to be tested for NULL. If this value is not NULL, it is also the value returned by the function.

expr2

Specifies a value to be returned when *expr1* is NULL.

Example

```
SQL> SELECT username, NVL(TO_CHAR(lock_date),'Not Locked')
  2  FROM dba_users;

USERNAME                       NVL(TO_CHAR(LOCK_
------------------------------ -----------------
```

```
SYS                       Not Locked
SYSTEM                    Not Locked
...
GNIS                      21-May-2000 17:18
```

SYS_CONTEXT

```
SYS_CONTEXT(namespace, attribute_name [,length])
```

Returns the value of an attribute in an application context namespace.

Parameters

namespace

Specifies the name of a namespace previously created using the CREATE CONTEXT statement. You may also specify the default namespace USERENV.

attribute

Specifies the name of an attribute within the namespace. That attribute's value is then returned by this function. Several predefined attributes are available for use with the default USERENV namespace. These attributes are listed in Table 5-6.

length

Specifies the length you want to allow for an attribute's return value. This optional parameter is only available beginning with Oracle 8.1.6, and only for the AUTHENTICATION_DATA attribute.

Table 5-6. Predefined Attributes in the USERENV Namespace

Attribute Name	Description	Max Length	Release Introduced
AUTHENTICATION_ DATA	The data used to authenticate a user. If authentication is via an X.503 certificate, the content of the certificate will be returned in hexadecimal format. This is the only option for which the SYS_CONTEXT function's LENGTH parameter may be used. The maximum length you can specify is 4000 bytes.	2564000	8.1.6
AUTHENTICATION_ TYPE	Indicates how the user was authenticated. One of the following values will be returned: DATABASE: a username and password were used. OS: operating system authentication was used. NETWORK: authentication was via a network protocol or the Advanced Networking Option (ANO). PROXY: authentication was by OCI (Oracle Call Interface) proxy.	30	8.1.6

Table 5-6. Predefined Attributes in the USERENV Namespace (continued)

Attribute Name	Description	Max Length	Release Introduced
BG_JOB_ID	If the current session was created by an Oracle background process, this attribute will be the job ID of the session. Otherwise, it will be NULL.	30	8.1.6
CLIENT_INFO	Returns up to 64 bytes of user session information stored using the DBMS_APPLICATION_INFO package.	64	8.1.6
CURRENT_SCHEMA	The current schema name. This usually matches the current username. However, if you log in as the INTERNAL user, or as SYSDBA or SYSOPER, your schema name will be SYS.	30	8.1.5
CURRENT_SCHEMAID	The ID number associated with the current schema.	30	8.1.5
CURRENT_USER	The current username. If a stored procedure has been invoked, this may not be the same as the login username returned by SESSION_USER.	30	8.1.5
CURRENT_USERID	The ID number associated with the current user.	30	8.1.5
DB_DOMAIN	The database domain as specified by the DB_DOMAIN initialization parameter.	256	8.1.6
DB_NAME	The database name as specified by the DB_NAME initialization parameter.	30	8.1.6
ENTRYID	Your auditing entry identifier. This attribute is not valid in distributed SQL statements. In addition, the AUDIT_TRAIL initialization parameter must be set to TRUE.	30	8.1.6
EXTERNAL_NAME	The external name of the database user. For users authenticated by SSL, this is the distinguished name (DN) from the user's V.503 certificate.	256	8.1.6
FG_JOB_ID	The session's job ID if the session was created by a client's foreground process. Otherwise, it is NULL.	30	8.1.6
HOST	The name of the machine from which the client is connecting.	54	8.1.6
INSTANCE	The number identifying the instance to which you are currently connected.	30	8.1.6
IP_ADDRESS	The user's IP address. This address only applies to TCP/IP connections.	30	8.1.5

Table 5-6. Predefined Attributes in the USERENV Namespace (continued)

Attribute Name	Description	Max Length	Release Introduced
ISDBA	Returns TRUE or FALSE, depending on whether or not the ISDBA role is enabled.	30	8.1.6
LANG	The ISO abbreviation for your current language name.	62	8.1.6
LANGUAGE	Your current language setting, territory setting, and database character set name.	52	8.1.6
NETWORK_ PROTOCOL	The name of the network protocol used for the connection. This name comes from the Net8 connect string's PROTO-COL attribute.	256	8.1.6
NLS_CALENDAR	The current NLS calendar name.	62	8.1.5
NLS_CURRENCY	The current NLS currency indicator.	62	8.1.5
NLS_DATE_ FORMAT	The current NLS date format.	62	8.1.5
NLS_DATE_ LANGUAGE	The current NLS date language.	62	8.1.5
NLS_SORT	The current sort base.	62	8.1.5
NLS_TERRITORY	The current NLS territory name.	62	8.1.5
OS_USER	The operating system username of the client process that initiated the database connection.	30	8.1.6
PROXY_USER	The name of the user who opened the current session on behalf of the current session user.	30	8.1.6
PROXY_USERID	The user ID of the user who opened the current session on behalf of the current session user.	30	8.1.6
SESSION_USER	The name with which the current user logged in. Note that this name does not change even when a stored procedure owned by another user is invoked.	30	8.1.5
SESSION_USERID	The ID number associated with the session user.	30	8.1.5
SESSIONID	Your auditing session identifier. This attribute is not valid in distributed SQL statements.	30	8.1.6

Table 5-6. Predefined Attributes in the USERENV Namespace (continued)

Attribute Name	Description	Max Length	Release Introduced
TERMINAL	The operating system identifier for the current session's client. In a distributed environment, this can only be used for remote SELECT statements and it returns the identifier for your local session.	10	8.1.6

Examples

```
SQL> SELECT SYS_CONTEXT('USERENV', 'SESSION_USER')
  2  FROM dual;

SYS_CONTEXT('USERENV','SESSION_USER')
----------------------------------------------------------------------
SYSTEM

SQL> SELECT SYS_CONTEXT('USERENV', 'NLS_SORT')
  2  FROM dual;

SYS_CONTEXT('USERENV','NLS_SORT')
---------------------------------------------------------------
BINARY
```

SYS_GUID

```
SYS_GUID()
```

Returns a 16-byte RAW value that can be used as a globally unique identifier. On most platforms, the value is a combination of the host ID, a process (or thread) ID, and a sequence number.

RAW values are converted to hexadecimal when displayed by SQL*Plus, so in the example, 32 rather than 16 characters are displayed in the result, since each character has been displayed using two hexadecimal digits.

Example

```
SQL> SELECT SYS_GUID() FROM dual;

SYS_GUID()
--------------------------------
```

6827BA0C1CF2D067E0300B0A100C0246

Unlike other functions, SYSGUID must be followed with parentheses even though no parameters are passed.

UID

UID

Returns an integer value that uniquely identifies the current database user. The value comes from the V$SESSION view's USER# column.

Example

```
SQL> SELECT UID FROM dual;

      UID
---------
       10
```

USER

USER

Returns the current username. Normally, USER returns the username used to log into the database. When invoked from within a stored procedure or function, however, USER returns the name of the procedure or function's owner. USER is also known as a pseudo-column. See Chapter 1 for more information.

When invoked from within a trigger, USER returns the login username.

Example

```
SQL> SELECT USER FROM dual;

USER
------------------------------
SYSTEM
```

USERENV

USERENV(*option*)

Returns information about the current user.

Parameter

option

> Specifies the exact piece of information to be returned, and must be one of the values listed in Table 5-7. The value returned by this function is always a VARCHAR2 character string.

 Beginning with the Oracle 8.1.6 release, the SYS_CONTEXT function may also be used to retrieve these user environment values.

Table 5-7. USERENV Option Values

Option	Description
ENTRYID	Returns an auditing entry identifier. The AUDIT_TRAIL initialization parameter must be TRUE for this option to be valid, and you cannot use this option in a distributed environment.
INSTANCE	Returns the instance identifier.
ISDBA	Returns TRUE or FALSE, depending on whether or not the ISDBA role is enabled.
LANG	Returns the abbreviation for the current ISO language.
LANGUAGE	Returns the user's current language and territory settings.
SESSIONID	Returns the auditing session identifier. The AUDIT_TRAIL initialization parameter must be TRUE for this option to be valid, and you cannot use this option in a distributed environment.
TERMINAL	Returns the current session's operating system terminal identifier.

Example

```
SQL> SELECT USERENV('INSTANCE'),USERENV('ISDBA') FROM dual;

USERENV('INSTANCE') USEREN
------------------- ------
                  1 FALSE
```

VSIZE

VSIZE(*expr*)

Returns the size, in bytes, of the value's internal representation.

Examples

```
SQL> SELECT VSIZE(SYSDATE) FROM dual;

VSIZE(SYSDATE)
--------------
             8

SQL> SELECT VSIZE(username) FROM dba_users;

VSIZE(USERNAME)
---------------
              3
              6
              5
```

6

SQL*Plus

SQL*Plus is Oracle's primary command-line interface to the database. It allows you to execute SQL statements and PL/SQL blocks and to format output. It also gives you a certain amount of operational control. SQL*Plus has been available since the earliest versions of Oracle (when it was called the *User Friendly Interface* (UFI)). SQL*Plus can execute the following types of statements:

- SQL statements (DDL and DML) corresponding to the ANSI SQL standard and Oracle extensions

- PL/SQL statements, a proprietary SQL language extension from Oracle

- SQL*Plus statements, proprietary formatting and operational statements from Oracle

In simple terms, this means that SQL*Plus works with source statements directly, without the need for separate compilation. SQL statements are sent to the Oracle server (locally or via Net8 or SQL*Net), where they are parsed and executed. PL/SQL blocks are also sent to the Oracle server, where they are compiled and executed. SQL*Plus statements are executed directly by the running copy of SQL*Plus.

Command-Line Syntax

SQL*Plus is a command-line utility and is usually invoked from a command prompt. The syntax for invoking SQL*Plus from a command prompt is as follows:

```
sqlplus [option] [username[/password][@hostname]] [@script] [parm1] [parm2] . . .
```

Keywords

option

Specifies an option that controls the operation of SQL*Plus and has the following syntax:

```
[-]
[-?]
[-M[ARKUP] HTML [ON | OFF]
  [HEAD text]
  [BODY text]
  [ENTMAP {ON | OFF}]
  [SPOOL {ON | OFF}]
  [PRE[FORMAT] {ON | OFF}]]
[-R[ESTRICT] {1 | 2 | 3}]
[-S[ILENT]] ]
```

- Displays the use and syntax of the SQL*Plus command line and then exits to the operating system.

-? Displays the version number for SQL*Plus and then exits to the operating system.

MARKUP HTML

Specifies that HTML output be generated for this SQL*Plus session.

ON

Specifies that HTML output be generated using the options specified.

OFF

Specifies that HTML output not be generated. This option is the default.

HEAD

Specifies that *text* be used as content for the <HEAD> tag. Heading text must be enclosed within quotes. By default, *text* is '<TITLE>SQL*Plus Report</TITLE>'.

BODY

Specifies that *text* be used as content for the <BODY> tag. Body text must be enclosed within quotes.

ENTMAP ON

Specifies that SQL*Plus display the special characters "<", ">", and "&" as the HTML entities <, >, and &, respectively.

ENTMAP OFF

Specifies that SQL*Plus not change display of the special characters "<", ">", and "&".

SPOOL ON

Specifies that SQL*Plus write HTML tags to the start and end of each file created by the SQL*Plus SPOOL command.

SPOOL OFF

Specifies that SQL*Plus not write HTML tags to the start and end of each file created by the SQL*Plus SPOOL command.

PREFORMAT ON

Specifies that SQL*Plus write output inside the HTML <PRE> tag.

PREFORMAT OFF

Specifies that SQL*Plus not write output inside the HTML <PRE> tag.

RESTRICT

Specifies that a restriction level, as indicated by 1, 2, or 3, be in effect for this session. Restriction levels disable certain SQL*Plus commands, as shown in Table 6-1.

SILENT

Specifies that all SQL*Plus information and prompt messages be suppressed, including the command prompt, the echoing of commands, and the banner normally displayed when you start SQL*Plus.

username

The Oracle username for the account to which you are connecting.

password

The username's password. If omitted, SQL*Plus will prompt for the password.

hostname

The hostname assigned to the database to which you are connecting. Typically, this hostname is resolved using *tnsnames.ora* or Oracle Names. If the hostname is omitted, SQL*Plus will attempt to take it from an environment variable or registry entry named LOCAL. If there is no LOCAL environment variable or registry entry, SQL*Plus will attempt a connection to the local database identified by your current ORACLE_SID setting.

script

The name of a SQL*Plus script to be executed upon successful connection to the database.

parm1, parm2 …

Optional parameters that will be passed to SQL*Plus and that may be referenced using substitution variables within a SQL*Plus script. String parameters containing spaces or other special characters must be enclosed in single quotes.

Table 6-1. Commands Disabled by Restriction Levels

Command	Level 1	Level 2	Level 3
EDIT	Yes	Yes	Yes
GET	No	No	Yes
HOST or !	Yes	Yes	Yes
SAVE	No	Yes	Yes
SPOOL	No	Yes	Yes
START or @ or @@	No	No	Yes
STORE	No	Yes	Yes

Examples

If you are connecting to a local database and you've set your ORACLE_SID environment variable properly, you can invoke SQL*Plus using the following simple command:

```
sqlplus
```

SQL*Plus will be started and you will be prompted to enter a username and password. You will then be connected to the default Oracle instance.

If you prefer, you can pass your username and password on the command line. The following command will connect you to your default instance and log you in as the user scott:

```
sqlplus scott/tiger
```

The command in the next example starts SQL*Plus and runs a SQL script named *report1.sql*. You'll be prompted for a username and password:

```
sqlplus @report1
```

The command in this final example starts SQL*Plus and connects you as the user scott to the Oracle instance pointed to by the Net8 service named test. The SQL script *report2.sql* is then executed. The values 1000 and 5000 represent command-line parameters that are passed to the script:

```
sqlplus scott/tiger@test @report2 1000 5000
```

The actual SQL*Plus executable name may vary from platform to platform and from release to release. For example, the executable name for the command-line version of SQL*Plus Version 8.0 under Windows 95/98 is *PLUS80.EXE*. The executable name for the GUI version on that platform is *PLUS80W.EXE*.

SQL*Plus Editing Commands

When a SQL*Plus session is started, you are presented with the SQL*Plus prompt, which indicates that SQL*Plus is ready to accept input. The default prompt is SQL>. Input is free-form, and can consist of: SQL statements (DML or DDL), PL/SQL code, and SQL*Plus commands.

SQL*Plus commands are executed immediately and not saved. SQL statements and PL/SQL blocks are stored in a memory buffer known as the *SQL*Plus buffer*. Buffer contents are organized into lines. As you enter a SQL statement or a PL/SQL block, a new buffer line is created each time you press the Enter key. The commands described in this section allow editing and related operations on the contents of the SQL*Plus buffer, and may be entered directly from the SQL> prompt. They may also be included in a SQL*Plus script.

Most editing commands operate on what is termed the *current line*. The current line is always the line that was most recently entered or displayed, and SQL*Plus always marks it with an asterisk. If the line you want to edit is not current, you can use the LIST command to make it so. Then you can execute other editing commands to enter changes that you wish to make.

APPEND

A[PPEND] *text*

Adds (appends) *text* to the end of the current line.

CHANGE

C[HANGE] /*old*/[*new*/]

Changes *old* to *new* in the current line. To delete text, supply an old value without a corresponding new value.

Examples

Change the string "abc" to "xyz":

    CHANGE /abc/xyz/

In the next example, because no new text was supplied, the specified text is simply removed from the line being edited:

    CHANGE /abc/

CLEAR

`CL[EAR] BUFF[ER]`

Deletes all lines from the buffer.

DEL

`DEL [line | *]`

Deletes the specified line, or the current line from the buffer.

`DEL {begin end | line * | * line}`

Deletes a specific range of lines from the buffer.

`DEL {line LAST | * LAST}`

Deletes all lines starting at a specific line, or the current line, from the buffer.

`DEL LAST`

Deletes the last line from the buffer.

Keywords

line

Specifies a line number.

* Specifies the current line.

begin

Specifies the first line to be deleted in a multiline delete. All lines from *begin* to *end* will be deleted.

end

Specifies the last line to be deleted in a multiline delete. All lines from *begin* to *end* will be deleted.

LAST

Specifies the last line in the buffer.

GET

`GET filename [LIS[T] | NOL[IST]]`

Places the contents of a file into the buffer.

Keywords

filename

Specifies the name of an operating system file whose contents will be placed into the buffer, replacing the current buffer contents.

LIST

Specifies that the file contents are to be listed to the display when the buffer is loaded. This option is the default.

NOLIST

Specifies that the contents of the file are not to be listed.

 The GET command is normally used only to load a file containing a single SQL statement because SQL*Plus cannot execute multiple statements from the buffer.

INPUT

`I[NPUT] [text]`

Adds one or more lines to the buffer. The new lines are inserted after the current line. The provided *text* will be entered into the buffer. If *text* is omitted, SQL*Plus will prompt for each new line of text to be entered until a null line is entered to terminate.

LIST

`L[IST]`

Displays all lines in the buffer.

`L[IST] line`

Displays a single line in the buffer.

`L[IST] *`

Displays the current line in the buffer.

`L[IST] LAST`

Displays the last line in the buffer.

`L[IST] {begin end | begin LAST | line LAST | * LAST}`

Displays a range of lines in the buffer.

Keywords

line

Specifies a line number.

*   Specifies the current line.

LAST

Specifies the last line in the buffer.

begin

Specifies the first line to be listed. All lines from *begin* to *end* will be listed.

end

Specifies the last line to be listed. All lines from *begin* to *end* will be listed.

SAVE

SAV[E] *filename* {<u>CREATE</u> | REPLACE | APPEND}

Saves the buffer contents into the specified file. The buffer contents are preserved.

Keywords

CREATE

Creates a new file. The file must not already exist if this option is specified. This option is the default.

REPLACE

Replaces the contents of an existing file. If the file does not exist, SQL*Plus will create it.

APPEND

Adds the buffer contents to the end of the specified file.

Only a single SQL statement or PL/SQL block will be contained in the buffer and saved to disk. No SQL*Plus commands will be stored, even if they have been previously executed, since they are not saved in the buffer. To create a script containing SQL*Plus commands, you must use a text editor.

Once the contents of the buffer are saved to a file, the GET command can be used to retrieve that file. The START command may be used to execute the command in that file.

Formatting SQL*Plus Output

While SQL*Plus provides some basic default formatting of output, you can also customize your output in various ways to produce "finished" reports. The following commands implement the formatting capabilities of SQL*Plus. You can enter these commands from a SQL*Plus prompt or include them in a SQL*Plus script.

BREAK (With Parameters)

`BRE[AK]  [ON column | expression | ROW | REPORT [action [action]]]. . .`

Specify where and how to change the formatting of a report. BREAK is often used with COMPUTE to generate totals and subtotals.

Keywords

column
> Causes the specified action to occur whenever the value of the specified column changes.

expression
> Causes the action to occur whenever the value of the specified expression (which must exactly match an expression in the SELECT statement) changes.

ROW
> Causes the action to occur whenever SQL*Plus returns a row.

REPORT
> Causes the corresponding COMPUTE command to be executed at the end of the report.

action
> Can be one or more of the following:

> *SKI[P]*
>> Skips *n* lines before printing the row on which the break occurred.

> *SKI[P] PAGE*
>> Skips the necessary number of lines to advance to a new page. If SET NEWPAGE 0 was specified, prints a formfeed character.

> *NODUP[LICATES]*
>> Causes blanks to be printed instead of the value of the break column when the value is the same as the value in the preceding row.

> *DUP[LICATES]*
>> Causes the value of the break column to be printed for every row, regardless of whether or not the value changes.

BREAK (Without Parameters)

`BREAK`

Lists all current BREAK definitions.

BTITLE (Controlling)

```
BTI[TLE] ON | OFF
```

Turns the printing of the bottom title ON or OFF without affecting its definition.

BTITLE (Defining)

```
BTI[TLE] [printspec [text | variable] . . . ]
```

Creates and formats a title that appears at the bottom of each page.

Keywords

printspec

> One or more of the following clauses used to place and format the text or variables in the title:

> *COL*

>> Starts *text* or *variable* in column *n*.

> *S[KIP]*

>> Skips *n* lines before printing *text* or *variable*. The default number of line to skip is 1.

> *TAB*

>> Skips *n* print positions forward (or backward if *n* is negative) before printing *text* or *variable*.

> *LE[FT]*

>> Prints *text* or *variable* aligned with the left margin.

> *CE[NTER]*

>> Prints *text* or *variable* centered on the page. The LINESIZE setting is used to calculate page width.

> *RI[GHT]*

>> Prints *text* or *variable* aligned with the right margin.

> *BOLD*

>> Prints *text* or *variable* in bold print.

> *FORMAT*

>> Formats *text* or *variable* according to the format model specified in *formatstring*. See Table 5-5 for available numeric formats.

text

> A character string to be printed on the page. Multiple words must be enclosed in single quotes.

variable
    A user variable or a system-maintained variable.

BTITLE (Displaying)

BTI[TLE]

Displays the current BTITLE definition.

CLEAR

CL[EAR] *option*

Resets or erases the current value of a SQL*Plus option.

Keyword

option
    May be one of the following:

BRE[AKS]
        Removes the definitions set by the BREAK command.

BUFF[ER]
        Clears all text from the buffer.

COL[UMNS]
        Resets column definitions set using the COLUMN command to their
        defaults.

COMP[UTES]
        Removes all definitions set by the COMPUTE command.

SCR[EEN]
        Clears the screen.

SQL
        Clears all text from the buffer.

TIMI[NG]
        Deletes all timing areas created by the TIMING command.

COLUMN

COL[UMN] {*column* | *expression*} [*option* . . .]

Specifies the display characteristics for a column or expression using one or more
options.

COL[UMN] {*column* | *expression*}

Displays the current display attributes for the named column or expression.

Keywords

column

A column name used in a SQL statement.

expression

An expression used in a SQL statement.

option

One or more of the following:

ALI[AS]

Assigns an alias name to the column or expression, which can then be used in subsequent BREAK, COMPUTE, or other COLUMN commands.

CLE[AR]

Resets attributes for this column or expression to their defaults.

FOLD_A[FTER]

Inserts a carriage return after the heading and after the column contents for each row of output displayed by SQL*Plus.

FOLD_B[EFORE]

Inserts a carriage return before the heading and before the column contents for each row of output displayed by SQL*Plus.

FOR[MAT]

Specifies a character string containing the format used to control how the column contents are displayed. See Table 5-4 for available date formats and Table 5-5 for available numeric formats. For character columns, use the format specifier A*xx* where *xx* is a number representing the column width in terms of characters. SQL*Plus cannot format DATE columns; those must be formatted in the SELECT statement using the TO_CHAR function.

HEA[DING]

Defines the column *string*. If *string* contains blanks or punctuation, it must be enclosed in either single or double quotes. The HEADSEP character, which is a vertical bar (|) by default, can be used to place line breaks in the heading.

JUST[IFY]

Aligns the heading as specified. By default, headings for NUMBER columns default to RIGHT alignment, and the headings for other column types default to LEFT alignment.

LIKE

Copies the display attributes of the named column, expression, or alias, and applies them to the column that you are formatting.

NEWL[INE]

Starts a new line before displaying the value for the *column* or *expression*.

NEW_V[ALUE]

Specifies that the column value be held in the specified variable, which can then be used in TTITLE and BTITLE commands.

NOPRI[NT]

Prevents the printing of a column or expression.

NUL[L] `text`

Specifies a character string to be displayed when the value of a column or expression is NULL.

OLD_V[ALUE]

Specifies that the previous value of a column or expression is to be held in the specified variable, which can then be used in TTITLE and BTITLE commands.

OFF

Disables the display attributes for a column or expression without affecting the attributes' definition.

ON

Enables the display attributes for a column or expression after they have previously been turned OFF.

TRU[NCATED]

Specifies that a value that is too long for the column is to be truncated.

WOR[D_WRAPPED]

Specifies that a value that is too long for the column is to be wrapped to the next line, starting with the first full word of the string that does not fit in the width of the column.

WRA[PPED]

Specifies that a value that is too long for the column is to be wrapped to the next line, starting with the first character of the string that does not fit in the width of the column.

COMPUTE

```
COMP[UTE] [function [LABEL text][ function [LABEL text]] . . . ]
 OF [{expr | column | alias} ...]
 ON {expr | column | alias | REPORT | ROW}
```

Causes SQL*Plus to calculate and display summary lines using standard computations on selected subsets of rows.

Keywords

function ...

> Is one or more of the following standard mathematical functions; if you specify more than one function name, use at least one space to separate the names:
>
> AVG
> COU[NT]
> MAX[IMUM]
> MIN[IMUM]
> NUM[BER]
> STD
> SUM
> VAR[IANCE]

LABEL

> Specifies that *text* be used as a label to be printed for the computed value. The label prints left-justified and is truncated to the column width or linesize, whichever is smaller. The maximum label length is 500 characters. If this keyword is omitted, *text* defaults to the unabbreviated function keyword.

The label for the computed value appears in the specified break column. To suppress the label, use the NOPRINT option of the COLUMN command on the break column.

OF

> Specifies the expression(s), column(s), or alias(es) to use in the computation. These options must also be listed in the SELECT statement to which the COMPUTE applies.

ON

> Specifies the entity which, when its value changes, triggers COMPUTE to display the computed value. ON must match a corresponding BREAK statement.

REPFOOTER (Controlling)

REPF[OOTER] ON | OFF

Turns the report footer ON or OFF without affecting its definition.

Keywords

ON

> Specifies that report footers are to be printed.

OFF

Specifies that report footers are not to be printed.

REPFOOTER (Defining)

REPF[OOTER] [PAGE] [printspec [text | variable] [printspec [text | variable] . . .]]

Places a report footer on the bottom of each report.

Keywords

PAGE

Specifies that a new page be started after printing the report footer.

printspec

Specifies that one or more of the following clauses are be used to place and format text or variables:

COL

Starts *text* or *variable* in column *n*.

S[KIP]

Skips *n* lines before printing *text* or *variable*. The default number of lines to skip is 1.

TAB

Skips *n* print positions forward (or backward, if *n* is negative) before printing *text* or *variable*.

LE[FT]

Prints *text* or *variable* aligned with the left margin.

CE[NTER]

Prints *text* or *variable* centered on the page. The LINESIZE setting is used to calculate page width.

RI[GHT]

Prints *text* or *variable* aligned with the right margin.

BOLD

Prints *text* or *variable* in bold print.

FORMAT

Formats *text* or *variable* according to the format model specified in *formatstring*. See Table 5-5 for available numeric formats.

text

A character string value to be printed as part of the report footer. Text containing spaces or punctuation characters must be enclosed in quotes.

variable

> A user or system-maintained variable (e.g., SQL.PNO for the page number). The variable's contents will be displayed as part of the report footer.

REPFOOTER (Displaying)

`REPF[OOTER]`

Displays the current report footer definition.

REPHEADER (Controlling)

`REPH[EADER] ON | OFF`

Turns the report header ON or OFF without affecting its definition.

REPHEADER (Defining)

`REPH[EADER] [PAGE] [printspec [text | variable] [printspec [text | variable]] . . .]`

Places a report header on the top of each report.

Keywords

PAGE

> Specifies that a new page be started after printing the report header.

printspec

> Specifies that one or more of the following clauses are to be used to place and format text or variables:

> *COL*

>> Starts *text* or *variable* in column *n*.

> *S[KIP]*

>> Skips *n* lines before printing *text* or *variable*. The default number of lines to skip is 1.

> *TAB*

>> Skips *n* print positions forward (or backward, if *n* is negative) before printing *text* or *variable*.

> *LE[FT]*

>> Prints *text* or *variable* aligned with the left margin.

> *CE[NTER]*

>> Prints *text* or *variable* centered on the page. The LINESIZE setting is used to calculate page width.

> *RI[GHT]*

>> Prints *text* or *variable* aligned with the right margin.

BOLD

>   Prints *text* or *variable* in bold print.

FORMAT

>   Formats *text* or *variable* according to the format model specified in *for-matstring*. See Table 5-5 for available numeric formats.

text

>   A character string value to be printed as part of the report header. Text containing spaces or punctuation characters must be enclosed in quotes.

variable

>   A user variable or system-maintained variable (e.g., SQL.PNO for the page number). The variable's contents will be displayed as part of the report header.

REPHEADER (Displaying)

`REPH[EADER]`

Displays the current report header definition.

TTITLE (Controlling)

`TTI[TLE] ON | OFF`

Turns the top title ON or OFF without affecting its definition.

TTITLE (Defining)

`TTI[TLE] [printspec [text | variable] . . .]`

Creates and formats a title that appears at the top of each page.

Keywords

printspec

>   Includes the following clauses used to place and format text or variables:

>   *COL*

>   >   Starts *text* or *variable* in column *n*.

>   *S[KIP]*

>   >   Skips *n* lines before printing *text* or *variable*. The default number of lines to skip is 1.

>   *TAB*

>   >   Skips *n* print positions forward (or backward, if *n* is negative) before printing *text* or *variable*.

LE[FT]

    Prints *text* or *variable* aligned with the left margin.

CE[NTER]

    Prints *text* or *variable* centered on the page. The LINESIZE setting is used to calculate page width.

RI[GHT]

    Prints *text* or *variable* aligned with the right margin.

BOLD

    Prints *text* or *variable* in bold print.

FORMAT

    Formats *text* or *variable* according to the format model specified in *formatstring*. See Table 5-5 for available numeric formats.

text

A character string value to be printed as part of the page title. Text containing spaces or punctuation characters must be enclosed in quotes.

variable

A user variable or system-maintained variable (e.g., SQL.PNO for the page number). The variable's contents will be displayed as part of the page title.

TTITLE (Displaying)

TTI[TLE]

Displays the current TTITLE definition.

*Miscellaneous SQL*Plus Commands*

The SQL*Plus commands described in this section are used to perform a variety of tasks. These commands may be entered directly from a SQL*Plus prompt, or they may be included in a SQL*Plus script.

@

@*filename*

Runs a series of SQL*Plus commands, and/or SQL and/or PL/SQL statements contained in a file. *filename* specifies the name of an operating system file containing SQL and/or PL/SQL statements.

This command is equivalent to specifying START *filename*.

Command files may be nested; in other words, a command file may contain another *@filename* command.

@@

`@@filename`

Runs a series of SQL*Plus commands, and/or SQL and/or PL/SQL statements contained in a file as a nested command. *filename* specifies the name of an operating system file containing SQL and/or PL/SQL statements that will be executed by SQL*Plus. When the script is complete, control will be passed back to the script that invoked it. If no path is specified, the file being invoked is expected to be in the same directory as its parent.

ARCHIVE LOG

```
ARCHIVE LOG {LIST |
            STOP |
            START    [TO destination] |
            NEXT     [TO destination] |
            ALL      [TO destination] |
            log_sequence [TO destination]
            }
```

Controls or displays information about archive logging. This command is intended for DBAs.

Keywords

LIST

Specifies that SQL*Plus is to display information about the current state of archiving.

STOP

Specifies that the automatic archiving of log files be stopped.

START

Specifies that the automatic archiving of log files be started. If TO *destination* is specified, all archived log files will be written to this destination.

NEXT

Specifies that the next redo log file group is to be archived manually (if it is filled). If TO *destination* is specified, the redo log file group will be written to this destination for this command only.

ALL

Specifies that all filled redo log file groups be archived manually. If TO *destination* is specified, the redo log file groups will be written to this destination for this command only.

log_sequence

Specifies that the log file group identified by *log_sequence* be manually archived. If TO *destination* is specified, the redo log file group will be written to this destination for this command only.

CONNECT

```
CONN[ECT] username[/password][@hostname] [AS {SYSOPER | SYSDBA}]
```

Connects to a database using the specified *username* and *password*.

```
CONN[ECT] /[@hostname] [AS {SYSOPER | SYSDBA}]
```

Connects to the database using operating system authentication.

```
CONN[ECT] INTERNAL[/password]
```

Connects to a database internally.

Keywords

username

The Oracle username to use while connecting to the database.

password

The password associated with the provided username. If omitted, SQL*Plus will prompt for a password.

hostname

The hostname assigned to the database to which you are connecting. This *hostname* is typically resolved using the *tnsnames.ora* file or Oracle Names.

AS SYSOPER

Specifies that the user will connect as an operator.

AS SYSDBA

Specifies that the user will connect as a database administrator.

/

Specifies that the operating system username under which you are already logged in will be concatenated with the current value of the *INIT.ORA* parameter OS_AUTHENT_PREFIX (by default OPS$). The resulting username must exist as a database user (created with CREATE USER *username* IDENTIFIED EXTERNALLY). For example, if OS_AUTHENT_PREFIX is set to the default value and you are logged into the operating system or network as SCOTT, an Oracle username OPS$SCOTT must exist and have the CONNECT privilege.

INTERNAL

Specifies that an internal connection be made.

COPY

```
COPY {FROM username[/password][@hostname] |
     TO username[/password]@hostname] |
     FROM username[/password][@hostname] TO username[/password][@hostname]}
{APPEND | CREATE | INSERT | REPLACE} destination_table [(column[,column . . .])]
USING query)
```

Copies data returned from a query to another table in either the local or remote database.

Keywords

username

The name of the user account (schema) from and/or to which data will be copied.

password

The password associated with the specified user account.

hostname

The SQL*Net or Net8 connect string for the database being connected to.

FROM

Specifies the username, password, and hostname for the database from which data will be copied. If omitted, the account SQL*Plus is currently logged into will be used.

TO

Specifies the username, password, and hostname for the database to which data will be copied. If omitted, the account SQL*Plus is currently logged into will be used.

APPEND

Causes rows to be inserted into *destination_table* if it exists; otherwise, *destination_table* is created.

CREATE

Creates *destination_table* before inserting rows. If *destination_table* already exists, an error results.

INSERT

Causes rows to be inserted into *destination_table*. If the table does not exist, an error results.

REPLACE

Causes *destination_table* to be deleted, if it exists, and a new version created before rows are copied.

destination_table

The name of the table that will receive the rows being copied.

column

The name of a column in *destination_table* where data will be inserted. If columns are specified, their number must match the number of columns being returned by query.

query

Any valid SQL SELECT statement. This statement is used to return the rows and columns that will be copied.

DESCRIBE

DESC[RIBE] {[schema.]object[@hostname] [column] | [schema.]object[.subobject]}

Lists the definition(s) for the specified database object.

Keywords

schema

Specifies the schema that contains the object to be described.

object

The name of the object to be described. The name can be for a table, view, synonym, function, procedure, or package.

hostname

The Net8 connect string for the database containing the object to be described.

column

The name of a column in a table (Oracle7 only).

subobject

The name of a function or procedure in a package.

DISCONNECT

DISC[ONNECT]

Commits any pending transactions and disconnects the current user from the database without exiting SQL*Plus.

EDIT

ED[IT] [*filename*]

Invokes the system editor (as specified by the value of the user variable _EDITOR). *filename* specifies the name of a file to be opened by the editor. If *filename* does not exist, it will be created. If the command is invoked without a *filename*, the current contents of the buffer are passed to the editor and are returned to the buffer when editing is complete.

EXECUTE

EXE[CUTE] *statement*

Executes a single PL/SQL statement; commonly used to execute a stored procedure.

Example

```
EXECUTE scott.funclib.do_calc;
```

EXIT

EXIT [SUCCESS | FAILURE | WARNING | *n* | *var* | :*bind_variable*]
     [COMMIT | ROLLBACK]

Commits all pending transactions (unless ROLLBACK is specified), passes a return code to the operating system, and exits SQL*Plus.

Keywords

SUCCESS

Exits normally with a return code indicating success. This option is the default behavior.

FAILURE

Exits with a return code indicating failure.

WARNING

Exits with a return code indicating a warning.

n

Exits with a specific numeric return code.

var

Exits using the value of the specified user-defined or system variable as the return code.

bind_variable

Exits using the value of the specified bind variable, created using the VARIABLE command, as the return code.

COMMIT

Commits pending changes to the database before exiting.

ROLLBACK

Rolls back pending changes before exiting.

HELP

`HELP [topic]`

Invokes the SQL*Plus help system and displays help information on *topic*, if specified; *topic* comes from the list of SQL*Plus topics; if no *topic* is specified, a list of topics is displayed.

 Help is not always available. The HELP command, for example, is not implemented for Windows platforms, and other platforms may require that the DBA specifically install the help feature.

HOST

`HO[ST] [command]`

Executes an operating system command without leaving SQL*Plus; *command* is any valid operating system command. If it is not specified, you'll be taken to a system prompt where you can execute system commands, and you'll remain at the system prompt until EXIT is entered.

PAUSE

`PAU[SE] [text]`

Displays an empty line, followed by a line containing *text* (if specified), and waits for the user to press the return key; *text* is the string (quotes are not necessary) that will appear on the output device.

RECOVER

```
RECOVER {[AUTOMATIC] [FROM location]
        {[STANDBY] DATABASE
         [UNTIL {CANCEL | CHANGE change_number | TIME time} |
            USING BACKUP CONTROLFILE |
         [STANDBY] DATAFILE filename[,filename ...]
           [UNTIL [CONSISTENT [WITH] CONTROLFILE |
         [STANDBY] TABLESPACE tablespace[,tablespace ...]
           [UNTIL [CONSISTENT [WITH] CONTROLFILE |
```

```
        TABLESPACE tablespace[,tablespace ...] |
        DATAFILE filename[,filename ...] |
        LOGFILE filename |
        CONTINUE [DEFAULT] |
        CANCEL
        } |
        MANAGED STANDBY DATABASE {TIMEOUT integer | CANCEL [IMMEDIATE]}
     }
  [PARALLEL integer | NOPARALLEL]
```

Performs media recovery on a database, tablespace, datafile, or logfile. This command is intended for DBAs.

Keywords

AUTOMATIC

Specifies that during a recovery operation, the name of the next required archived log file will be automatically generated using the LOG_ARCHIVE_ DEST (or LOG_ARCHIVE_DEST_1) and LOG_ARCHIVE_FORMAT parameters from the *INIT.ORA* initialization file. If this keyword is omitted and LOGFILE is not specified, the user will be prompted for the name of each archived log file as required.

FROM

Specifies the location of archived log files to be read. *location* must be provided in an operating system-dependent form (typically a fully qualified directory name), and if this keyword is specified, the value of *location* overrides the value of the LOG_ARCHIVE_DEST or LOG_ARCHIVE_DEST_1 parameters in the *INIT.ORA* file.

STANDBY

Specifies that the standby database, which must be mounted and not open, will be recovered using the control file, and that archived redo log files will be copied from the primary database.

DATABASE

Specifies that the entire database be recovered.

UNTIL CANCEL

Specifies that an incomplete, cancel-based recovery be performed. Recovery proceeds by prompting with the suggested filenames of archived redo log files, and recovery completes when "CANCEL" is entered instead of a filename.

UNTIL CHANGE

Specifies that incomplete, change-based recovery be performed. *integer* is the System Change Number (SCN) following the last change to be recovered.

UNTIL TIME

Specifies that incomplete, time-based recovery be performed up to the time provided in *time*, which must be enclosed in single quotes using the format 'YYYY-MM-DD:HH24:MI:SS'.

USING BACKUP CONTROLFILE

Specifies that recovery be performed using a backup control file instead of the current control file.

DATAFILE

Specifies that a lost or damaged datafile be recovered. If STANDBY is specified, a datafile on the standby database is to be recovered using the control file and archived redo log files copied from the primary database. Any number of datafiles may be listed for recovery.

UNTIL CONSISTENT WITH CONTROLFILE

Specifies that the recovery of a standby datafile (or tablespace) is to use the current standby database control file.

TABLESPACE

Specifies that the tablespace named *tablespace* be recovered. Up to 16 tablespaces may be listed for recovery.

LOGFILE

Specifies that recovery be continued by applying the logfile identified by *logfile*.

CONTINUE

Specifies that multi-instance recovery is to continue after it has been interrupted to disable a thread.

DEFAULT

Specifies that recovery is to continue using the redo log file that would be automatically generated if no other logfile was specified. This keyword is equivalent to specifying AUTOMATIC, except that Oracle does not prompt for a filename.

CANCEL

Specifies that cancel-based recovery (using the UNTIL CANCEL keyword) is to be stopped.

MANAGED STANDBY DATABASE

Specifies that sustained standby recovery, which assumes that the standby database is an active component of an overall standby database architecture, is to be performed. The primary database actively archives its redo log files to the standby site, where they are used for a managed standby recovery operation.

TIMEOUT

Specifies, in *integer* minutes, the time that the sustained recovery operation waits for a requested archived log redo to be available for writing to the standby database. If the redo log file does not become available within that time, the recovery process terminates with an error message. The statement can be issued again to return to sustained standby recovery mode. If this keyword is not specified, the database remains in sustained standby recovery mode until the statement is reissued with the RECOVER CANCEL clause, or until instance shutdown or failure.

CANCEL IMMEDIATE

Specifies that the sustained recovery operation is to be terminated after applying all the redo records in the current archived redo file or after the next redo log file is read, whichever comes first.

PARALLEL integer

Specifies that recovery be performed using a degree of parallelism (the number of parallel threads used in parallel operations) equal to the number of CPUs available on all participating instances, multiplied by the value of the PARALLEL_THREADS_PER_CPU parameter in the *INIT.ORA* file. If *integer* is provided, that degree of parallelism will be used instead of the automatic calculation. The PARALLEL keyword overrides the RECOVERY_PARALLELISM initialization parameter in *INIT.ORA*.

NOPARALLEL

Specifies that recovery be performed serially, and not in parallel. This option is the default.

This command is equivalent to the RECOVER command in Server Manager, and is available starting with SQL*Plus Version 8.1. Recovery can be very complex, and should be attempted only by an experienced DBA. For more information, see Oracle's *Oracle8i Backup and Recovery Guide*.

REMARK

`REM[ARK] [text]`

Indicates that all characters following on the same line be treated as a comment.

SET

`SET system_variable value`

Set a SQL*Plus system variable to the specified value.

Keywords

system_variable

> The name of a valid SQL*Plus system variable (see "SQL*Plus System Variables" later in this chapter).

value

> A valid value for the system variable.

SHOW

```
SHO[W] [var]
```

Lists the value of a specific SQL*Plus setting, or of all settings.

```
SHO[W] ERR[ORS] [type] [[schema.]name]
```

Displays compilation errors from an attempt to create or replace a stored PL/SQL program unit.

Keywords

var

> May be one of the following:
>
> > ALL
> > BTI[TLE]
> > LABEL (obsolete beginning with Oracle8*i*)
> > LNO
> > PARAMETERS
> > PNO
> > REL[EASE]
> > REPF[OOTER]
> > REPH[EADER]
> > SGA
> > SPOO[L]
> > SQLCODE
> > TTI[TLE]
> > USER
>
> In addition to these specific items, you can also use any SQL*Plus system variables that can be used with the SET command.

ERRORS

> When specified without an additional keyword, displays the errors for the most recently compiled PL/SQL procedure. When *type* and *name* are included, errors are shown for the most recent compilation of that object.

type

May be one of the following:

FUNCTION
PROCEDURE
PACKAGE
PACKAGE BODY
TRIGGER
VIEW
TYPE
TYPE BODY

schema

Specifies the name of the schema that contains the named object. If omitted, the current schema is assumed.

name

Specifies the name of the stored object for which errors are to be displayed.

SHUTDOWN

```
SHUTDOWN [NORMAL | IMMEDIATE | TRANSACTIONAL | ABORT]
```

Shuts down an Oracle instance. This command is intended for DBAs.

Keywords

NORMAL

Specifies that a normal shutdown is to be performed. A normal shutdown will prevent new user logins and wait for all users to disconnect before shutting down the instance.

IMMEDIATE

Specifies that an immediate shutdown is to be performed. An immediate shutdown prevents new user logins and disconnects each user when the currently executing SQL statement is complete. When all users are disconnected, the instance will be shut down.

TRANSACTIONAL

Specifies that a transactional shutdown is to be performed. A transactional shutdown prevents new user logins and disconnects any user whose transaction is complete (i.e., no COMMIT is pending). As each remaining user completes the current transaction via a COMMIT or ROLLBACK statement, the session is disconnected. When all users are disconnected, the instance will be shut down.

ABORT

    Specifies that the instance is to be shut down without regard to pending trans-actions. No rollback information is written and dirty buffers are not written to disk before the shutdown. Crash recovery will be performed when the database is started.

 This command is equivalent to the SHUTDOWN command in Server Manager and is available starting with Oracle Version 8.1.

SPOOL

SPOOL

Displays the current spooling status.

```
SPO[OL] [filename[.extension]] | [OFF | OUT]
```

Spools all subsequent SQL*Plus output to a file.

Keywords

filename[.extension]

    The filename and optional extension for the file to which the output will be written. If an *extension* is not supplied, *.LIS* or *.LST* (depending on the platform) will be used as the extension.

OFF

    Stops spooling.

OUT

    Stops spooling, and sends the output file to the default printer. This option is not supported on all platforms. For example, it is not supported under Windows.

 The SPOOL OFF command must be supplied when spooling is complete or the spooled file will not be saved.

START

```
STA[RT] filename [arg1 [arg2...]]
```

Runs a series of SQL*Plus commands, and/or SQL and/or PL/SQL statements contained in a file.

Keywords

filename

Specifies the name of an operating system file containing SQL and/or PL/SQL statements.

arg

One or more arguments to be passed to the script. These arguments may be referenced within the SQL or PL/SQL script as &1, &2, etc. Arguments are positional and are separated by spaces.

 This command is equivalent to specifying @*filename.*

Command files may be nested; in other words, a command file may contain another START *filename* command.

STARTUP

```
STARTUP [FORCE] [RESTRICT]
[PFILE=filename]
{MOUNT | OPEN [database_name] | NOMOUNT}
[EXCLUSIVE | {PARALLEL | SHARED} [RETRY]]
```

Starts an Oracle instance. This command is intended for DBAs.

Keywords

FORCE

Specifies that the instance is to be forced to start. If the instance is already running, this keyword forces a SHUTDOWN ABORT, followed by the specified STARTUP.

RESTRICT

Specifies that the database is to be opened in restricted mode, which allows only users with the RESTRICTED SESSION privilege to connect.

PFILE

Specifies that the instance should be started using parameters contained in the file provided by *pfilename.* This file must be available on the machine running SQL*Plus.

MOUNT

Specifies that the instance is to be started and the database is to be mounted, but not opened.

OPEN

Specifies that the instance is to be started and the database is to be mounted and opened. This option is the default.

database_name

Specifies the name of the database and overrides the value of the parameter DB_NAME in the initialization file.

NOMOUNT

Specifies that the instance is to be started, but the database is not to be mounted or opened.

EXCLUSIVE

Specifies that the database is to be mounted and/or opened only by this instance, and cannot be shared by any other instance.

PARALLEL

Specifies that the database is to be mounted and/or opened so other instances can access it simultaneously. This keyword is a synonym for SHARED.

SHARED

Specifies that the database is to be mounted and/or opened so other instances can access it simultaneously. This keyword is a synonym for PARALLEL.

RETRY

Specifies that if another instance is performing a recovery on this database, Oracle will retry the open operation every five seconds until the database recovery is complete and the operation is successful.

 This command is equivalent to the STARTUP command in Server Manager, and is available starting with Oracle Version 8.1.

STORE

```
STORE SET filename [CRE[ATE] | REP[LACE] | APP[END]]
```

Saves attributes of the current SQL*Plus environment in a file as a list of SET commands.

Keywords

filename

Specifies the name of an operating system file that will contain the SET commands.

CREATE

    Creates a new file; the filename must not exist if this option is specified.

REPLACE

    Replaces the contents of any existing file; if the filename does not exist, it is created.

APPEND

    Adds the contents of the buffer to the end of the specified file.

TIMING

`TIMING`

Lists the number of active timers.

`TIMI[NG] [START text | SHOW | STOP]`

Starts, stops, or lists elapsed timers.

Keywords

START

    Sets up a timer and names it *text*.

SHOW

    Lists the current timer's name and timing data.

STOP

    Lists the current timer's name and timing data, then deletes the timer.

Don't confuse the TIMING command with the SET TIMING ON and SET TIMING OFF commands. The TIMING command controls active timers, while the SET TIMING command controls the automatic reporting of elapsed time for individual SQL statements.

WHENEVER OSERROR

```
WHENEVER OSERROR {EXIT {SUCCESS | FAILURE | n | var | :bind_variable}
                 [COMMIT | ROLLBACK] |
              CONTINUE [COMMIT | ROLLBACK | NONE]
              }
```

Specifies the action to be taken by SQL*Plus if an operating system error occurs.

Keywords

EXIT

    Directs SQL*Plus to exit as soon as an operating system error is detected.

COMMIT

Directs SQL*Plus to execute a COMMIT before exiting or continuing after an operating system error occurs.

CONTINUE

Turns off the EXIT option.

FAILURE

Exits with a return code indicating failure.

n

Exits and returns the specified numeric return code.

NONE

Directs SQL*Plus to take no action after an operating system error.

ROLLBACK

Directs SQL*Plus to execute a ROLLBACK before exiting or continuing after an operating system error occurs.

SUCCESS

Exits normally with a return code indicating success. This option is the default behavior.

var

A user-defined or system variable, the value of which will be used as the return code.

bind_variable

A bind variable, created in SQL*Plus with the VARIABLE command, the value of which will be used as a return code.

WARNING

Exits with a return code indicating a warning status.

WHENEVER SQLERROR

```
WHENEVER SQLERROR {EXIT {SUCCESS | FAILURE | n | var | :bind_variable}
                   [COMMIT | ROLLBACK] |
                   CONTINUE [COMMIT | ROLLBACK | NONE]
                  }
```

Specifies the action to be taken by SQL*Plus if an error is generated by a SQL statement or a PL/SQL block.

Keywords

EXIT

Directs SQL*Plus to exit as soon as a SQL or PL/SQL error is detected.

COMMIT

Directs SQL*Plus to execute a COMMIT before exiting or continuing after a SQL or PL/SQL error is detected.

CONTINUE

Turns off the EXIT option.

FAILURE

Exits with a return code indicating failure.

n

A specific numeric return code to be returned.

NONE

Directs SQL*Plus to take no action after a SQL or PL/SQL error.

ROLLBACK

Directs SQL*Plus to execute a ROLLBACK before exiting or continuing after a SQL or PL/SQL error is detected.

SUCCESS

Exits normally with a return code indicating success. This option is the default behavior.

var

A user-defined or system variable, the value of which will be used as the return code.

bind_variable

A bind variable, created in SQL*Plus with the VARIABLE command, the value of which will be used as a return code.

WARNING

Exits with a return code indicating a warning status.

SQL*Plus Variables and Related Commands

SQL*Plus provides a mechanism for the creation and use of user variables. The commands and constructs described in this section are used to manipulate SQL*Plus user variables. You can enter these commands and constructs directly from a SQL*Plus prompt, or include them in a SQL*Plus script.

&

&*n*

Inserts a command-line parameter.

&var

Creates a SQL*Plus variable *var* and prompts for a value each time *&var* is encountered.

Keywords

n

Specifies the position on the command line for the parameter that will be inserted. Each occurrence of &*n* is replaced with the corresponding parameter from the command line. For example, &1 would be replaced with the value of the first parameter specified on the command line.

var

Specifies the name of a SQL*Plus variable that will be replaced by a value supplied at the time the statement or command is executed. The terminal session running SQL*Plus will be prompted for the value.

&&

&&var

Creates a SQL*Plus variable that is replaced with a value that is retained for subsequent use. *var* specifies the name of a SQL*Plus variable that is replaced by a value supplied at the time the statement or command is executed. The terminal session running SQL*Plus is prompted for the value the first time *&&var* is encountered, and the value is retained until the end of the SQL*Plus session, or until *var* is undefined.

ACCEPT

```
ACC[EPT] var [type] [FORMAT formatstring] [DEFAULT default] [PROMPT text | NOPROMPT]
   [HIDE]
```

Reads a line of input and stores it in a variable.

Keywords

var

Specifies the name of a variable that will hold the supplied value.

type

Restricts the type of input allowed, and may be either NUMBER, CHAR, or DATE.

FORMAT

Specifies that *formatstring* will be used as the input format for the input. See Table 5-5 for available numeric formats.

DEFAULT
>   Specifies that *default* will be used as a value if no input is supplied.

PROMPT
>   Specifies the text to be displayed as a prompt before accepting input.

HIDE
>   Specifies that the value input not be displayed on the screen.

DEFINE

```
DEF[INE] var = text
```

Creates a variable and assigns a text string to it.

```
DEF[INE] [var]
```

Lists the current value of a specified user variable or of all user variables.

Keywords

var
>   Specifies the name of a SQL*Plus variable.

text
>   Specifies a string of CHAR text that will be stored in var.

PRINT

```
PRI[NT] bind_variable
```

Displays the current value of a variable. *bind_variable* specifies the name of a bind variable (created with the VARIABLE command) to be displayed.

UNDEFINE

```
UNDEF[INE] var
```

Deletes a user variable; *var* specifies the name of the user variable to be deleted.

VARIABLE

```
VAR[IABLE] bind_variable
  [NUMBER | CHAR | VARCHAR2 | NVARCHAR2 | CLOB | NCLOB | REFCURSOR]
```

Declares a bind variable that can be referenced in PL/SQL.

```
VAR[IABLE]
```

Displays a list of all declared bind variables.

Keywords

bind_variable
> Specifies the name of a bind variable to be created.

NUMBER
> Specifies that *bind_variable* be a NUMBER variable.

CHAR
> Specifies that *bind_variable* be a CHAR variable.

VARCHAR2
> Specifies that *bind_variable* be a VARCHAR2 variable.

NVARCHAR2
> Specifies that *bind_variable* be an NVARCHAR2 variable.

CLOB
> Specifies that *bind_variable* be a CLOB variable.

NCLOB
> Specifies that *bind_variable* be an NCLOB variable.

REFCURSOR
> Specifies that *bind_variable* be a REFCURSOR variable.

See Chapter 7, *PL/SQL*, for more information about these PL/SQL variable types.

SQL*Plus System Variables

The SQL*Plus system-level variables described in this section control various aspects of SQL*Plus' operation, and may be referenced in the SQL*Plus SET and SHOW commands.

APPINFO

`APPI[NFO]{ON | OFF | text}`

Controls the automatic registering of command files through the built-in DBMS_APPLICATION_INFO package to enable the performance and resource usage of each command file that will be monitored by the DBA.

Keywords

ON

> Specifies that automatic registration be enabled.

OFF

> Specifies that automatic registration be disabled.

text

> Specifies that text be registered if no command file is being run or if APPINFO is set to OFF.

ARRAYSIZE

`ARRAY[SIZE] {n}`

Sets the number of rows that SQL*Plus will fetch from the database at one time; *n* specifies the number of rows to be fetched at one time. Valid values are 1 to 5000; the default is 15.

AUTOCOMMIT

`AUTO[COMMIT] {ON | OFF | IMM[EDIATE] | n}`

Controls when Oracle commits pending changes to the database.

Keywords

ON

> Commits pending changes to the database after each successful SQL statement or PL/SQL block is executed.

OFF

> Suppresses automatic committing so that you must commit changes manually. This option is the default.

IMMEDIATE

> Functions the same as ON.

n

> Commits after every *n* successful SQL statements or PL/SQL blocks.

AUTOPRINT

`AUTOP[RINT] {ON | OFF}`

Controls the automatic printing of bind variables.

Keywords

ON

Specifies that bind variables be automatically printed after each PL/SQL block or SQL statement in which they are referenced.

OFF

Specifies that bind variables not be printed automatically. This option is the default.

AUTORECOVERY

AUTORECOVERY {ON | OFF}

Controls whether the RECOVER command runs without user intervention. This variable is intended for DBAs.

Keywords

ON

Specifies that autorecovery be used. Autorecovery allows the RECOVER command to be run automatically, as long as the archived log files are located in the destination to which the *INIT.ORA* file's LOG_ARCHIVE_DEST parameter points.

OFF

Specifies that autorecovery is not enabled and that user intervention is required to specify log file names when using the RECOVER command. This option is the default.

AUTOTRACE

AUTOT[RACE] {ON | OFF | TRACE[ONLY]} [EXP[LAIN]] [STAT[ISTICS]]

Causes SQL*Plus to display a report on the execution of successful SQL DML statements.

Keywords

ON

Causes a trace report to be displayed after each execution of a DML statement.

OFF

No trace report is displayed. This option is the default.

TRACEONLY

Causes a trace report to be displayed, but suppresses the printing of query data.

EXPLAIN

Causes SQL*Plus to show the query execution plan for each SQL DML statement that is executed. The EXPLAIN PLAN statement is used to get the execution plan, and your plan table must have a schema for this option to work.

STATISTICS

Causes SQL*Plus to display execution statistics for each executed statement.

BLOCKTERMINATOR

`BLO[CKTERMINATOR] [c]`

Sets the nonalphanumeric character used to end PL/SQL blocks; *c* specifies the character that terminates entry of a PL/SQL block, but does not cause it to be executed. To execute the block, you must subsequently issue a RUN or / (slash) command. The default value is a period.

CLOSECURSOR

`CLOSECUR[SOR] ON | OFF`

Controls whether SQL*Plus closes the cursor after a SQL statement is executed.

This variable is obsolete beginning with Oracle8*i*.

CMDSEP

`CMDS[EP] {c | ON | OFF}`

Sets the character used to separate multiple SQL*Plus commands entered on one line.

Keywords

c

Specifies the character (which must not be alphanumeric) used to separate SQL*Plus commands. The default is a semicolon (;).

ON

Turns on the ability to enter multiple commands on one line and automatically sets the command separator character to a semicolon (;).

OFF

Turns off the ability to enter multiple commands on a line.

COLSEP

COLSEP *text*

Sets the text to be printed between columns returned by a query. The default for *text* is one space.

COMPATIBILITY

COM[PATIBILITY] V7 | V8 | <u>NATIVE</u>

Specifies the version of Oracle to which a session is currently connected.

Keywords

V7

Specifies that the SQL*Plus session is connected to an Oracle7 database, or that if the SQL*Plus session is connected to an Oracle8 database, the behavior should emulate that of Oracle7.

V8

Specifies that the SQL*Plus session is connected to an Oracle8 database.

NATIVE

Indicates that you wish the database to determine the setting. If connected to Oracle8, for example, compatibility would default to V8.

CONCAT

CON[CAT] *c* | ON | OFF

Sets the character used to terminate a substitution variable reference.

Keywords

c Specifies a character to terminate a substitution variable reference, if you wish to immediately follow the variable reference with a character that SQL*Plus would otherwise interpret as a part of the substitution variable name. The default is a period.

ON

Resets the value of CONCAT to a period.

OFF

Specifies that no CONCAT character be set.

COPYCOMMIT

COPYC[OMMIT] *n*

Controls the number of batches after which the COPY command commits changes to the database; *n* specifies the number of batches to be copied by the COPY command before a commit is issued. Since the size of a batch is controlled by ARRAY-SIZE, the number of rows copied before each commit will be ARRAYSIZE * *n*. If COPYCOMMIT is set to zero (the default), COPY performs a commit only at the end of a copy operation.

COPYTYPECHECK

COPYTYPECHECK <u>ON</u> | OFF

Controls whether or not SQL*Plus checks to be sure that source and destination datatypes match when you use the COPY command to copy data from one table to another.

DEFINE

DEF[INE] *c* | <u>ON</u> | OFF

Sets the character used to prefix substitution variables.

Keywords

c

Changes the value of the define character to this character.

ON

Changes the value of the define character back to the default "&", and enables the define feature.

OFF

Turns off the define feature.

ECHO

ECHO ON | <u>OFF</u>

Controls whether SQL*Plus, when executing the START command, lists each statement in a command file as it is executed.

EDITFILE

EDITF[ILE] *filename*

Sets the default filename for the EDIT command. *filename* specifies the name of a file that will be executed when the EDIT command is issued. For more information about the EDIT command, see EDIT in this chapter.

EMBEDDED

EMB[EDDED] ON | OFF

Controls where on a page each report begins.

Keywords

ON

Allows a report to begin anywhere on a page. Page numbering will continue from one report to another.

OFF

Forces each report to start at the top of a new page. Page numbering will begin with 1 for each report. This option is the default.

ESCAPE

ESC[APE] *c* | ON | OFF

Defines the character to use as the escape character, which indicates that SQL*Plus should treat a substitution character as an ordinary character rather than as a request for variable substitution.

Keywords

c

Changes the value of the escape character to this character.

ON

Changes the value of the escape character back to the default backslash ("\"), and enables the escape feature.

OFF

Turns off the escape feature. This option is the default.

FEEDBACK

FEED[BACK] {<u>6</u> | *n* | OFF | ON}

Specifies a threshold for when the number of records returned by a query is to be displayed.

Keywords

n

> Specifies the number of records required to be returned before a feedback number is displayed. The default is 6.

ON

> Enables the feedback display and sets *n* to 1.

OFF

> Turns off the feedback display.

FLAGGER

FLAGGER <u>OFF</u> | ENTRY | INTERMED[IATE] | FULL

Checks to make sure SQL statements conform to the ANSI/ISO SQL-92 standard.

Keywords

OFF

> Turns off the FIPS flagging feature. This option is the default.

ENTRY

> Specifies that SQL should be checked at the SQL-92 Entry standard.

INTERMED[IATE]

> Specifies that SQL should be checked at the SQL-92 Intermediate standard.

FULL

> Specifies that SQL should be checked at the SQL-92 Full standard.

You may execute SET FLAGGER even if you are not connected to a database. FIPS flagging will remain in effect across SQL*Plus sessions until a SET FLAGGER OFF (or ALTER SESSION SET FLAGGER = OFF) command is successful or until you exit SQL*Plus. When FIPS flagging is enabled, SQL*Plus displays a warning for the CONNECT, DISCONNECT, and ALTER SESSION SET FLAGGER commands, even if they are successful.

FLUSH

`FLU[SH]` `ON` | `OFF`

Controls when output is sent to the user's display device.

Keywords

ON

> Specifies that output may be buffered before being sent to the display device. This option is the default.

OFF

> Specifies that output be displayed immediately.

HEADING

`HEA[DING]` `ON` | `OFF`

Controls printing of column headings in reports.

Keywords

ON

> Prints column headings in reports. This option is the default.

OFF

> Suppresses column headings.

HEADSEP

`HEADS[EP]` `c` | `ON` | `OFF`

Defines the heading separator character.

Keywords

c

> Changes the value of the heading separator character to this character.

ON

> Changes the value of the heading separator character back to the default " | " and enables the head separator feature. This option is the default.

OFF

> Turns off the head separator feature.

Headings are interpreted when they are defined, so subsequent changes to HEADSEP won't affect existing heading definitions.

INSTANCE

INSTANCE *instance_name* | LOCAL

Specifies a default database to connect to when using the CONNECT command.

Keywords

instance_name

Specifies the Net8 service name for the instance.

LOCAL

Specifies that the default instance is the local database. This option is the default.

The local database is determined by an operating system–specific setting. In Windows, for example, it is set using the LOCAL parameter in the registry file.

LINESIZE

LIN[ESIZE] *n*

Sets the total number of characters SQL*Plus displays on one line; *n* specifies the total number of characters that will be displayed on one line before wrapping to a new line. The default is 80.

When spooling output to a file, LINESIZE determines the record length of the output records produced. Note, however, that additional characters (for example, a carriage return and linefeed) may be appended, depending on the operating system.

LOBOFFSET

LOBOF[FSET] *n*

Sets the starting position from which CLOB and NCLOB data is retrieved and displayed; *n* specifies that CLOB and NCLOB data be retrieved starting at character position *n*. The default is 1.

LONG

LONG *n*

Sets the maximum width for displaying LONG, CLOB, and NCLOB values and for copying LONG values; *n* specifies the maximum width in bytes. The default is 80.

LONGCHUNKSIZE

LONGC[HUNKSIZE] *n*

Sets the size of the increments in which SQL*Plus retrieves a LONG, CLOB, or NCLOB value; *n* specifies the size of a long chunk in bytes. The default is 80.

MARKUP HTML

```
MARK[UP] HTML [ON | OFF]
   [HEAD text]
   [BODY text]
   [ENTMAP {ON | OFF}]
   [SPOOL {ON | OFF}]
   [PRE[FORMAT] {ON | OFF}]
```

Controls whether SQL*Plus will generate HTML output. This command is available starting with SQL*Plus 8.1.6.

Keywords

ON

   Specifies that HTML output be generated using the specified options.

OFF

   Specifies that HTML output not be generated. This option is the default.

HEAD

   Specifies that the *text* be used as content for the <HEAD> tag. Heading text must be enclosed within quotes. By default, *text* is '<TITLE>SQL*Plus Report</TITLE>'.

BODY

   Specifies that text be used as content for the <BODY> tag. Body text must be enclosed within quotes.

ENTMAP ON

> Specifies that SQL*Plus display the special characters "<", ">", and "&" as the HTML entities <, > and &, respectively.

ENTMAP OFF

> Specifies that SQL*Plus not change display of the special characters "<", ">", and "&".

SPOOL ON

> Specifies that SQL*Plus write HTML tags to the start and end of each file created by the SQL*Plus SPOOL command.

SPOOL OFF

> Specifies that SQL*Plus not write HTML tags to the start and end of each file created by the SQL*Plus SPOOL command.

PREFORMAT ON

> Specifies that SQL*Plus write output inside the HTML <PRE> tag.

PREFORMAT OFF

> Specifies that SQL*Plus not write output inside the HTML <PRE> tag.

NEWPAGE

NEWP[AGE] *n* | NONE

Sets the number of blank lines printed between the top of each page and the top title.

Keywords

n

> Specifies the number of blank lines printed at the top of a new page. If the value is zero, the formfeed character will be used to mark the beginning of each page (including the first page). A formfeed character will clear the screen on most terminals. The default is 1.

NONE

> Specifies that SQL*Plus will print neither blank lines nor a formfeed character between report pages.

NULL

NULL *text*

Sets the text used to represent a null value when displaying the results of a SQL SELECT statement.

Keyword

text

> Specifies the text representing the value of NULL when displaying the results of a SELECT statement.

NUMFORMAT

`NUMF[ORMAT]` *formatstring*

Sets the default format for displaying numbers; *formatstring* specifies the number format used by default when displaying numeric data. See Table 5-5 for available number formats.

NUMWIDTH

`NUM[WIDTH]` *n*

Sets the default width for displaying numbers; *n* specifies the number of digits to be displayed for numeric data. The default is 10.

 NUMFORMAT overrides NUMWIDTH, so SET NUMWIDTH 5, followed by SET NUMFORMAT –999,999.99, results in an 11-character wide column.

PAGESIZE

`PAGES[IZE]` *n*

Sets the number of lines in each page; *n* specifies the number of lines to be printed on each page.

 PAGESIZE can be set to zero to suppress all headings, pagebreaks, titles, the initial blank line, and other formatting information. This option can be useful when spooling output to a file.

PAUSE

`PAU[SE]` ON | OFF | *text*

Controls scrolling of displayed data.

Keywords

OFF

> Specifies that the output is not paused while displaying. This option is the default.

ON

> Specifies that the output be paused at the beginning of each output page. The user must press the <ENTER> key to resume output.

text

> Specifies that output be paused at the beginning of each output page. The string specified by *text* will be displayed, and the user must press the ENTER key to resume output. *text* may include terminal control sequences to control functions like color or inverse video.

RECSEP

```
RECSEP WR[APPED] | EA[CH] | OFF
```

Controls how records are separated.

Keywords

WRAPPED

> Causes SQL*Plus to print a record separator (which consists of a single line consisting of the RECSEPCHAR character repeated LINESIZE times) only after wrapped lines.

EACH

> Causes SQL*Plus to print a record separator (which consists of a single line consisting of the RECSEPCHAR character repeated LINESIZE times) after each row.

OFF

> Prevents SQL*Plus from printing any record separators.

RECSEPCHAR

```
RECSEPCHAR {' ' | c}
```

Defines the record separator character; *c* specifies the character to be used as the record separator character.

SERVEROUTPUT (Oracle7 Syntax)

```
SERVEROUT[PUT] ON | OFF} [SIZE n]
```

Controls whether SQL*Plus displays the output of stored procedures or PL/SQL blocks executed from the SQL*Plus prompt. Such output is most often generated by the DBMS_OUTPUT.PUT_LINE procedure.

Keywords

ON

Displays the output.

OFF

Suppresses the output of DBMS_OUTPUT.PUT_LINE. This option is the default.

SIZE

Sets the number of output bytes that can be buffered within the server. The default for *n* is 2000, and *n* must be between 2000 and 1,000,000.

SERVEROUTPUT (Oracle8 Syntax)

```
SERVEROUT[PUT] {ON | OFF}
  [SIZE n]
  [FOR[MAT] {WRA[PPED] | WOR[D_WRAPPED] | TRU[NCATED]}]
```

Controls whether or not SQL*Plus displays the output of stored procedures or PL/SQL blocks executed from the SQL*Plus prompt. Such output is most often generated by the DBMS_OUTPUT.PUT_LINE procedure.

Keywords

ON

Displays the output.

OFF

Suppresses the output of DBMS_OUTPUT.PUT_LINE. This option is the default.

SIZE

Sets the number of output bytes that can be buffered within the server. The default for *n* is 2000, and *n* must be between 2000 and 1,000,000.

WRAPPED

Specifies that output is to be wrapped within the current linesize. Line breaks can occur in the middle of words.

WORD WRAPPED

Specifies that output is to be word-wrapped within the current linesize. Line breaks will occur between words.

TRUNCATED

Specifies that any line longer than the linesize will be truncated.

SHIFT

SHIFT[INOUT] {VIS[IBLE]|<u>INV[ISIBLE]</u>}

Allows correct alignment for terminals that display shift characters.

Keywords

VIS[IBLE]
> Displays shift characters.

INV[ISIBLE]
> Does not display shift characters. This option is the default.

 The SET SHIFTINOUT command is useful for terminals, such as the IBM 3270 terminal, that display shift characters together with data.

SHOWMODE

SHOW[MODE] ON | <u>OFF</u>

Controls whether SQL*Plus lists the old and new settings of a SQL*Plus system variable when the SET command is used.

Keywords

ON
> Causes SQL*Plus to list settings when a change is made. (This option results in the same behavior as the now obsolete SHOWMODE BOTH command.)

OFF
> Suppresses listing of old and new settings when a change is made. This option is the default.

SQLBLANKLINES

SQLBL[ANKLINES] ON | <u>OFF</u>

Controls whether SQL*Plus allows blank lines to be embedded within a SQL command.

SQLCASE

SQLC[ASE] <u>MIX[ED]</u> | LO[WER] | UP[PER]

Controls the case conversion of SQL statements and PL/SQL blocks (including any quoted text literals) just prior to execution.

Keywords

MIX[ED]
    Specifies that case will not be changed.

LO[WER]
    Specifies that all characters will be converted to lowercase.

UP[PER]
    Specifies that all characters will be converted to uppercase.

SQLCONTINUE

SQLCO[NTINUE] *text*

Sets the character sequence SQL*Plus displays as a prompt after a SQL*Plus command is continued beyond one line. The default for *text* is ">".

SQLNUMBER

SQLN[UMBER] <u>ON</u> | OFF

Controls whether SQL*Plus uses the line number as part of the prompt when you enter a multi-line SQL statement.

Keywords

ON
    The line number is made part of the prompt. This is the default setting.

OFF
    The line number is not made part of the prompt.

SQLPREFIX

SQLPRE[FIX] *c*

Sets the SQL*Plus prefix character; *c* specifies the character to be used as the SQL*Plus prefix. While you enter a SQL command or PL/SQL block, you can enter a SQL*Plus command on a separate line, prefixed by this character, and that command will be executed without disturbing the SQL statement you enter. The SQL*Plus prefix character must be nonalphanumeric, and the default is "#".

SQLPROMPT

`SQLP[ROMPT] {SQL> | text}`

Sets the SQL*Plus command prompt.

SQLTERMINATOR

`SQLT[ERMINATOR] c | ON | OFF`

Sets the character used to end and execute SQL commands.

Keywords

c

Changes the terminator character's value to this character.

ON

Changes the value of the terminator character back to the default ";" and enables the SQL terminator feature.

OFF

Turns off the SQL terminator feature.

SUFFIX

`SUF[FIX] text`

Sets the default file extension that SQL*Plus uses in commands referring to command files; *text* specifies the extension to use when referring to SQL command files and when the operating system supports file extensions. The default is *.SQL.*

 SUFFIX does not control the extension used for spool files, but is used in conjunction with START, GET, etc.

TAB

`TAB ON | OFF`

Controls how SQL*Plus formats whitespace in terminal output.

Keywords

ON

Specifies that SQL*Plus uses TAB characters when inserting large amounts of whitespace into terminal output.

OFF

   Specifies that SQL*Plus uses spaces to format whitespace in the output.

TERMOUT

`TERM[OUT] ON | OFF`

Controls whether SQL*Plus displays the output generated by commands executed from a command file or the terminal screen.

TIME

`TI[ME] ON | OFF`

Controls whether time is displayed as part of the current prompt.

 The displayed time will be taken from the clock on the machine on which SQL*Plus is currently running, which may not necessarily be the server the session is connected to. For example, if you are running SQL*Plus on a workstation in London (set to local time) and you are connected to an Oracle server in Moscow, London time will be displayed.

TIMING

`TIMI[NG] ON | OFF`

Controls display of timing statistics.

Keywords

ON

   Specifies that timing information (elapsed time and CPU time, when available) will be displayed after the completion of each SQL statement.

OFF

   Specifies that no timing information will be displayed. This option is the default.

TRIMOUT

`TRIM[OUT] ON | OFF`

Controls whether SQL*Plus allows trailing blanks at the end of each line displayed on the terminal.

Keywords

ON

Causes SQL*Plus to remove blanks from the end of each line. This option improves performance, especially when accessing SQL*Plus from a slow dial-up connection. This option is the default.

OFF

Causes SQL*Plus to display any trailing blanks that might be contained on a line.

TRIMSPOOL

TRIMS[POOL] ON | OFF

Controls whether SQL*Plus allows trailing blanks at the end of each line written to a spool file.

Keywords

ON

Causes SQL*Plus to remove trailing blanks from the end of each line written to a spool file.

OFF

Causes SQL*Plus to include trailing blanks when writing output to a spool file. This option is the default.

UNDERLINE

UND[ERLINE] c | ON | OFF

Sets the character used to underline column headings.

Keywords

c

Changes the value of the underline character to this character.

ON

Changes the value of the underline character back to the default "-" and enables the underline feature.

OFF

Turns off underlining.

VERIFY

VER[IFY] <u>ON</u> | OFF

Controls whether SQL*Plus lists the text of a modified line of a SQL or PL/SQL block before and after SQL*Plus replaces substitution variables with values.

Keywords

ON

>   Specifies that the line containing modified text be displayed. This is the default.

OFF

>   Specifies that the line containing modified text not be displayed. Note that this option affects display only; the substitution will still occur.

WRAP

WRA[P] <u>ON</u> | OFF

Controls how SQL*Plus displays data output if it is too long for the current line width.

Keywords

ON

>   Specifies that the row's display should be continued (wrapped) on one or more subsequent lines. This option is the default.

OFF

>   Specifies that if a row is longer than the current line width, the display of the row should be truncated.

7

PL/SQL

The power, flexibility, and utility of the SQL language are undeniable. However, as Oracle and its developers became more sophisticated, SQL's inherent limitations, particularly its lack of procedural control, became apparent. SQL is a fourth-generation language, which means that the programmer specifies *what* is to be done, but not *how*. Other languages, like C, are known as third-generation languages. With these languages, the programmer maintains control over exactly how the program operates. Each approach is useful and each has its own set of advantages and disadvantages.

In response to the need for third-generation type procedural capabilities, particularly within Oracle's development tools, Oracle created the PL/SQL language. PL/SQL, which stands for "Procedural Language extensions to SQL," first appeared with Oracle Version 6, and the language has been updated and improved with each subsequent release of Oracle.

The PL/SQL language looks a lot like ADA, the third-generation language developed for the United States Department of Defense. PL/SQL is also based on SQL and allows the use of standard SQL statements. In fact, PL/SQL can be used to write 3GL-like procedural code, but can also contain SQL statements and reference database objects.

PL/SQL is used in virtually every Oracle tool available today, and provides the developer with a rich array of procedural and nonprocedural capabilities. PL/SQL code can be developed to run "standalone" from SQL*Plus, as part of an Oracle form or report, as a component of a web application, or even stored in and executed by the Oracle database itself. This chapter focuses only on the basics of PL/SQL.*

The Structure of PL/SQL

PL/SQL code is built in blocks, which are logical units of work. Multiple blocks may be arranged sequentially (one after the other) to perform tasks in sequence, or blocks may be nested; a PL/SQL block may contain another block of PL/SQL code, for example.

A PL/SQL block consists of up to four distinct sections:

Block header

> This optional section identifies a block name and type (e.g., procedure, function, anonymous). If omitted, the block will be considered an anonymous block with no name.

Declaration section

> This optional section defines (and optionally initializes) variables and cursors used in the block. It is not required if no variables or cursors are used.

Execution section

> This optional section contains the PL/SQL (and SQL) executable statements executed by the PL/SQL runtime engine.

Exception section

> This section contains instructions that customize the handling of errors encountered during execution of the block.

Figure 7-1 shows the structure of a PL/SQL block.

Figure 7-2 shows the code for a simple PL/SQL block that will give a 10 percent raise to all employees who were hired over 90 days ago.

You can use PL/SQL to create several different types of modular structures, each of which has a particular purpose:

Anonymous block

> An unnamed PL/SQL block that can perform one or more PL/SQL actions. Anonymous blocks are most often used to impose structure on a larger collection of PL/SQL code. An anonymous block does not contain a block header.

Named block

> An anonymous block that has been given a name, but is otherwise the same as an anonymous block.

---

* Entire books have been written on PL/SQL, and we will not try to duplicate them here. For a more complete discussion of PL/SQL, I strongly urge you to refer to *Oracle PL/SQL Programming, Second Edition* (O'Reilly & Associates) by Steven Feuerstein and Bill Pribyl.

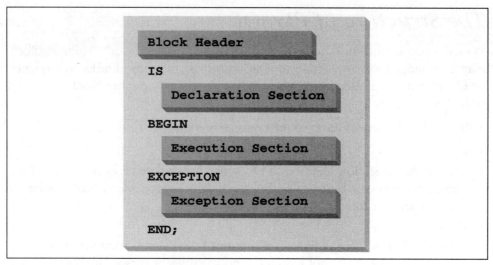

Figure 7-1. The structure of a PL/SQL block

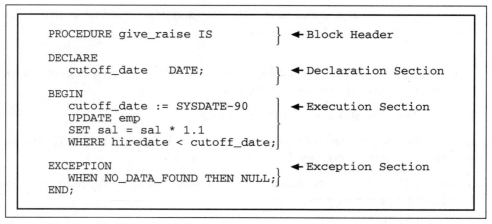

Figure 7-2. A sample PL/SQL block

Function

A named PL/SQL block that performs some action and returns a single value. A function can accept one or more parameters.

Procedure

A named PL/SQL block that performs one or more actions. A parameter list may be used to pass values into and/or out of the procedure.

Package

A named collection of PL/SQL functions and/or procedures. A package may also include variables.

Block Header

Except for anonymous blocks, all PL/SQL blocks begin with a block header. The general syntax of the PL/SQL block header is:

```
{{PROCEDURE | FUNCTION} name IS |   <<name>> }
```

Keywords

PROCEDURE

Indicates that the block is a PL/SQL procedure.

FUNCTION

Indicates that the block is a PL/SQL function.

name

Specifies the name to be assigned to the block. If used to create a named block, then the *name* appears within pairs of angle brackets (<< >>) and the IS keyword is omitted.

Declaration Section

The declaration section is required if any variables are to be used in a PL/SQL block. The declaration section also defines cursors, types, local procedures, and functions that are used in a block. If no variables or other elements need to be declared, then this section may be omitted.

 A PL/SQL variable is not the same as a table column. A column name, which may appear, for example, in a SELECT statement or WHERE clause, is not a variable and does not need to be declared. However, the target of a SELECT...INTO... statement is a variable, and must be declared.

Declaring Variables

Several different types of variables may be defined in a PL/SQL block. You can use simple, scalar variables to hold numeric, character string, and date values. You can declare record variables that allow you to manipulate several related values together. You can even declare in-memory tables and arrays.

The syntax for declaring a scalar variable is shown here:

```
variable_name type [CONSTANT] [NOT NULL] [:=initial_value]
```

Declares a variable explicitly.

```
variable_name [schema.] table_name.column_name%TYPE
```

Declares a variable by reference to an existing database column.

```
variable_name pl/sql_variable%TYPE
```

Declares a variable by reference to a previously defined PL/SQL variable.

Keywords

variable_name

> Specifies the variable's name. A valid name may be up to 30 characters long, must begin with a letter, and may contain the letters A to Z, digits 0 to 9, underscores, dollar signs, and pound signs. Variable names are normally case-insensitive, but may be made case-sensitive by enclosing them in double quotes. Reserved words cannot be used as variable names except within double quotes.

type

> Specifies the datatype of the variable. Table 7-1 lists the available datatypes.

CONSTANT

> Specifies that an initial value is specified for this variable and that the value cannot be changed.

NOT NULL

> Specifies that an initial value is specified for this variable and that the variable may not be set to NULL.

initial_value

> Specifies the variable's initial value. If omitted, the initial value of the variable will be NULL. Note that an initial value must be specified if either CONSTANT or NOT NULL is specified.

schema

> Specifies the name of a schema in the database. If omitted, the current schema is used.

table_name

> Specifies the name of a table in the specified schema of the database.

column_name

> Specifies the name of a column in the specified table.

pl/sql_variable

> Specifies the name of a previously declared PL/SQL variable.

Variable datatypes

Table 7-1 summarizes the valid PL/SQL datatypes.

Table 7-1. PL/SQL Datatypes

Datatype	Description
Numeric	
BINARY_INTEGER	Two's complement signed binary representation of integer values.
DEC	Decimal number; equivalent to NUMBER.
DECIMAL	Decimal number; equivalent to NUMBER.
DOUBLE PRECISION	Double-precision decimal number; equivalent to NUMBER.
FLOAT	Floating-point decimal number; equivalent to NUMBER.
INT	Integer number; equivalent to NUMBER, but with no scale specified.
INTEGER	Integer number; equivalent to NUMBER, but with no scale specified.
NATURAL	Equivalent to BINARY INTEGER, but restricted to values of 0 through 2,147,483,647.
NUMBER	Oracle's internal representation of decimal or integer numeric values, which is optimized for precision and storage efficiency.
NUMERIC	Equivalent to NUMBER.
PLS_INTEGER	Stores signed integers between –2,147,483,647 and 2,147,483,647. Used for faster computation than that obtained by NUMBER.
POSITIVE	Equivalent to BINARY INTEGER, but restricted to values of 1 through 2,147,483,647.
REAL	Real number; equivalent to NUMBER.
SMALLINT	Small integer; equivalent to NUMBER.
Character	
CHAR	Fixed-length character string.
CHARACTER	Fixed-length character string.
LONG	A PL/SQL-specific character string essentially like a VARCHAR2, with a maximum length of 32,760 bytes. Note that this length is shorter than a LONG database column.
LONG RAW	Similar to LONG, but will not be converted between character sets.
NCHAR	Fixed-length NLS (National Language Support) character data, with a maximum length of 32,767 bytes.
NVARCHAR2	Variable-length NLS character data, with a maximum length of 32,767 bytes.
RAW	Similar to CHAR, but will not be converted between character sets.
ROWID	Binary internal representation of the physical location of a data row. This should be used for Oracle7 and Oracle7 compatibility only.

Table 7-1. PL/SQL Datatypes (continued)

Datatype	Description
UROWID	Universal Row ID, a binary internal representation of the physical, logical, or non-Oracle location of a data row. UROWID, rather than ROWID, should be used with Oracle8 forward.
STRING	Equivalent to VARCHAR2.
VARCHAR	Equivalent to VARCHAR2.
VARCHAR2	Variable-length character string, with a maximum length of 32,767 bytes. Note that this length is longer than the VARCHAR database column type, which has a maximum length of 4000 (2000 in Oracle7).
Boolean	
BOOLEAN	Boolean data, with values of TRUE, FALSE, or NULL.
Date/Time	
DATE	Oracle internal date format.
Large Object	
BFILE	Stores the location of large binary objects contained in operating system files.
BLOB	Stores a locator for a large binary object.
CLOB	Stores a locator for a large block of single-character data.
NCLOB	Stores a locator for a large block of NLS character data.

In addition to the datatypes listed in Table 7-1, PL/SQL allows variables to have their types defined by reference to an existing database column or to a previously declared PL/SQL variable, as shown in the earlier declaration syntax.

Variable scope

The scope of a variable refers to the portion of the entire PL/SQL program in which the variable is available for use. PL/SQL variables become available in the declaration section where they are declared and remain available for the entire block, including any nested blocks. Figure 7-3 illustrates two variables in a PL/SQL program consisting of two blocks.

In Figure 7-3, the variable "aaa" is available for the entire program, including the inner block. The variable "bbb", however, is declared in the inner block, so it is available only within that block. It is not available in the outer block.

```
DECLARE                    ◄ Beginning of outer block
    aaa     NUMBER;
BEGIN
    DECLARE                ◄ Beginning of inner block
        bbb      NUMBER;
    BEGIN
    ...
    END;
...
END;
```

Figure 7-3. The scope of PL/SQL variables

Declaring Records

In PL/SQL, you can declare a record type when you want to manipulate a number of related variables as a unit. For example, you might want to treat the columns empno, ename, sal, and comm as a single unit (or record) within a PL/SQL program. This PL/SQL type is similar to a structure in C. To use a record, you must first define a record type. You can then declare record variables based on that type.

Declaring a Record Type

```
TYPE type_name IS RECORD (
    variable_name type [NOT NULL] [:=initial_value]
    [, variable_name type [NOT NULL] [:=initial_value] ...])
```

Declares a record type.

Keywords

type_name
Specifies the name of the record type.

variable_name
Specifies the name of a PL/SQL variable.

type
Specifies the datatype of the variable. See Table 7-1 for a list of valid PL/SQL datatypes.

NOT NULL
Specifies that an initial value be specified for the variable, and that the variable may not be set to NULL.

initial_value

Specifies the initial value of the variable. If omitted, the initial value of the variable will be NULL. Note that an initial value must be specified if either CONSTANT or NOT NULL is specified.

Declaring a Record Based on a Type

record_name type_name

Once a record type is declared, you can declare one or more record variables of that type using this syntax.

Keywords

record_name

The name to be assigned to the new instance of the record type.

type_name

The name of a record type. This type may be defined using the TYPE statement, or it may be a %ROWTYPE.

Examples

A record type may be declared as follows:

```
DECLARE
    TYPE Emp_Rec_Type IS RECORD  (
        Empno NUMBER(4) NOT NULL,
        Ename VARCHAR2(10),
        Hiredate DATE,
        Sal NUMBER(7,2),
        Comm NUMBER(7,2));
```

Instances of the record type Emp_Rec_Type can then be declared as follows:

```
old_emp Emp_Rec_Type;
new_emp Emp_Rec_Type;
```

 Records can be the target of a SQL SELECT statement by using the INTO clause.

Referencing Fields in a Record

record_name.variable_name

Individual fields of a record can be referenced using the *dot notation* syntax shown here.

Keywords

record_name
> Specifies the name of the record.

variable_name
> Specifies the name of a variable in the record.

Example

The following PL/SQL statement places the current date and time into a record, in the field named hiredate:

```
new_emp.hiredate := SYSDATE;
```

%ROWTYPE

record_name [schema.]table_name%ROWTYPE

Often, a record needs to be declared with the same structure as a table in the database. PL/SQL provides the simple syntax shown here to define such a record.

Keywords

record_name
> Specifies the name of the record.

schema
> Specifies the name of a schema in the database. If omitted, the current schema is used.

table_name
> Specifies the name of a table in the specified schema.

%ROWTYPE
> Specifies that a record be created where the names and datatypes of the fields in the record match the names and datatypes of a row in the table.

Index-by Tables

You can declare index-by tables when you need to work with multiple occurrences of a variable. These tables are similar to, but not quite the same as, arrays in C. An index-by table type must be declared before you can declare an index-by table based on that type.

TYPE (Index-by Tables)

```
TYPE tabletype_name IS TABLE OF
   {type | variable%TYPE |[schema.]table_name%ROWTYPE}
   INDEX BY BINARY_INTEGER;
```

Declares an index-by table type.

Keywords

tabletype_name
   Specifies the name of the index-by table type.

type
   Specifies a valid PL/SQL datatype. Each element of the resulting table represents an occurrence of the specified type.

variable
   Specifies the name of a PL/SQL variable that was previously defined. The *variable*%TYPE syntax allows you to create a table based on an existing variable declaration.

schema
   The name of the schema containing *table_name*. If omitted, the current schema is used.

table_name
   Identifies a database table. The *table_name*%ROWTYPE syntax allows you to easily create an index-by table where each element represents an occurrence of a record that matches the structure of the specified table.

INDEX BY BINARY_INTEGER
   A string required for an index-by table type declaration.

The result of a table-type declaration is an in-memory table with two columns:

   KEY (always a BINARY_INTEGER)
   VALUE (whatever type was defined in the declaration statement)

Declaring an Index-by Table

```
table_name tabletype_name;
```

Once an index-by table type has been declared, you can declare and work with variables of that type by using the standard PL/SQL declare syntax shown here to declare an index-by table based on an existing type.

```
table_name(key)
```

After a table is declared, you can reference individual elements using this syntax.

Keywords

table_name
   Specifies the name of the table.

key
   Specifies the index to a specific row of the table. This index must be an integer value.

Example

This code declares a table of VARCHAR2 values that can be used to hold employee names:

```
DECLARE
    TYPE ename_table_type IS TABLE OF varchar2(10)
        INDEX BY BINARY_INTEGER;

    ename_table ename_table_type;
```

Once you've declared the ename_table, the following statement assigns a value of "KING" to one of the table's elements:

```
ename_table(10) := 'KING';
```

 Index-by tables may be sparsely populated. You can have a table where element 1 and element 1000 exist, but where elements 2 through 999 do not exist. If you reference an element of an index-by table that does not exist, PL/SQL will raise a NO_DATA_FOUND exception. In your code, you should either write an exception handler to trap that exception, or use the EXISTS method to verify that an element exists before you reference it. Later sections describe these language elements.

Index-by Table Methods

PL/SQL index-by table types have methods associated with them that may be referenced in PL/SQL statements. Table 7-2 lists the available methods, along with the type of the return value (if any).

Table 7-2. Methods Available with PL/SQL Index-by Tables

Method	Return Value Type	Description
COUNT	NUMBER	Returns the number of rows in the table
DELETE		Deletes all rows from the table
DELETE(x)		Deletes the row with key x from the table
DELETE(x,y)		Deletes all rows with keys between x and y from the table
EXISTS(x)	BOOLEAN	Returns TRUE if a row with key x exists in the table; otherwise, returns FALSE
FIRST	BINARY_INTEGER	Returns the key of the row of the table with the lowest key
LAST	BINARY_INTEGER	Returns the key of the row of the table with the highest key

Table 7-2. Methods Available with PL/SQL Index-by Tables (continued)

Method	Return Value Type	Description
NEXT(*x*)	BINARY_INTEGER	Returns the key of the row of the table with the lowest key that is higher than the supplied key
PRIOR(*x*)	BINARY_INTEGER	Returns the key of the row of the table with the highest key that is lower than the supplied key

 The DELETE method is only available in Oracle8 and above. Prior to that version, no mechanism was available for deleting rows from an index-by table.

Methods are referenced using the following syntax:

```
table_name.method[(x[,y...])]
```

Keywords

table_name
> Specifies the name of the table.

method
> Specifies the method, as listed in Table 7-2.

(x[,y...])
> Specifies one or more arguments if required for the method (see Table 7-2).

Examples

This example checks for the existence of a table element with a key of 10, and changes its case to initial capitals if it exists in the table. If it does not exist, the literal "Missing" is inserted:

```
IF ename_table.EXISTS(10) THEN
    ename_table(10) := INITCAPS(ename_table(10));
ELSE
    ename_table(10) := 'Missing';
END IF;
```

In this example, the FIRST, NEXT, and LAST methods are used to iterate through all the existing rows in a table:

```
t_key := ename_table.FIRST;

LOOP
    ename_table(t_key) := INITCAPS(ename_table(t_key));
    EXIT WHEN t_key = ename_table.LAST;

    t_key := ename_table.NEXT(t_key);
END LOOP;
```

In the loop, each element of the table is converted to initial caps. The current key is checked against the highest key, and the loop is exited when those two values match. Otherwise, the next key is obtained using the NEXT method. Note that the current key is passed to the method for use as a starting point. NEXT starts with the element specified by the current key and searches for the next nonempty table element.

Variable-sized Arrays

Variable-sized arrays are a collection type with a specific number of elements. Unlike the situation with index-by tables, the maximum number of elements in an array is fixed when the array is declared. Variable-sized arrays are also called VARRAYs, and they may be used to hold the contents of a VARRAY column in a database table. As with the other collection types, you must first declare a variable array type, then you may declare variables of that type.

 Variable-sized arrays are only available with Oracle8*i* Enterprise Edition. They are not available in the Standard Edition.

TYPE (VARRAY)

```
TYPE vartype_name IS {VARRAY | VARYING ARRAY} (maxsize)
OF data_type [NOT NULL]
```

Declares a VARRAY array type.

Keywords

vartype_name
   The name you want to give the type.

maxsize
   Specifies the maximum number of entries you want the variable-sized array to hold.

data_type
   Specifies the datatype for the elements of the array.

Once a type for a variable-sized array is declared, you can declare variables of that type using the following syntax:

```
varray_name vartype_name;
```

Before values can be assigned to array elements, you must initialize the array by calling its constructor function, whose name is identical to the name of the underlying type name.

Example

The following example shows two VARRAYs being created. One is initialized as an empty array; no parameters are passed to its constructor method. The other is initialized as an array of three elements:

```
DECLARE
    TYPE num_array IS VARRAY (100) OF NUMBER;

    num1 num_array;
    num2 num_array;
BEGIN
    --Call the constructor methods
    num1 := num_array();
    num2 := num_array(1,2,3);

    --Extend each array in order to add one value.
    num1.extend;
    num1(1) := 1;

    num2.extend;
    num2(4) := 4;
END;
```

 VARRAYs cannot be extended beyond their maximum declared size.

VARRAY Array Methods

Table 7-3 shows the methods available with PL/SQL variable-sized arrays.

Table 7-3. Methods Available with PL/SQL Variable-sized Arrays

Method	Return Value Type	Description
COUNT	INTEGER	Returns the number of rows in the table.
DELETE		Deletes all rows from the table.
DELETE(x)		Deletes the row with index x from the table.
DELETE(x,y)		Deletes all rows from the table with indexes between x and y, inclusively.
EXISTS(x)	BOOLEAN	Returns TRUE if the index x represents a valid entry in the table; otherwise, returns FALSE.

Table 7-3. Methods Available with PL/SQL Variable-sized Arrays (continued)

Method	Return Value Type	Description
FIRST	INTEGER	Returns the lowest used index value for the table.
LAST	INTEGER	Returns the highest used index value for the table.
NEXT(x)	INTEGER	Returns the next valid index subsequent to the index you specify as an input parameter.
PRIOR(x)	INTEGER	Returns the highest valid index prior to the index you specify as an input parameter.
TRIM	None	Deletes the entry with the highest index value.
TRIM(x)	None	Deletes the specified number of entries from the end of the table. These entries will be the x highest entries.
EXTEND	None	Adds one entry to the nested table.
EXTEND(x)	None	Adds x entries to the nested table.
EXTEND(x,y)	None	Adds x entries to the nested table and makes them all copies of the entry for index y.
LIMIT	INTEGER	Returns the maximum declared size for the array.

Declaring Cursors

PL/SQL cursors allow a SELECT statement that returns multiple rows to be executed; you can then iterate through each of those rows using a loop. SQL statements for cursors do not need to be parsed each time the cursor is opened. To work with the cursors that you declare, you must use the OPEN, FETCH, and CLOSE statements. These statements are described in the "Execution Section" section later this chapter.

CURSOR

```
CURSOR cursor_name IS
select_statement
[FOR UPDATE [OF column[,column...]] [NOWAIT]];
```

Declares a cursor.

Keywords

CURSOR

A required keyword indicating that a PL/SQL cursor is being declared.

cursor_name

A valid PL/SQL name used to identify the cursor.

select_statement

A valid SQL SELECT statement. This statement may reference PL/SQL variables in the WHERE clause, as long as these variables have been declared and are available in the block.

FOR UPDATE

Specifies that when a row is selected as a result of a FETCH operation's using this cursor, an exclusive row lock will be acquired on that row so that it may later be updated. If the row is locked, PL/SQL will wait for the lock to be released (unless NOWAIT is specified). The WHERE CURRENT OF clause of the UPDATE or DELETE statement may be used to update or delete the row most recently returned by a cursor fetch operation.

OF column[, column...]

Specifies one or more columns that will be updated following the FETCH.

NOWAIT

Specifies that if the retrieved row is locked by another process, Oracle will not wait for the lock to be released and will return the error, "ORA-00054: resource busy and acquire with NOWAIT specified."

The SELECT statement associated with a cursor may not include the INTO clause. Instead, data is retrieved into PL/SQL variables using a FETCH statement. See the "Executing Cursors" section later in this chapter.

Example

The following cursor declaration includes a SELECT statement that retrieves all rows from the scott.emp table with a salary greater than the current value of the PL/SQL variable t_sal, which must already have been declared:

```
CURSOR emp_cursor IS
    SELECT sal, comm
    FROM scott.emp
    WHERE sal > t_sal;
```

Declaring Exceptions

Exceptions are used by PL/SQL to handle errors and other conditions that may occur during the execution of a PL/SQL program. Oracle has predefined exceptions that it throws for common errors. You can also define your own.

EXCEPTION

exception_name EXCEPTION

Declares an exception of your own.

Keywords

exception_name
>   A valid PL/SQL name for the exception.

EXCEPTION
>   A keyword required to indicate that this declaration is for a user-defined
>   exception.

>   If you declare a named exception without tying it to a specific error
>   number using the PRAGMA EXCEPTION_INIT statement (described
>   next), then the only way that exception will be raised is by raising it
>   manually in your code.

PRAGMA EXCEPTION_INIT

PRAGMA EXCEPTION_INIT (*exception_name, ora_number*);

Associates an exception with a specific Oracle error number.

Keywords

PRAGMA EXCEPTION_INIT
>   Invokes a compiler directive that associates a named exception with a specific
>   Oracle error number.

exception_name
>   A valid PL/SQL name for the exception.

ora_number
>   The Oracle error number you want to tie to the named exception.

>   Oracle error numbers are almost always negative. If you want to trap
>   the error ORA-02292, use -2292 as your *ora_number* value.

After declaring an exception, you can associate your exception with a specific Oracle error number so that when the specified error occurs, Oracle will automatically raise the exception.

If you declare a named exception without using PRAGMA EXCEPTION_INIT to tie it to a specific error number, the only way that exception will ever be raised is if you raise it manually in your code.

Execution Section

The execution section of a PL/SQL block is the only required section. It contains the PL/SQL code that actually performs some action; the exception section also performs an action, but only after being triggered by an action in the execution section. The general syntax of the execution section is:

```
BEGIN
    {assignment_statement    |
      proc_call    |
      control_statement    |
      PL/SQL_block    |
      SQL
    };
    [{assignment_statemanet    |
      proc_call    |
      control_statement    |
      PL/SQL_block    |
      SQL
    }; . . . ]
END;
```

Keywords

BEGIN

A required keyword marking the beginning of the execution section.

assignment_statement

Any valid PL/SQL assignment statement. These statements normally consist of a variable and an expression separated by an := operator.

proc_call

A call to a PL/SQL procedure or function.

control_statement

Any valid PL/SQL control statement. These statements are described later in this chapter.

PL/SQL_block

Any complete PL/SQL block. A PL/SQL block contained with an execution section is called a *nested block*.

SQL

Any valid SQL DML statement, such as SELECT, INSERT, UPDATE, DELETE, ROLLBACK, or COMMIT.

END

A required keyword marking the end of the execution section.

Assignment Statements

An assignment statement provides a value to a PL/SQL variable. The general syntax of a PL/SQL assignment statement is:

```
variable := expression;
```

Keywords

variable

Any previously declared PL/SQL variable.

:=

The PL/SQL symbol for assignment. Note the difference between := and the typical = used in many other languages.

expression

Any valid PL/SQL expression.

Expressions

PL/SQL expressions consist of one or more PL/SQL variables optionally combined with one or more PL/SQL operators. In PL/SQL, an expression may appear in one of the following locations:

- On the right side of an assignment statement

- As part of a control statement

- As part of a SQL statement

The PL/SQL operators that may be used in expressions, along with their relative precedence (where 1 is the highest) are listed in Table 7-4.

Table 7-4. PL/SQL Operators

Operator	Description	Type	Precedence
||	Concatenate two character strings	Character	4
+	Addition	Numeric	4
+	Unary identity (when used as a positive sign)	Numeric	2
-	Subtraction	Numeric	4
-	Unary negation (when used as a negative sign)	Numeric	2

Table 7-4. PL/SQL Operators (continued)

Operator	Description	Type	Precedence
*	Multiplication	Numeric	3
**	Exponentiation	Numeric	1
/	Division	Numeric	3
=	Equality	Numeric	5
!=	Non-equality	Boolean	5
<>	Non-equality	Boolean	5
~=	Non-equality	Boolean	5
<	Less than	Boolean	5
>	Greater than	Boolean	5
<=	Less than or equal to	Boolean	5
>=	Greater than or equal to	Boolean	5
IS NULL	Test for NULL value	Boolean	5
LIKE	Test equality of character strings using mask	Boolean	5
BETWEEN	Test inclusion in range	Boolean	5
IN	Test inclusion in list	Boolean	5
AND	Logical AND evaluation	Boolean	6
OR	Logical OR evaluation	Boolean	7
NOT	Logical negation	Boolean	1

Control Statements

PL/SQL control statements are used to control the execution behavior of a PL/SQL block. The existence of control statements provides PL/SQL with its procedural, or third-generation, capabilities. These capabilities distinguish it from SQL.

IF-THEN-ELSE

```
IF expression THEN
    statement;[statement; ...]
[ELSIF expression THEN
    statement;[statement; ...]
[ELSIF expression THEN
    statement;[statement; ...] ...]
]
[ELSE
    statement;[statement; ...]]
END IF;
```

Executes one or more statements based on the logical evaluation of Boolean expressions.

Keywords

IF

Required keyword that indicates the beginning of conditional processing.

expression

Any valid PL/SQL expression returning a Boolean result.

THEN

A required keyword indicating that the statement(s) to follow will be executed if *expression* evaluates to TRUE.

statement

Any valid PL/SQL assignment statement, SQL statement, procedure call, or function call.

ELSIF

Optional keyword indicating an alternative expression to be evaluated if the primary expression is FALSE. If the ELSIF expression is evaluated and is TRUE, the statements following the ELSIF will be executed. As many alternate conditions (ELSIF) may be specified as are required.

ELSE

Optional keyword preceding statements to be executed in the event that none of the IF or ELSIF expressions evaluate to TRUE.

END IF

Required keyword that indicates the end of the IF statement. Each IF must be ended by only one END IF keyword.

 Only one set of statements will be executed in an IF-THEN-ELSE statement. Once an expression evaluates to TRUE, the associated statements are executed and control is transferred to the statement following the END IF keyword.

Example

In the following example, salaries are adjusted and bonuses are awarded according to the initial value of an employee's salary per pay period. If the salary is less then $1000, a 10 percent raise is given (salary * 1.10), but no bonus is awarded. Salaries between $1001 and $1500 get an 8 percent raise and a $500 bonus. Salaries between $1501 and $2000 get a 5 percent raise and a $750 bonus. Everyone else—those with salaries over $2000—gets a 2 percent raise and a $1000 bonus:

```
IF salary < 1000 THEN
   salary := salary * 1.10;
   bonus := 0;
ELSIF salary BETWEEN 1001 AND 1500 THEN
```

```
    salary := salary * 1.08;
    bonus := 500;
ELSIF salary BETWEEN 1501 AND 2000 THEN
    salary := salary * 1.05;
    bonus := 750;
ELSE
    salary := salary * 1.02;
    bonus := 1000;
END IF;
```

LOOP

```
[<<label>>]
LOOP
[EXIT;]
[EXIT WHEN condition;]
statement;[statement;...]
END LOOP [<<label>>];
```

Performs one or more statements repetitively, optionally terminating execution when a condition is met or when an explicit EXIT command is issued. Each statement between LOOP and END LOOP is executed sequentially. If an EXIT command has not been encountered, control is passed back to the first statement in the loop.

Keywords

<<label>>

Specifies an optional label for the loop. The loop is labeled by a *<<label>>* preceding the LOOP statement and the corresponding END LOOP statement may then optionally reference the same label.

LOOP

Required keyword indicating that subsequent statements, until the END LOOP keyword is reached, be performed repetitively.

EXIT

Optional keyword that causes control to be passed to the next statement after the END LOOP keyword. EXIT is actually an executable statement that usually appears after an IF statement embedded in the loop. This keyword may appear in any statement between the LOOP and END LOOP keywords, and may appear multiple times. Note that EXIT is not strictly a component of the LOOP syntax, but is included here for clarity, since it is often used in LOOP programming.

EXIT WHEN

Optionally specifies a condition which, when it evaluates to TRUE, causes control to be transferred to the next statement after the END LOOP keyword. This keyword may appear in any statement between the LOOP and END

LOOP keywords, and may appear multiple times. The specified exit condition is evaluated when the EXIT WHEN statement is encountered. Note that EXIT WHEN is not strictly a component of the LOOP syntax, but is included here for clarity, since it is often used in LOOP programming.

statement

Any valid PL/SQL assignment statement, SQL statement, procedure call, or function call.

END LOOP

Required keyword indicating the end of the LOOP structure.

 It is perfectly legal to have a loop structure without an EXIT or EXIT WHEN keyword. However, such a loop will run forever, which is probably not what you intended!

Example

In this example, which uses a PL/SQL table, the loop continues until one of two conditions occur: if a row of the table is NULL, the loop immediately exits. The loop is also ended when the value of loop_counter reaches 100.

```
loop_counter := 0;
LOOP
   EXIT WHEN loop_counter = 100;
   loop_counter := loop_counter+1;
   IF salary_table(loop_counter) IS NULL THEN EXIT;
   salary_table(loop_counter) := salary_table(loop_counter) * 1.1;
END LOOP;
```

WHILE Loop

```
[<<label>>]
WHILE condition LOOP
statement; [statement;...]
END LOOP [<<label>>];
```

Performs one or more statements repetitively until a condition is not met. When the last statement is executed, control is passed back to the first statement for execution. This iterative execution continues until *condition* evaluates to FALSE.

Keywords

<<label>>

Specifies an optional label for the loop. The loop is labeled by a *<<label>>* preceding the WHILE statement, and the corresponding END LOOP statement may then optionally reference the same label.

WHILE ... LOOP

Specifies that this is a WHILE loop that will execute as long as *condition* evaluates to TRUE. When *condition* evaluates to FALSE, the keyword will cause control to be transferred to the next statement following the END LOOP keyword. The condition is tested before each execution of the loop body.

statement

Any valid PL/SQL assignment statement, SQL statement, procedure call, or function call.

END LOOP

Required keyword indicating the end of the LOOP structure.

 The condition is evaluated prior to each iteration of the loop. If the condition is TRUE, all statements in the loop are executed; if it evaluates to FALSE, control is passed to the next statement after the END LOOP keyword.

Example

This example is similar to that shown earlier with the LOOP command, and demonstrates how the same result can be accomplished using different methods. Here, two statements are repeatedly executed (one to increment the variable loop_counter and one to update the corresponding element of the salary table) until the value of loop_counter reaches 100. At that point, it is no longer less than 100, and the loop terminates:

```
loop_counter := 0;
WHILE loop_counter < 100 LOOP
    loop_counter := loop_counter+1;
    salary(loop_counter) := salary(loop_counter) * 1.1;
END LOOP;
```

FOR Loop

```
[<<label>>]
FOR counter IN [REVERSE] start .. end LOOP
statement; [statement;...]
END LOOP [<<label>>];
```

Performs a sequence of statements a defined number of times.

Keywords

<<label>>

Specifies an optional label for the loop. The loop is labeled by a *<<label>>* preceding the FOR statement, and the corresponding END LOOP statement may then optionally reference the same label.

counter

    Specifies the name of a variable used to hold the count of iterations through the loop. After each iteration of the loop, *counter* is incremented by 1, unless REVERSE is specified, in which case *counter* is decremented by 1. This variable is automatically defined as a BINARY_INTEGER and does not need to be declared in the block. If a variable of the same name is declared and available in the block, its declaration is temporarily overridden while the FOR loop is active, unless it is explicitly referenced using *blockname.variable* notation.

REVERSE

    Specifies that *counter* will be decremented from *end* to *start* when the FOR loop is executed.

start

    Specifies the beginning value for *counter*, unless REVERSE is specified. If REVERSE is specified, *start* represents the ending value for the counter.

end

    Specifies the last value for *counter*; that is, when *counter* reaches this value, the FOR loop is terminated and control is passed to the executable statement immediately following the END LOOP statement. If REVERSE is specified, *end* specifies the initial value of *counter*, which is then decremented by 1 until *start* is reached.

statement

    Any valid PL/SQL assignment statement, SQL statement, procedure call, or function call.

END LOOP

    Required keyword indicating the end of the LOOP structure.

Example

This example performs the same operation as the example shown for the WHILE loop, but is written using a FOR loop. Here the first 99 elements of the salary table are updated:

```
FOR loop_counter IN 1..99 LOOP
    salary(loop_counter) := salary(loop_counter) * 1.1;
END LOOP;
```

GOTO

```
GOTO label;
```

Transfers program control to the executable statement immediately following *label*. The following rules must be observed when using the GOTO statement:

*   You can't jump into a block from outside a block.

*   You can't jump into the middle of a loop.

- You can't jump into the middle of an IF statement.

- You can't jump out of an exception handler and back into the code.

Example

In this example, when salary is greater than 1000, control is passed to the label no_raise, and the next statement to be executed assigns the current date to the variable up_date:

```
IF salary > 1000 THEN
    GOTO no_raise;
END IF;
Salary := salary * 1.1;

<<no_raise>>
up_date := SYSDATE;
```

NULL

```
NULL;
```

The NULL statement does absolutely nothing. It can be used as a placeholder when developing new code or to replace the contents of a deeply nested portion of an IF statement that you no longer want to execute.

Example

In the following example, NULL has been used as a placeholder for code that needs to be written later:

```
IF emp_sal < 0 THEN
    --Write this later when the specs are finished
    NULL;
ELSE
    print_paycheck(emp_no, emp_sal);
END IF;
```

SQL Statements

The ability to use SQL within a PL/SQL program is one of PL/SQL's major strengths. By adding the ability to use variables in SQL code, PL/SQL becomes a powerful and robust language that can take full advantage of complex Oracle databases.

There are some limitations to the use of SQL in PL/SQL, however. Most notable is that only Data Manipulation Language (DML) and control statements are permitted in PL/SQL. The following SQL statements are permitted in a PL/SQL block:

SELECT
INSERT

UPDATE
DELETE
COMMIT
ROLLBACK
SET CONSTRAINTS
SET ROLE
SET TRANSACTION
SAVEPOINT
LOCK TABLE

Data Definition Language (DDL) statements, including session and system control statements, are not allowed in PL/SQL. EXPLAIN PLAN is also not allowed.

 There is a way to execute DDL statements from PL/SQL through the use of the DBMS_SQL built-in package. The use of this package (and the other built-in packages) is beyond the scope of this book. For more information about the use of DBMS_SQL, refer to the *Oracle Built-in Packages* (O'Reilly & Associates) by Steven Feuerstein, Charles Dye, and John Beresniewicz.

SQL used in a PL/SQL program differs from "standard" SQL in the following important ways:

- The INTO keyword permits data to be read from a database table and placed into a PL/SQL variable or record.

- PL/SQL variables may be used anywhere a constant or expression would be permitted, including in the WHERE clause. Thus, although the names of tables and columns must be known when the code is written, the values for columns and other expressions need not be.

- SQL statements executed in PL/SQL do not return data to the screen or other output device.

The specific syntax for each permitted SQL statement is presented below, with two exceptions. COMMIT and ROLLBACK are the same as in standard SQL, so their syntax is not repeated.

SELECT

```
SELECT select_list
INTO {pl/sql_record | variable [, variable…]}
FROM table_list
[WHERE where_clause];
```

Selects data from an Oracle table (or view), and places the result in a PL/SQL record or into one or more PL/SQL variables.

Keywords

select_list

Specifies the list of columns to be retrieved by the statement. See Chapter 3 for more information.

pl/sql_record

Specifies the name of a PL/SQL record to receive the data returned by the SELECT statement. The record must contain exactly the same number of variables as are listed in the select list, and their types must be compatible. If the datatype of a field in the record differs from the corresponding column in the select list, the two types must be compatible enough for Oracle to implicitly convert from one to the other.

table_list

Specifies the name of one or more tables from which data will be selected.

variable

Specifies the name of a previously declared PL/SQL variable. There must be exactly the same number of variables as columns in the select list, and each must be of the same (or compatible) type.

where_clause

Specifies the WHERE conditions for this SELECT. Expressions in the WHERE clause may include previously declared PL/SQL variables.

 This syntax description is for the basic form of the SELECT statement. Keep in mind that there are additional clauses available. These clauses include the GROUP BY and ORDER BY clauses. See Chapter 3, *Data Manipulation and Control Statements,* for the full syntax of the SELECT statement, including descriptions of all the clauses.

Example

This example retrieves KING's row from the emp table and places the values for hiredate, sal, and comm into the corresponding PL/SQL variables:

```
DECLARE
    t_hiredate DATE;
    t_salary NUMBER;
    t_commission NUMBER;
BEGIN
    SELECT hiredate, sal, comm
```

```
        INTO t_hiredate, t_salary, t_commission
        FROM scott.emp
        WHERE ename = 'KING';
    END;
```

INSERT

```
INSERT INTO [schema.]table (column[,column..])
VALUES ({expression[,expression..]  |  select_statement});
```

Inserts a new data row into the specified table, providing values for each specified column. Alternatively takes the results from a query, and inserts them into the specified table.

Keywords

schema

The name of the schema that contains *table*. If omitted, the current schema is used.

table

Specifies the name of a table into which new rows will be inserted.

column

Specifies the name of a column in *table* that will receive data specified in the VALUES clause.

expression

Specifies a valid PL/SQL expression, which may contain a previously declared PL/SQL variable or record type.

select_statement

Specifies that the data to be inserted is the result of this SELECT statement. The SELECT statement must return one column for each column listed in the INSERT INTO clause, and the types must be compatible.

Example

The code in the following PL/SQL block inserts a new row into the emp table:

```
BEGIN
    INSERT INTO emp (empno, ename, sal)
    VALUES (1111, 'Gennick', 2500);
END;
```

UPDATE

```
UPDATE [schema.]table
SET {column = expression[,column = expression..]  |
        column[,column..] = (select_statement)
    }
```

```
WHERE {where_clause | CURRENT OF cursor_name};
```

Updates one or more rows of a table.

Keywords

schema

The name of the schema that contains *table*. If omitted, the current schema is used.

table

Specifies the name of a table for which rows will be updated.

column

Specifies the name of a column in the table being updated.

expression

Any valid SQL expression.

select_statement

Any valid SELECT statement, which must return the appropriate number and type of data elements. SELECT statements used in the SET clause must be enclosed within parentheses.

where_clause

Specifies the WHERE conditions for this update. Expressions in the WHERE clause may include previously declared PL/SQL variables.

CURRENT OF

Specifies that the update be applied to the row most recently fetched and locked by the named cursor.

cursor_name

Specifies the name of a PL/SQL cursor used to fetch data from the table being updated.

Example

The following example updates the records of all employees who work for employee number 7788 and doubles their salaries:

```
BEGIN
   UPDATE emp
      SET sal = sal * 2
   WHERE mgr = 7788;
END;
```

The following, more complex UPDATE statement, sets the salary of each employee to 90 percent of their manager's salary. Employees without managers do not receive a salary adjustment:

```
BEGIN
   UPDATE emp e
```

```
       SET sal = (SELECT sal * 0.90
                  FROM emp m
                  WHERE e.mgr = m.empno)
   WHERE mgr IS NOT NULL;
END;
```

DELETE

```
DELETE FROM [schema.]table
WHERE {where_clause | CURRENT OF cursor_name};
```

Deletes one or more rows of a table.

Keywords

schema

The name of the schema that contains *table*. If omitted, the current schema is used.

table

Specifies the name of a table from which rows will be deleted.

where_clause

Specifies the WHERE conditions for this delete. Expressions in the WHERE clause may include previously declared PL/SQL variables.

CURRENT OF

Specifies that the delete be applied to the row most recently fetched via the named cursor.

cursor_name

Specifies the name of a PL/SQL cursor used to fetch data from the specified table.

Example

The following example deletes managers who make too much money:

```
BEGIN
    DELETE FROM emp m
    WHERE empno IN (SELECT mgr FROM emp)
     AND sal * 0.90 > (SELECT MAX(sal)
                       FROM emp e
                       WHERE e.mgr = m.empno);
END;
```

In this case, "too much money" is defined as any salary that is still greater than the highest salary of that manager's subordinate employees when multiplied by 90 percent. Those managers are history.

Executing Cursors

PL/SQL cursors provide a method of accessing multiple rows of data from an Oracle database and maintaining complete control of program execution for each row. You must perform the following four steps to use a PL/SQL cursor:

1. Declare the cursor (see the "Declaring Cursors" section earlier in this chapter).

2. Open the cursor.

3. Issue FETCH statements to retrieve the data.

4. Close the cursor.

The following sections show the general syntax of the PL/SQL statements required during cursor execution.

OPEN

```
OPEN cursor_name;
```

Opens a PL/SQL cursor for use within the current block. This cursor must not already be open.

FETCH

```
FETCH cursor_name INTO {variable_list | record};
```

Reads a row of data from the cursor result set into the specified PL/SQL variable(s). Each successive FETCH will read a new row of data from the result set until no more rows remain to be read.

Keywords

FETCH
>   Specifies that a row be returned from the SQL statement associated with *cursor_name*.

cursor_name
>   Specifies the name of a cursor that has previously been declared and opened.

variable_list
>   One or more previously declared PL/SQL variables into which column values returned by the SELECT statement associated with the cursor will be placed.

record
>   A previously declared PL/SQL record into which columns returned by the SELECT statement associated with the cursor will be placed. The fields in the record must match those in the underlying SQL statement's select list.

CLOSE

```
CLOSE cursor_name;
```

Closes a cursor and frees associated resources. The cursor must have previously been declared and opened.

Cursor FOR Loops

```
FOR {variable_list | record}
IN {cursor_name | (select_statement)} LOOP
   [pl/sql_statement; ...]
END LOOP;
```

While it is usually necessary to explicitly OPEN a cursor, FETCH from it, and then CLOSE the cursor, PL/SQL provides a shortcut to perform this processing. This shortcut is called the *cursor FOR loop*, and it is useful when you want to do a simple iteration through all the rows returned by a cursor's underlying SQL SELECT statement.

Keywords

variable_list

One or more previously declared PL/SQL variables into which column values returned by the SELECT statement associated with *cursor_name* will be placed.

record

A previously declared PL/SQL record into which column values returned by the SELECT statement associated with *cursor_name* will be placed.

cursor_name

Specifies the name of a cursor that has previously been declared. The cursor is implicitly opened when the statement is executed.

select_statement

As an alternative to specifying a cursor name, you may provide a SELECT statement as part of the FOR loop syntax. If you do, you must enclose the SELECT statement within parentheses.

END LOOP

Indicates the end of the cursor FOR loop. When all the data has been fetched, the loop ends and the cursor is implicitly closed.

When a cursor FOR loop is executed, the cursor associated with it is opened and rows of data are fetched. After each row is fetched, the PL/SQL statements between the FOR ... IN statement and the END LOOP statement are executed. When all rows have been fetched, the cursor is closed and execution continues with the statement following the END LOOP.

Example

The following example shows a cursor FOR loop used to iterate through the records returned by the cursor named emp_cursor:

```
BEGIN
    FOR v_emp_data IN emp_cursor LOOP /*Begin the loop and open the cursor*/
        -- a row is implicitly fetched, so now process it
        bonus := v_emp_data.sal * 1.12;     /*Assign a 12% bonus*/
        INSERT INTO bonus (empno, bonus)
        VALUES (v_emp_data.empno, bonus);

        -- now the loop will check for more rows, and fetch another if possible
    END LOOP;
    COMMIT;
                                            /* Continue with other processing*/
END;
```

This second example does the same thing as the first, except that the SELECT statement to be executed is made part of the FOR loop:

```
BEGIN
    FOR v_emp_data IN (SELECT * FROM emp) LOOP
        -- a row is implicitly fetched, so now process it
        bonus := v_emp_data.sal * 1.12;
        INSERT INTO bonus (empno, bonus)
        VALUES (v_emp_data.empno, bonus);

        -- now the loop will check for more rows,
        -- and fetch another if possible
    END LOOP;
    COMMIT;

END;
```

The definition of the record v_emp_data used in these two examples must match the number and datatypes of the columns returned by each cursor's underlying SQL statement. In the second example, since SELECT * was used, you could declare the record as v_emp_data emp%ROWTYPE.

Referencing Cursor Attributes

Once a cursor is declared, four attributes can be used to get information about that cursor. These attributes, together with the possible values that they can return, are summarized in Table 7-5.

Table 7-5. Attributes of PL/SQL Cursors

Attribute	Description	Value	Meaning
%FOUND	Indicates whether a row of data has been returned.	TRUE	The previous FETCH returned a data row.
		FALSE	The previous FETCH did not return a data row; all rows have been retrieved.
		NULL	The cursor has been opened but no FETCH has been executed.
%NOTFOUND	Indicates that a data row has not been returned. This attribute is the opposite of %FOUND.	TRUE	The previous FETCH did not return a data row; all rows have been retrieved.
		FALSE	The previous FETCH returned a data row.
		NULL	The cursor has been opened but no FETCH has been executed.
%ISOPEN	Indicates whether the cursor is opened.	TRUE	The cursor has been opened.
		FALSE	The cursor has not been opened or has been closed.
%ROWCOUNT	Indicates the number of rows returned by this cursor so far.	0	The cursor has been opened but no FETCH has been executed.
		Positive integer	The number of rows that have been retrieved by FETCHs from this cursor.

Cursor Attributes

`cursor_name.attribute`

References a cursor attribute.

Keywords

cursor_name

> The name of a previously declared PL/SQL cursor. This cursor may be closed or open. If referencing an attribute associated with an implicit cursor (i.e., single-row SELECT, INSERT, DELETE, or UPDATE), the name of the implicit cursor is SQL.

attribute

> The name of the attribute to be referenced.

Example

The following example declares a cursor that selects rows from the scott.emp table that have a value for the sal column greater than 100. The executable block reads each row (using a FETCH within a LOOP) into the salary variable and increments a variable named sal_total until all rows have been read. The %NOTFOUND attribute is used to detect the point at which all rows have been processed:

```
DECLARE
    sal_total NUMBER :=0;    /*Variable for salary sum */
    salary emp.sal%TYPE      /*Variable for salary FETCHed by cursor */
    CURSOR emp_cursor IS     /*Declare the cursor */
          SELECT sal FROM scott.emp WHERE sal > 100;
BEGIN
    OPEN emp_cursor;         /* Open the cursor */

    LOOP
       FETCH emp_cursor INTO salary;   /*Read a row into salary */
       EXIT WHEN emp_cursor%NOTFOUND;  /*See if all rows have been read */
       sal_total := sal_total + salary;  /*Add salary to total */
    END LOOP;                /*Go back to the top of the loop */

    CLOSE emp_cursor;        /*Close the cursor */
END;
```

Exception Section

Even the best-written PL/SQL programs encounter errors or unexpected events. PL/SQL provides a powerful and flexible method for handling both expected and unexpected events through the use of exceptions and exception handlers. Any Oracle error (those reported with Oracle error numbers in the form ORA-*xxxxx*) PL/SQL runtime error, or user-defined condition (not necessarily an error), can be handled.

> PL/SQL compile errors are not handled by PL/SQL exception handling, since these errors occur prior to execution of the PL/SQL program.

PL/SQL error handling is fairly straightforward. When an error occurs in a running PL/SQL program, an exception is raised and the appropriate exception handler takes control.

Types of Exceptions

PL/SQL handles two types of exceptions: predefined and user-defined. User-defined exceptions must be declared in the DECLARE section (see the "Declaring Exceptions" section earlier in this chapter) of a PL/SQL block. Predefined exceptions are supplied to handle the most common types of errors and are summarized in Table 7-6.

Table 7-6. Predefined PL/SQL Exceptions

Exception	Oracle Error	Description
CURSOR_ALREADY_OPEN	ORA-06511	An attempt was made to open a cursor that was already open.
DUP_VAL_ON_INDEX	ORA-00001	A unique constraint was violated.
INVALID_CURSOR	ORA-01001	An illegal operation, such as an attempt to close an already closed cursor, was attempted with a cursor.
INVALID_NUMBER	ORA-01722	An implicit or explicit conversion from character to numeric failed in a SQL statement.
LOGIN_DENIED	ORA-01017	A login was denied because of an invalid username or password.
NO_DATA_FOUND	ORA-01404	A query returned no rows.
NOT_LOGGED_ON	ORA-01012	The session is not connected to Oracle.
OTHERS		An error occurred that was not predefined.
PROGRAM_ERROR	ORA-06501	An internal PL/SQL error occurred.
ROWTYPE_MISMATCH	ORA-06504	The types of a host cursor variable and a PL/SQL cursor variable did not match.
STORAGE_ERROR	ORA-06500	The process ran out of memory.
TIMEOUT_ON_RESOURCE	ORA-00051	A resource was requested, but the operation timed out. This event often occurs while waiting for a lock.
TOO_MANY_ROWS	ORA-01422	A SELECT statement returned more than one row.
TRANSACTION_BACKED_OUT	ORA-00061	A deadlock condition forced a ROLLBACK.
VALUE_ERROR	ORA-06502	A conversion error occurred in a procedural statement.
ZERO_DIVIDE	ORA-01476	A division by 0 was attempted.

When an exception occurs, it is said to be "raised." Predefined exceptions are raised when the exception event occurs. User-defined exceptions are raised by the explicit execution of a RAISE command (described in the later section, "Exception Handling Statements"). In either case, when an exception is raised, execution is immediately transferred to the appropriate exception handler. This transfer is one-way; there is no method available to return to the executable section.

You can easily work around this limitation on returns by using nested PL/SQL blocks; once an exception is handled, control can pass to the outer block to continue execution.

Exception Handling

The exception section of a PL/SQL block has the following syntax:

```
EXCEPTION
    [WHEN exception_name THEN
        pl/sql_statements
    [WHEN exception_name THEN
        pl/sql_statements...]]
     [WHEN OTHERS THEN
         pl/sql_statements]
END;
```

Keywords

exception_name

The name of a predefined exception or a previously declared user-defined exception.

pl/sql_statements

One or more valid SQL or PL/SQL statements to be executed when the specified exception is raised.

WHEN OTHERS

Defines a catch-all exception handler that is executed when no other handlers apply.

END

Marks the end of the exception section and the end of the block.

Example

The code in this example attempts to retrieve the salary and name for a specific employee (if there is no record of the specified employee, a row is inserted into an error log table):

```
DECLARE
    emp_name emp.ename%type;
    emp_sal emp.sal%type;
    empno_to_find NUMBER := 9999;
BEGIN
    SELECT ename, sal
    INTO emp_name, emp_sal
    FROM emp
    WHERE EMPNO = empno_to_find;
EXCEPTION
    WHEN NO_DATA_FOUND THEN
        INSERT INTO error_log (empno, error_message)
        VALUES (empno_to_find, 'Missing employee record');
END;
```

Exception handling functions

Table 7-7 lists the two PL/SQL built-in functions provided to make error handling more convenient, particularly if the WHEN OTHERS exception handler is executed.

Table 7-7. Exception Handling Functions

Function	Returns
SQLCODE	Oracle error number encountered
SQLERRM	Text of Oracle error encountered

Raising exceptions

Exceptions may be raised in a PL/SQL block in one of the following three ways:

- An Oracle error may occur, triggering an exception automatically.
- A RAISE statement may be used to explicitly raise an exception.
- A call may be made to the RAISE_APPLICATION_ERROR procedure.

Exceptions raised as the result of an Oracle error are automatic, and not much more needs to be said about them. The other two methods must be implemented with code that you write.

Exception Handling Statements

You can use the RAISE statement and the RAISE_APPLICATION_ERROR procedure in the execution section of a PL/SQL block to raise an exception. You can also include them in an exception handler to reraise an exception or raise a new exception.

RAISE

```
RAISE exception_name
```

Raises an exception. Usually the RAISE statement is used to raise a previously defined user-defined exception, but it can also raise one of the predefined exceptions.

 When you issue RAISE from within the execution portion of a PL/SQL block, you must always specify the name of the exception that you want to raise. You can also use RAISE from within an exception handler to reraise an exception to the parent PL/SQL block. When you do that, you can omit the exit name, causing the current exception to be raised again.

Example

The following example illustrates one use of the RAISE statement (when you try to use the create_emp procedure to create a new employee and you fail to specify a salary other than zero dollars, the procedure fails with an error):

```
CREATE OR REPLACE
PROCEDURE create_emp (emp_no IN NUMBER,
                      emp_name IN VARCHAR2,
                      emp_sal IN NUMBER)
IS
    --Declare a user-defined exception, and associate it with
    --an error code of -20000.
    no_salary EXCEPTION;
    PRAGMA EXCEPTION_INIT(no_salary,-20000);
BEGIN
    --Raise an exception if salary zero or null.
    IF NVL(emp_sal,0) = 0 THEN
       RAISE no_salary;
    END IF;

    INSERT INTO emp (empno, ename, sal)
    VALUES (emp_no, emp_name, emp_sal);
EXCEPTION
    WHEN no_salary THEN
       --Reraise the exception
       RAISE;
END;
```

When an attempt is made to use create_emp to insert a record with a zero salary, a no_salary exception is raised. That exception causes control to jump to the associated exception handler. In the exception handler, the RAISE statement raises the same exception again, propagating it to the code that invoked the procedure.

RAISE_APPLICATION_ERROR

```
RAISE_APPLICATION_ERROR (error_number,error_text[,keep_errors]);
```

Provides a method to define error numbers and messages for conditions not handled by standard Oracle errors.

Keywords

error_number

> The number you want to use for the error being raised. This number should be between -20,000 and -20,999 to avoid conflict with Oracle error numbers. That range was set aside by Oracle for user-defined error numbers.

error_text

> A character string between 1 and 2048 bytes in length providing text to be associated with the error being raised.

keep_errors

> A Boolean value, either TRUE or FALSE. If TRUE is specified, the error will be added to a list of errors that have been raised. If FALSE, this error will replace previous errors on the error stack. The default behavior is that specified by FALSE.

> RAISE_APPLICATION_ERROR is often useful from within a trigger. If you decide in a trigger that you want the triggering SQL statement to fail, all you need to do is call RAISE_APPLICATION_ERROR. For more information about triggers, see the discussion in the "Triggers" section later in this chapter.

Example

The following code shows RAISE_APPLICATION_ERROR used in a trigger to prevent a new employee record from being inserted without a name:

```
CREATE OR REPLACE TRIGGER emp_insert
BEFORE INSERT ON emp
FOR EACH ROW
BEGIN
   IF :new.ename IS NULL THEN
       RAISE_APPLICATION_ERROR(-20000,'Employees must have a name.');
   END IF;
END;
```

The code in this trigger checks to see if the employee name in the new record is NULL. If the new name is NULL, a call to RAISE_APPLICATION_ERROR is made. Raising an error in a BEFORE trigger always causes the triggering statement to fail.

Now there certainly are easier ways to enforce a NOT NULL constraint, but this code clearly illustrates the potential use of RAISE_APPLICATION_ERROR.

Procedures and Packages

Most third-generation languages include the ability to create discrete program units, called *subprograms*, that can be executed by other programs. PL/SQL also includes this capability. Using PL/SQL, you can implement two types of subprograms: *procedures* and *functions*. The characteristics of each are summarized in Table 7-8.

Table 7-8. Characteristics of PL/SQL Procedures and Functions

Characteristic	Procedure	Function
Can accept input parameters	Yes	Yes
Can return parameter values	Yes	Yes
Returns a single value	No	Yes
Can be referenced in an expression	No	Yes
Is stored in the database in compiled form	Yes	Yes

As you can see from Table 7-8, the primary difference between a procedure and a function is that functions return a single value, and can thus be used in a PL/SQL expression anywhere a PL/SQL variable or constant may be used. PL/SQL procedures, on the other hand, do not return values and cannot form part of an expression.

Procedures

A PL/SQL procedure is much like a subroutine, or subprogram, in other languages. It can accept one or more parameters or arguments as input, can operate on these parameters, and may replace the values in one or more of these parameters with new values. The program that invoked the procedure (the calling program) can then access these new values. PL/SQL procedures are created and maintained using the SQL DDL statements CREATE PROCEDURE, ALTER PROCEDURE, and DROP PROCEDURE.

CREATE PROCEDURE

```
CREATE [OR REPLACE] PROCEDURE [schema.]procedure_name
[(argument [IN | OUT | IN OUT] [NOCOPY] datatype
[,argument [IN | OUT | IN OUT] [NOCOPY] datatype ...])]
```

```
[AUTHID {CURRENT_USER | DEFINER}]
{IS | AS} {plsql_code |
          LANGUAGE {JAVA NAME 'string' |
          C [NAME name] LIBRARY libname [WITH CONTEXT] [PARAMETERS parms}}
```

Creates a stored procedure or replaces an existing version of a stored procedure with a new version.

Keywords

OR REPLACE

Specifies that an existing stored procedure be replaced.

schema

The name of the schema to contain the procedure. Storing the procedure in your current schema is the default.

procedure_name

The name you want to give this procedure.

argument

The name of an argument to the procedure.

IN

Specifies that the argument is an input that must be supplied when the procedure is called. This specification is the default. Within the procedure, you won't be allowed to assign a value to an input argument.

OUT

Specifies that the argument is an output and will be set by the procedure before control is returned to the calling program. Within the procedure, you will be allowed to store a value into an output variable, but you won't be allowed to refer to that value.

IN OUT

Specifies that the argument is both an input and an output. A value must be supplied when the procedure is called, and another value may be set by the procedure prior to its return.

NOCOPY

Specifies that the argument should be passed by reference rather than by value. Passing an argument by value requires that a copy be made. Passing an argument by reference requires only that a memory address be passed, thereby providing significantly enhanced performance. This keyword affects OUT and IN OUT arguments, and it is the default for IN arguments.

datatype

The argument's datatype, which can be any datatype supported by PL/SQL.

AUTHID

Specifies whose privileges the function will execute under.

CURRENT_USER

Specifies that the privileges and schema of the current user will be used when executing this function.

DEFINER

Specifies that the privileges and schema of the function owner will be used when executing this function; this is the default behavior.

plsql_code

The PL/SQL code to implement this procedure.

LANGUAGE

Specifies that the PL/SQL procedure is mapped to a Java or C method.

JAVA NAME

Specifies that the function is mapped to a Java method.

string

Specifies the Java implementation of the method.

C [NAME]

Specifies that the function is mapped to a C method.

name

Specifies the name of the C routine.

libname

Specifies the name of the library containing the C routine.

WITH CONTEXT

Specifies that a context pointer be passed to the C routine.

parms

Specifies the parameter(s) to be passed to the C routine.

 If you are creating a procedure from SQL*Plus and the procedure does not compile correctly, use the SQL*Plus command SHOW ERRORS to see specific error messages that were generated.

Example

The procedure created by the CREATE PROCEDURE statement in the following example reads a row from the emp table and gives an employee a raise. The first parameter is p_ename, and it identifies the employee by name. The procedure calculates a new salary and passes it back in the second parameter, newsal:

```
CREATE OR REPLACE PROCEDURE give_raise
(p_ename IN VARCHAR2,
 newsal OUT NUMBER)
```

```
AS
    t_sal NUMBER;
    t_deptno NUMBER;
BEGIN
    SELECT sal, deptno
    INTO t_sal, t_deptno
    FROM emp
    WHERE ename = p_ename;

    IF t_deptno = 10 THEN
        newsal := t_sal*1.1;
    ELSIF t_deptno =20 THEN
        newsal := t_sal*1.08;
    ELSE
        newsal := t_sal*1.05;
    END IF;
END;
```

The keywords CREATE [OR REPLACE] PROCEDURE ... [AS|IS] replace the DECLARE label that is normally found at the beginning of a PL/SQL code block. In this case, the DECLARE is implied and the declarations follow the procedure header

The following example shows the output from a PL/SQL block, executed from SQL*Plus, which demonstrates how the give_raise procedure can be called. In the first call to give_raise, a string literal is used to pass the employee name to the procedure. In the second call, the employee name is assigned to a variable, and that variable is then passed as a parameter to give_raise:

```
SQL> SET SERVEROUTPUT ON
SQL> DECLARE
  2      emp_name emp.ename%type;
  3      new_salary NUMBER;
  4  BEGIN
  5      give_raise('KING', new_salary);
  6      DBMS_OUTPUT.PUT_LINE('King''s new salary is ' ||
  7                          TO_CHAR(new_salary,'$999,999.99'));
  8
  9      emp_name:='SCOTT';
 10      give_raise(emp_name, new_salary);
 11      DBMS_OUTPUT.PUT_LINE('Scott''s new salary is ' ||
 12                          TO_CHAR(new_salary,'$999,999.99'));
 13  END;
 14  /
King's new salary is     $5,500.00
Scott's new salary is    $3,240.00

PL/SQL procedure successfully completed.
```

ALTER PROCEDURE

`ALTER PROCEDURE [schema.]procedure_name COMPILE [DEBUG]`

Recompiles a procedure already stored in the Oracle database.

Keywords

schema

> The name of the schema containing the procedure. If omitted, the current schema is assumed.

procedure_name

> The name of the existing procedure to be recompiled.

COMPILE

> Causes the procedure to be recompiled.

DEBUG

> Causes the PL/SQL compiler to generate debugging code for use by the PL/SQL debugger.

 This command first causes the recompilation of all objects upon which the procedure is dependent. If any of those objects are invalid, the procedure being recompiled will also be marked invalid.

Example

The following example explicitly recompiles the procedure called give_raise in schema scott:

```
ALTER PROCEDURE scott.give_raise COMPILE
```

DROP PROCEDURE

`DROP PROCEDURE [schema.]procedure_name`

Removes a procedure from the database.

Keywords

schema

> The name of the schema containing the procedure to be dropped. If omitted, the current schema is assumed.

procedure_name

> Specifies the name of the procedure to be dropped.

Example

The following example removes the procedure give_raise from the database:

```
DROP PROCEDURE give_raise
```

In this case, since the schema name was not explicitly specified in the DROP PRO-CEDURE command, you need to log in as the procedure owner for the procedure to be dropped.

Functions

PL/SQL functions are similar to functions in many other languages. Like PL/SQL procedures, PL/SQL functions are created and maintained with SQL DDL statements, which are listed in this section. As I mentioned previously, a function is very much like a procedure: it can have arguments that are passed to the function as well as arguments that can be passed back from the function (and arguments that can do both); it is built as one or more blocks of PL/SQL code with the same structure as other PL/SQL blocks, and can be stored in the database. There is, however, one crucial distinction: a PL/SQL function returns a single value and therefore is used as part of a PL/SQL expression.

PL/SQL functions are created and maintained using the SQL DDL statements CRE-ATE FUNCTION, ALTER FUNCTION, and DROP FUNCTION.

CREATE FUNCTION

```
CREATE [OR REPLACE] FUNCTION [schema.]function_name
[(argument [IN | OUT | IN OUT] [NOCOPY] datatype
[,argument [IN | OUT | IN OUT] [NOCOPY] datatype..])]
RETURN datatype
[AUTHID {CURRENT_USER | DEFINER}]
[DETERMINISTIC]
[PARALLEL_ENABLE]
{IS|AS} {plsql_code |
  LANGUAGE {JAVA NAME 'string` |
            C [NAME name] LIBRARY libname [WITH CONTEXT] [PARAMETERS parms}}
```

Creates a stored function.

Keywords

OR REPLACE

Specifies that an existing stored function be replaced.

schema

The name of the schema to contain the function. If omitted, the current user's schema is assumed.

function_name

The name for the function being created.

argument

The name of an argument to the function.

IN

Specifies that the argument is an input that must be supplied when the function is called; this is the default argument type.

OUT

Specifies that the argument is an output that will be set by the function prior to its return.

IN OUT

Specifies that the argument is both an input and an output. A value can be supplied when the function is called, and the function may in turn change that value prior to returning.

NOCOPY

Specifies that the argument be passed by reference rather than by value. Passing an argument by value requires that a copy be made. Passing an argument by reference requires only that a memory address be passed, thereby providing significantly enhanced performance. This keyword affects OUT and IN OUT arguments, and it is the default for IN arguments.

datatype

The argument's datatype, which can be any datatype supported by PL/SQL.

RETURN datatype

Specifies the datatype of the value returned by the function.

AUTHID

Specifies under whose privileges the function will execute.

CURRENT_USER

Specifies that the current user's privileges and schema will be used when executing the function.

DEFINER

Specifies that the privileges and schema of the function's owner will be used when executing the function; this is the default behavior.

DETERMINISTIC

Tells the Oracle optimizer that the function will always return the same result for any given input. The query optimizer can then use this information to avoid redundant calls to the function. Do not use DETERMINISTIC if there are any factors other than the input parameters that can affect the function's result.

PARALLEL_ENABLE

Specifies that the query optimizer may execute this function in parallel as part of a parallel query operation. Only specify PARALLEL_ENABLE if the function does not use any package variables or other session-specific information.

plsql_code

The PL/SQL code to implement the function.

LANGUAGE

Specifies that the function is mapped to a Java or C method.

JAVA NAME

Specifies that the function is mapped to a Java method.

string

Specifies the Java implementation of the method.

C [NAME]

Specifies that the function is mapped to a C method.

name

Specifies the name of the C routine.

libname

Specifies the name of the library containing the C routine.

WITH CONTEXT

Specifies that a context pointer be passed to the C routine.

parms

Specifies the parameter(s) to be passed to the C routine.

As with stored procedures, if you are creating a function from SQL*Plus and that function does not compile correctly, you can use the SQL*Plus SHOW ERRORS command to see the specific error messages.

Examples

The CREATE FUNCTION statement in the following example creates a function to return the salary of an employee from the scott user's emp table. The employee number is used to identify the employee, and it is passed to the function as an argument:

```
CREATE FUNCTION get_sal
(emp_num IN NUMBER)
RETURN NUMBER
IS
  emp_sal NUMBER (8,2);
```

```
BEGIN
  SELECT sal
  INTO emp_sal
  FROM scott.emp
  WHERE emp_num = empno;
  RETURN emp_sal;
END;
```

After creating the get_sal function, you can use the following code to get the salary for a specific employee:

```
SQL> select get_sal(7788) from dual;

GET_SAL(7788)
-------------
         3000
```

In the scott demo schema, employee number 7788 is named SCOTT. His salary, as you can see from this example, is $3000.

ALTER FUNCTION

ALTER FUNCTION [*schema.*]*function_name* COMPILE [DEBUG]

Recompiles a stored function.

Keywords

schema
> The name of the schema containing the function. If omitted, the current user's schema is assumed.

function_name
> The name of the function to be recompiled.

COMPILE
> Causes the function to be recompiled.

DEBUG
> Causes the compiler to insert debug code for use by the PL/SQL debugger.

Example

The following example shows how to use ALTER FUNCTION to recompile the function get_sal:

```
ALTER FUNCTION get_sal COMPILE
```

DROP FUNCTION

DROP FUNCTION [*schema.*]*function_name*

Removes a function from the database.

Keywords

schema

> The name of the schema containing the function to be dropped. If omitted, the current user's schema is assumed.

function_name

> The name of the function to be dropped.

Example

Use the following statement to drop the function get_sal:

```
DROP FUNCTION get_sal
```

Packages

It's often desirable to create a number of related PL/SQL procedures and functions and to maintain and store them together. PL/SQL packages are designed to do just that. A PL/SQL package is a collection of related functions, procedures, and variables that are created together with a single set of commands, and are stored together within the database.

A package may contain functions, procedures, variables, types, and cursors. In general, anything that can appear in the DECLARE section of a PL/SQL program can be included in a package.

One benefit of using packages is that they give you a mechanism for implementing global PL/SQL variables. Packages maintain their state throughout a database session, so once you set a package variable to a value, that value becomes accessible to code in any other PL/SQL block executed as part of the same session. In essence, package variables can function as global variables.

Unlike functions and procedures, which can be created with a single CREATE statement, packages are created in two distinct steps:

1. Create the package specification, sometimes referred to as the package header.

2. Create the package body.

The package specification can be considered a "table of contents" for a package. It contains information about the package, such as procedure and function declarations, but it does not contain any actual PL/SQL code.

The package body contains all the PL/SQL code used to implement the functions and procedures that are declared in the package specification. Note that this code includes the specifications for the functions and/or procedures (i.e., name, parameters, and parameter modes), even though these specifications have already been included in the package specification. Furthermore, these specifications must be the same in both the package specification and the package body.

PL/SQL packages are created and maintained using the SQL DDL statements CREATE PACKAGE, CREATE PACKAGE BODY, ALTER PACKAGE, and DROP PACKAGE.

CREATE PACKAGE

```
CREATE [OR REPLACE] PACKAGE [schema.]package_name
[AUTHID {CURRENT_USER | DEFINER}]
{IS | AS} plsql_package_spec
```

Creates a PL/SQL package specification.

Keywords

OR REPLACE

Specifies that an existing package specification be replaced.

schema

The name of the schema containing this package. If omitted, the current user's schema is assumed.

package_name

The name of the package to be created.

AUTHID

Specifies under whose privileges the functions and procedures in the package will execute.

CURRENT_USER

Specifies that the privileges and schema of the current user will be used when executing the functions and procedures in this package.

DEFINER

Specifies that the privileges and schema of the package owner will be used when executing the functions and procedures in this package; this specification is the default behavior.

plsql_package_spec

The PL/SQL package specifications, which may include procedure and function specifications, variable declarations, cursor declarations, and type declarations.

The SQL*Plus SHOW ERRORS command can be used to display details about compilation errors that occur when creating a package specification.

Examples

The following example creates a package specification for a package named emp_ pkg in the scott user's schema:

```
CREATE OR REPLACE PACKAGE scott.emp_pkg AS
    FUNCTION emp_sal (empnum IN NUMBER) RETURN NUMBER;
    PROCEDURE update_sal (empnum IN NUMBER, pct_increase IN NUMBER,
                          update_count OUT NUMBER);
    PROCEDURE add_bonus (empnum IN NUMBER, bonus_amt IN NUMBER);
END emp_pkg;
```

CREATE PACKAGE BODY

```
CREATE [OR REPLACE] PACKAGE BODY [schema.]package_name
{IS | AS}
plsql_declaration [plsql_declaration ...]
[BEGIN
  pl/sql_initialization_code]
END [package_name];
```

Creates a PL/SQL package body.

Keywords

OR REPLACE

Specifies that an existing package body should be replaced.

schema

The name of the schema to contain the package. If omitted, the current schema is assumed.

package_name

The name of the package whose body you are creating.

plsql_declaration

A PL/SQL declaration, which may be a procedure, function, variable, type, or cursor.

plsql_initialization_code

A block of PL/SQL code that will be executed when the package is first loaded into memory by an Oracle session.

The package specification should already exist before a package body can be created; otherwise, Oracle will issue a warning message.

Examples

The following example shows a CREATE PACKAGE BODY statement that creates a body for the emp_pkg package in the scott user's schema:

```
CREATE OR REPLACE PACKAGE BODY scott.emp_pkg AS
--Declare package-level variables
update_count NUMBER;

FUNCTION emp_sal (empnum IN NUMBER)
RETURN NUMBER IS
   emp_sal NUMBER (8,2);
BEGIN
  SELECT sal
  INTO emp_sal
  FROM scott.emp
  WHERE empnum = empno;
  RETURN emp_sal;
END;

PROCEDURE update_sal
(empnum IN NUMBER, pct_increase IN NUMBER, update_count OUT NUMBER)
IS
BEGIN
  UPDATE scott.emp
  SET sal = sal+ sal*pct_increase
  WHERE empnum = empno;
  update_count := update_count + 1;
END;

PROCEDURE add_bonus (empnum IN NUMBER, bonus_amt IN NUMBER) is
BEGIN
  UPDATE scott.emp
  SET comm = comm + bonus_amt
  WHERE empnum = empno;
  update_count := update_count + 1;
END;
BEGIN
  --Here is the package initialization code.
  update_count := 0;
END emp_pkg;
```

This CREATE PACKAGE BODY statement corresponds to the CRE-ATE PACKAGE statement shown in the previous section. Each function or procedure defined in the CREATE PACKAGE statement was also defined here in the CREATE PACKAGE BODY statement. Also note that those declarations are identical, down to the function parameter names and types. Those items must be identical. If you provide different names for a parameter in the specification and the body of a function, PL/SQL won't recognize the two as a match.

ALTER PACKAGE

```
ALTER PACKAGE [schema.]package_name
COMPILE [DEBUG] [PACKAGE | SPECIFICATION | BODY]
```

Recompiles a stored package specification, body, or both.

Keywords

schema

The name of the schema containing the package. If omitted, the current schema is assumed.

package_name

The name of the package to be recompiled.

COMPILE

Causes the package to be recompiled.

DEBUG

Causes the PL/SQL compiler to create debug information for use with the PL/SQL debugger.

PACKAGE

Specifies that both the package specification and the package body be recompiled; this is the default behavior.

SPECIFICATION

Specifies that only the package specification be recompiled.

BODY

Specifies that only the package body be recompiled.

Examples

The following statement explicitly recompiles the specification and the body of the emp_pkg package in the scott user's schema:

```
ALTER PACKAGE scott.emp_pkg COMPILE PACKAGE
```

The following statement recompiles only the body for the package:

```
ALTER PACKAGE emp_pkg COMPILE BODY
```

DROP PACKAGE

```
DROP PACKAGE [BODY][schema.]package_name
```

Removes a package from the database.

Keywords

schema
> The name of the schema containing the package to be dropped. If omitted, the current schema is assumed.

package_name
> The name of the package to be dropped.

BODY
> Specifies that only the package body, and not the specification, be dropped.

 If DROP PACKAGE is used without the BODY qualifier, both the package specification and the package body will be dropped.

Examples

The following statement drops both the package specification and the package body for the package named emp_pkg:

```
DROP PACKAGE emp_pkg
```

The following statement drops only the emp_pkg package body:

```
DROP PACKAGE BODY emp_pkg
```

Triggers

A *trigger* represents a special type of PL/SQL block that you can tie to an event. When a trigger is executed by the Oracle database, it is said to "fire." The most commonly used types of triggers are Data Manipulation Language (DML) triggers that fire in response to INSERT, UPDATE, and DELETE statements. There are 15 different DML trigger types, listed in Table 7-9.

Table 7-9. Oracle's DML Trigger Types

Trigger Event	Triggered for Each	Description
BEFORE INSERT	Statement	Executes code before an INSERT statement is executed on the target table
BEFORE INSERT	Row	Executes code before each row is INSERTed into the target table
AFTER INSERT	Statement	Executes code after an INSERT statement is executed on the target table
AFTER INSERT	Row	Executes code after each row is INSERTed into the target table
INSTEAD OF INSERT	Row	Executes code instead of the INSERT for each row on which an INSERT is attempted
BEFORE UPDATE	Statement	Executes code before an UPDATE statement is executed on the target table
BEFORE UPDATE	Row	Executes code before each row of the target table is UPDATEd
AFTER UPDATE	Statement	Executes code after an UPDATE statement is executed on the target table
AFTER UPDATE	Row	Executes code after each row of the target table is UPDATEd
INSTEAD OF UPDATE	Row	Executes code instead of the UPDATE statement for each row for which an UPDATE is attempted
BEFORE DELETE	Statement	Executes code before a DELETE statement is executed on the target table
BEFORE DELETE	Row	Executes code before a row is DELETEd from the target table
AFTER DELETE	Statement	Executes code after a DELETE statement is executed on the target table
AFTER DELETE	Row	Executes code after a row is DELETEd from the target table
INSTEAD OF DELETE	Row	Executes code instead of the DELETE statement for each row for which a DELETE is attempted

 Along with the DML triggers described in Table 7-9, Oracle8*i* introduced triggers on database events that allow you to run code automatically on instance startup, instance shutdown, and when users connect. Each of these new trigger categories represents a large subject in its own right. In this book, I focus only on the DML triggers, the triggers that SQL programmers are most likely to encounter. For information on database triggers, see *Oracle PL/SQL Programming Guide to Oracle8i Features* (O'Reilly & Associates, 1999) by Steven Feuerstein.

A trigger can include any legal PL/SQL statement(s) with the following exceptions:

- A trigger may not issue a COMMIT, ROLLBACK, or SAVEPOINT statement, and may not call any function or procedure that issues one of these statements.

- A trigger may not declare a LONG or LONG RAW variable.

- A trigger may not perform DML operations on the table for which it is defined.

The following sections show the SQL syntax for the DDL statements used to work with triggers.

Triggers are created and maintained using the SQL DDL statements CREATE TRIGGER, ALTER TRIGGER, and DROP TRIGGER.

CREATE TRIGGER

```
CREATE [OR REPLACE]  TRIGGER [triggerschema.]triggername
{BEFORE | AFTER | INSTEAD OF}
{INSERT | DELETE | UPDATE [OF column[,column ...]]}
[OR {INSERT | DELETE | UPDATE [OF column[,column …]]}…]
ON [tableschema.]{tablename | viewname}
   [REFERENCING [OLD [AS] old ] [NEW [AS] new]]
   [FOR EACH ROW [WHEN condition]]
   plsql_block
```

Creates a trigger, a stored PL/SQL block associated with a table or view, which is automatically executed in response to a particular SQL statement or set of statements.

Keywords

triggerschema
> The name of the schema to contain the trigger. If omitted, the current schema is assumed.

triggername
> The name of the trigger to be created.

BEFORE
> Specifies that the trigger is to be fired before executing the triggering statement.

AFTER
> Specifies that the trigger is to be fired after executing the triggering statement.

INSTEAD OF
> Specifies that the code associated with this trigger, instead of the event that originally fired the trigger, is to be executed.

INSERT
> Specifies that the trigger is to be fired when an INSERT statement adds a row to the table.

DELETE

> Specifies that the trigger is to be fired when a DELETE statement removes a row from the table.

UPDATE OF

> Specifies that the trigger is to be fired when an UPDATE statement changes the value in one of the columns specified in the OF clause. If the OF clause is omitted, an UPDATE to any column will cause the trigger to fire.

ON

> Introduces the clause that specifies the name of the table on which the trigger is to be created.

tableschema

> The name of the schema containing the table on which the trigger is to be defined. This name defaults to the current user's schema.

tablename

> The name of the table on which the trigger is defined. This table must exist within the specified schema.

viewname

> The name of the view on which the trigger is defined. This view must exist within the specified schema.

REFERENCING

> Specifies correlation names. This specification allows code in the PL/SQL block to refer to old and new values from the rows affected by DML statements that cause the trigger to fire. The default values are OLD and NEW.

FOR EACH ROW

> Specifies that this trigger is to be a row trigger, which is fired once for each row that is affected by the triggering mechanism and that meets the conditions specified in the WHEN clause. If FOR EACH ROW is omitted, the trigger will be fired once for each execution of the triggering statement.

WHEN

> Specifies a SQL condition that must be true in order for the trigger to fire.

plsql_block

> The PL/SQL block that will be executed when the trigger fires. This block may not contain COMMIT, ROLLBACK, or SAVEPOINT statements.

Example

The statements in the following example create an audit table named track_sal_ changes and a trigger on the scott user's emp table. The trigger fires in response to INSERT statements and in response to UPDATE statements that result in salary changes. The trigger then logs the old salary value to the audit table:

```
CREATE TABLE track_sal_changes (
    empno NUMBER,
    sal NUMBER)
/
CREATE OR REPLACE TRIGGER scott.empaud
    BEFORE INSERT OR UPDATE OF sal
    ON scott.emp
    FOR EACH ROW WHEN (
        (new.sal <> old.sal)
        OR ((new.sal IS NOT NULL) AND (old.sal IS NULL)))

    BEGIN
    /* Write the record */
        INSERT INTO track_sal_changes
        VALUES (:new.empno, :old.sal);
    END;
```

ALTER TRIGGER

```
ALTER TRIGGER [schema.]triggername {ENABLE | DISABLE}
```

Enables or disables a database trigger.

Keywords

schema

> The name of the schema containing the trigger. If omitted, the current schema is assumed.

triggername

> Specifies the name of the trigger to alter.

ENABLE

> Specifies that this trigger is to be fired when a triggering statement is issued.

DISABLE

> Specifies that this trigger is not to be fired when a triggering statement is issued.

 Unlike other ALTER commands, the ALTER TRIGGER statement does not change the definition or structure of a trigger; this change must be done with a CREATE OR REPLACE TRIGGER statement. A trigger is automatically enabled when it is created. The ENABLE ALL TRIGGERS and DISABLE ALL TRIGGERS clauses of the ALTER TABLE statement may also perform this function.

Example

The following statement disables the scott user's empaud trigger:

```
ALTER TRIGGER scott.empaud DISABLE
```

DROP TRIGGER

```
DROP TRIGGER [schema.]trigger_name
```

Removes a trigger from the database.

Keywords

schema

> The name of the schema containing the trigger to be dropped. If omitted, the current schema is assumed.

triggername

> Specifies the name of the trigger to be dropped.

Example

The following statement removes the empaud trigger from the database:

```
DROP TRIGGER empaud
```

8

SQL Statement Tuning

If you work with Oracle, it won't be long before you are confronted with the need to tune SQL statements. You will write a "simple" query that ends up with a projected run time of about a week. You wrote it, so you should be able to fix it. Or someone will write a query that takes too long to execute. You will be seen as the source of all Oracle knowledge (after all, you did get that week-long query to run in under a minute!), and, consequently, you will be handed the job of making that query run faster. Tuning SQL statements goes hand-in-hand with writing SQL statements.

You need to understand Oracle's approach to executing a SQL statement before you will be able to tune it effectively. Then you have to determine whether there is a better approach. Finally, assuming there is a better approach, you need to get Oracle to use it. To help you do these things, Oracle has built the following features into its software:

EXPLAIN PLAN statement
> You can use this statement to determine Oracle's execution plan for a SQL statement.

SQL Trace facility
> Not only gets you the execution plan, but also collects vital statistics related to a statement's execution.

SQL*Plus SET AUTOTRACE command
> Causes SQL*Plus to automatically display the query plan and execution statistics for statements as you execute them.

SQL*Plus TIMING command
> Allows you to measure elapsed execution time.

Optimizer hints

Allow you to tell Oracle how you want it to execute a particular query.

Tuning often centers on SELECT statements, and those statements are the basis for all the examples in this chapter. Note, though, that INSERT, DELETE, and UPDATE statements may be tuned in the same manner as SELECT statements.

Using EXPLAIN PLAN

When faced with the task of making a slow SQL statement run faster, you first need to find out how Oracle is currently executing that statement. Whenever you execute a statement, a part of Oracle known as the *optimizer* constructs a list of steps that will be used to execute the statement. This list of steps is referred to as an *execution plan*. For example, if you select data from a table to print a report, one possible execution plan is to read all the rows in a table. Most execution plans are a bit more complex than that, and involve such tasks as reading indexes, joining tables, and sorting data.

 Oracle includes two optimizers—one rule-based, the other cost-based. The rule-based optimizer is old, and Oracle discourages its use. The cost-based optimizer makes decisions based on statistics collected by the ANALYZE statement. The OPTIMIZER_MODE initialization parameter controls the default optimizer choice for an instance. You can override it at the session level using the ALTER SESSION statement, and at the statement level using hints.

You can discover the execution plan Oracle is going to use for a SQL statement by using Oracle's EXPLAIN PLAN statement. That statement is prepended to the statement you are interested in tuning. For example:

```
EXPLAIN PLAN
  SET STATEMENT_ID = 'emp_report'
  FOR
  SELECT empno, ename
  FROM emp
  ORDER BY hiredate;
```

When you use EXPLAIN PLAN, Oracle doesn't display its execution strategy on the screen; instead, it inserts rows into a table. This table is referred to as the *plan table*, and you must query it properly to see the results. Of course, the plan table must exist too, so if you've never used EXPLAIN PLAN before, you may need to create the plan table first.

Creating the Plan Table

Oracle provides a script to create the plan table. The script is named *utlxplan.sql*, and on Linux or Unix systems, it resides in your *$ORACLE_HOME/rdbms/admin* directory. On a Windows system, the directory will be something like *E:\ORACLE\ ORA81\RDBMS\ADMIN* or *C:\ORANT\RDBMS80\ADMIN*. You can run the script from SQL*Plus, as shown in this example:

```
SQL> @$ORACLE_HOME/rdbms/admin/utlxplan.sql

Table created.
```

The resulting plan table will look like this:

```
SQL> DESCRIBE plan_table
 Name                                       Null?     Type
 ------------------------------------------ --------  ------------------------
 STATEMENT_ID                                         VARCHAR2(30)
 TIMESTAMP                                            DATE
 REMARKS                                              VARCHAR2(80)
 OPERATION                                            VARCHAR2(30)
 OPTIONS                                              VARCHAR2(30)
 OBJECT_NODE                                          VARCHAR2(128)
 OBJECT_OWNER                                         VARCHAR2(30)
 OBJECT_NAME                                          VARCHAR2(30)
 OBJECT_INSTANCE                                      NUMBER(38)
 OBJECT_TYPE                                          VARCHAR2(30)
 OPTIMIZER                                            VARCHAR2(255)
 SEARCH_COLUMNS                                       NUMBER
 ID                                                   NUMBER(38)
 PARENT_ID                                            NUMBER(38)
 POSITION                                             NUMBER(38)
 COST                                                 NUMBER(38)
 CARDINALITY                                          NUMBER(38)
 BYTES                                                NUMBER(38)
 OTHER_TAG                                            VARCHAR2(255)
 PARTITION_START                                      VARCHAR2(255)
 PARTITION_STOP                                       VARCHAR2(255)
 PARTITION_ID                                         NUMBER(38)
 OTHER                                                LONG
 DISTRIBUTION                                         VARCHAR2(30)
```

The name of the table does not have to be plan_table, but that's the default and it's usually easiest to leave it that way. If you don't have access to the *utlxplan.sql* script, you can create the table manually. Just be sure that the column names and datatypes match those shown here.

The question sometimes comes up regarding the number of plan tables you should have in any given database. In theory, you could create just one plan table, grant all your users access to it, and have everyone share it. In practice, it's usually easiest to let each user create his own plan tables.

The columns in the plan table change somewhat from one release of Oracle to the next. Often, this change is made to support new features that have been added. The three partition-related columns, for example, were added when partitioning was introduced in Oracle8. If you have an old plan table that's been around for a while, you may want to drop and recreate it to ensure that you have the latest version.

Explaining a Query

Once you have a plan table, you are ready to use the EXPLAIN PLAN statement. There are three things that you need to do in order to explain a plan:

1. Decide on a statement ID for the statement that you are explaining. This ID may be any character string up to 30 characters in length.
2. Delete any existing plan table records with the same statement ID.
3. Execute the EXPLAIN PLAN statement.

When you execute the EXPLAIN PLAN statement, Oracle inserts several records into the plan table to describe the execution plan for the statement being explained. The plan table may hold execution plans for many statements at one time. The statement ID that you supply identifies the records for a given statement and differentiates them from records for other statements. Use of a statement ID is optional, but encouraged.

The EXPLAIN PLAN statement does not clear existing records from the plan table. If you are explaining a statement for a second time, plan table records from the first time will remain in the table. If you use the same statement ID both times, you'll get unusable results. These results often appear to repeat the same step, or sequence of steps, several times. To be safe, delete existing records with the statement ID you are about to use.

The syntax is for EXPLAIN PLAN is very simple. Just put the keywords EXPLAIN PLAN, plus a few clauses, in front of the SQL statement of interest. The complete syntax looks like this:

```
EXPLAIN PLAN
    SET STATEMENT_ID = 'text'
    [INTO [schema.]tablename[@dblink]]
    FOR SQL_statement
```

For a complete description of the EXPLAIN PLAN syntax, refer to Chapter 3, *Data Manipulation and Control Statements.*

The following example demonstrates how EXPLAIN PLAN is used. The SELECT statement being explained runs against tables in the scott schema, and produces a list of employees, their departments, and their salary grades. The results are sorted highest salary first. Notice that a DELETE is used first to clear out old records with the statement ID we are about to use:

```
SQL> DELETE
  2  FROM PLAN_TABLE
  3  WHERE statement_id = 'emp_report';

8 rows deleted.

SQL>
SQL> EXPLAIN PLAN
  2  SET STATEMENT_ID = 'emp_report'
  3  FOR
  4  SELECT e.empno, e.ename, d.dname, e.sal, sg.grade
  5  FROM emp e, dept d, salgrade sg
  6  WHERE e.deptno = d.deptno
  7  AND e.sal > sg.losal
  8  AND e.sal < sg.hisal
  9  ORDER BY sal DESC;

Explained.
```

Other than seeing the word "Explained," you won't see any output when you execute this EXPLAIN PLAN statement because Oracle stores the query plan in the plan table. Retrieving and interpreting the results is your next task.

Viewing the Execution Plan

Execution plans are hierarchical in nature. That is, the task of executing a query is one large step, which can be broken down into one or more smaller steps. Each of those steps might then be broken down further into even smaller steps. This division continues until the bottom is reached. To look at such an execution plan, you need to execute a hierarchical query such as the one shown here:

```
SELECT LPAD(' ', 2*(level-1)) ||
       operation || ' ' || options
       || ' ' || object_name || ' ' ||
       DECODE(id, 0, 'Cost = ' || position)
       "Query Plan"
FROM plan_table
START WITH id = 0 AND statement_id
```

```
              = 'statement_id'
CONNECT BY PRIOR id = parent_id
       AND statement_id = 'statement_id';
```

 The START WITH and CONNECT BY clauses in this query are used to organize the results in a hierarchy. The ID and PARENT_ID fields in the plan table determine that hierarchy; each step is indented underneath its parent. The LPAD expression in the query's select list is used to indent the results to reflect the hierarchy. Each plan table record contains an ID and a PARENT_ID column. The results of each step are fed as input into the parent step, which is identified by the PARENT_ID.

If this query is used to view the plan for the emp_report statement that was explained in the previous section, the following results will be displayed:

```
Query Plan
-------------------------------------
SELECT STATEMENT    Cost = 9
  SORT ORDER BY
    HASH JOIN
      MERGE JOIN CARTESIAN
        TABLE ACCESS FULL DEPT
        SORT JOIN
          TABLE ACCESS FULL SALGRADE
      TABLE ACCESS FULL EMP
```

The step that is indented the most is executed first. In this example, the first step is a full table scan of the salgrade table. The results from this step are then fed as input into the parent step. Table 8-1 explains each step of this plan in detail. The different possible plan operations are explained in Table 8-2.

Table 8-1. The emp_report Execution Plan Explained

Execution Plan Step	Explanation
SORT JOIN TABLE ACCESS FULL SALGRADE	The SORT JOIN operation sorts a rowset to prepare for a merge join. In this case, the rowset consists of all rows in the SALGRADE table.

MERGE JOIN CARTESIAN
  TABLE ACCESS FULL DEPT
  SORT JOIN
    TABLE ACCESS FULL SALGRADE
	The Cartesian product of the DEPT and SALGRADE tables is the result of this step. Oracle reads the entire DEPT table, combines that rowset with the results of the previous SORT JOIN operation, and produces a rowset consisting of all possible combinations of DEPT and SALGRADE rows.

HASH JOIN
  MERGE JOIN CARTESIAN
  . . .
  TABLE ACCESS FULL EMP
	The results of the merge join are then joined with the EMP table. This time, Oracle uses a hashing algorithm to join the two rowsets. Many rows from the Cartesian product will be eliminated in this operation because only a few relate to an EMP record.

Table 8-1. The emp_report Execution Plan Explained (continued)

Execution Plan Step	Explanation

SORT ORDER BY
  HASH JOIN
   ...
	The results of the hash join are fed into a sort operation. This sort orders the result set according to the ORDER BY clause specified in the query.

SELECT STATEMENT   Cost = 9
  SORT ORDER BY
   ...
	The results of the sort operation are fed back to the user or application as the results of the SELECT statement itself.

When two steps in an execution plan are indented by the same amount, it is not possible to know which will execute first. It really doesn't matter, because the end result is the same in terms of the resources used to execute the statement.

The cost for an execution plan comes from the POSITION field in the record with an ID value of 0. In this example, the cost was 9. Query cost should never be looked at as an absolute value. Query cost is always relative to other queries against the same database. A query with a cost of 9 requires half the I/O and CPU resources of a query with a cost of 18, but you won't know if that's half a minute or half an hour until you actually execute the query.

Query costs are estimated only when the cost-based optimizer is used. You also must have statistics on at least one of the tables involved in the query. If you have no statistics for your tables, Oracle will fall back on the rule-based optimizer, and won't compute a cost.

Keep your statistics up-to-date. Out-of-date statistics will result in an inaccurate cost. They may also result in Oracle's choosing a suboptimal execution plan.

Interpreting the Results

The execution plan returned by the query shown in the previous section includes three columns of information for each step:

OPERATION column

Identifies the major operation to be performed

OPTIONS column

Further qualifies how that operation is to be performed. There are several types of sorts, for example.

OBJECT_NAME column

Where applicable, identifies the object on which the operation will be performed. The object will usually be a table or index. If the OBJECT_NAME for an operation is blank, the object consists of one or more rowsets returned by the operation's children.

Table 8-2 describes the various operations and options you might see in an execution plan.

Table 8-2. EXPLAIN PLAN Operations

Operation	Options	Description
AND-EQUAL		This step will have two or more child steps, each of which returns a set of ROWIDs. The AND-EQUAL operation selects only the ROWIDs that are returned by all the child operations.
BITMAP	CONVERSION TO ROWIDS	Converts a bitmap from a bitmap index to a set of ROWIDs that can be used to retrieve the actual data.
	CONVERSION FROM ROWIDS	Converts a set of ROWIDs into a bitmapped representation.
	CONVERSION COUNT	Counts the number of rows represented by a bitmap.
	INDEX SINGLE VALUE	Retrieves the bitmap for a single key value. For example, if the field was a YES/NO field, and your query wanted only rows with a value of "YES", this operation would be used.
	INDEX RANGE SCAN	Similar to BITMAP INDEX SINGLE VALUE, but bitmaps are returned for a range of key values.
	INDEX FULL SCAN	Scans the entire bitmapped index.
	MERGE	Merges two bitmaps together and returns one bitmap as a result. This is an OR operation between two bitmaps. The resulting bitmap will select all rows from the first bitmap, plus all rows from the second bitmap.
	MINUS	This operation is the opposite of a MERGE, and may have two or three child operations that return bitmaps. The bitmap returned by the first child operation is used as a starting point. All rows represented by the second bitmap are subtracted from the first. If the column is nullable, all rows with NULL values are also subtracted.
	OR	Takes two bitmaps as input, ORs them together, and returns one bitmap as a result. The returned bitmap will select all rows from the first, plus all rows from the second.

Table 8-2. EXPLAIN PLAN Operations (continued)

Operation	Options	Description
CONNECT BY		Rows are retrieved hierarchically, because the query was written with a CONNECT BY clause.
CONCATENATION		Combines multiple sets of rows into one set, essentially a UNION ALL.
COUNT		Counts the number of rows that have been selected from a table.
	STOPKEY	The number of rows to be counted is limited by the use of ROWNUM in the query's WHERE clause.
FILTER		Takes a set of rows as input, and eliminates some of them based on a condition from the query's WHERE clause.
FIRST ROW		Retrieves only the first row of a query's result set.
FOR UPDATE		Locks retrieved rows. This operation would be the result of specifying FOR UPDATE in the original query.
HASH JOIN		Joins two tables using a hash join method.
INDEX	UNIQUE	The lookup of a unique value from an index. You would only see this value when the index (e.g., the index used to enforce a primary key or a unique key) is unique.
	RANGE SCAN	An index is being scanned for rows that fall into a range of values. The index is scanned in ascending order.
	RANGE SCAN DESCENDING	Same as RANGE SCAN, but the index is scanned in descending order.
INLIST ITERATOR		One or more operations are to be performed once for each value in an IN predicate.
INTERSECTION		Takes two rowsets as input, and returns only rows that appear in *both* sets.
MERGE JOIN		Joins two rowsets based on a common value. Both rowsets will first have been sorted by this value. This operation is an inner join.
	OUTER	Similar to a MERGE JOIN, but performs an outer join.
	ANTI	Indicates that an anti-join is being performed.
	SEMI	Indicates that a semi-join is being performed.
MINUS		This operation is the result of the MINUS operator. Two rowsets are taken as inputs. The resulting rowset contains all rows from the first input that do not appear in the second.

Table 8-2. EXPLAIN PLAN Operations (continued)

Operation	Options	Description
NESTED LOOPS		This operation has two children, each returning a rowset. For every row returned by the first child, the second child operation will be executed.
	OUTER	Represents a nested loop used to perform an outer join.
PARTITION		Executes an operation for one or more partitions. The PARTITION_START and PARTITION_STOP columns give the range of partitions over which the operation is performed.
	SINGLE	Indicates that the operation will be performed on a single partition.
	ITERATOR	Indicates that the operation will be performed on several partitions.
	ALL	Indicates that the operation will be performed on all partitions.
	INLIST	Indicates that the operation will be performed on the partitions, and is driven by an IN predicate.
PROJECTION		Takes multiple queries as input and returns a single set of records. This operation is used with INTERSECTION, MINUS, and UNION operations.
REMOTE		Indicates that a rowset is being returned from a remote database.
SEQUENCE		Indicates that an Oracle sequence is being accessed.
SORT	AGGREGATE	Applies a group function, such as COUNT, to a rowset, and returns only one row as the result.
	UNIQUE	Sorts a rowset and eliminates duplicates.
	GROUP BY	Sorts a rowset into groups. This operation is the result of a GROUP BY clause.
	JOIN	Sorts a rowset in preparation for a join. See MERGE JOIN.
	ORDER BY	Sorts a rowset according to the ORDER BY clause specified in the query.
TABLE ACCESS	FULL	Indicates that Oracle will read all rows in the specified table.
	CLUSTER	Indicates that Oracle will read all rows in a table that match a specified index cluster key.
	HASH	Indicates that Oracle will read all rows in a table that match a specified hash cluster key.

Table 8-2. EXPLAIN PLAN Operations (continued)

Operation	Options	Description
	BY ROWID	Indicates that Oracle will retrieve a row from a table based on its ROWID.
UNION		Takes two rowsets, eliminates duplicates, and returns the result as one set.
VIEW		Executes the query behind a view and returns the resulting rowset.

Once you understand the execution plan Oracle is using for a query, you can look for ways to improve the results. See the section "Improving Query Performance" later in this chapter.

Using Oracle's SQL Trace Facility

The information from EXPLAIN PLAN is useful, but it tells only half the story. Knowing the execution plan for a statement is one thing, but properly tuning a query requires correlating that execution plan with resource usage, and Oracle's built-in SQL Trace facility allows this action. Using SQL Trace, statistics can be generated showing the resources consumed by SQL statements that are executed. SQL Trace tracks the following information for each SQL statement that is executed:

- The number of executions
- The number of times the statement was parsed
- The number of rows returned
- The number of physical reads
- The number of logical reads
- The elapsed time spent executing the statement
- The CPU time spent executing the statement

This information is valuable for two reasons:

1. It allows you to identify those statements consuming the most resources. Those statements are the ones you need to tune.

2. It provides concrete data by which you can measure your tuning efforts. You can see the effect that a changed execution plan has on physical I/O counts and CPU time immediately.

From a high level, the process of using SQL Trace looks like this:

1. Set key initialization file parameters, notably TIMED_STATISTICS.

2. Enable tracing for the database session.

3. Run the SQL statements that are being tuned.

4. Disable tracing for the session.

5. Find the trace files.

6. Format the trace file using the tkprof utility.

7. Review the tkprof output.

You can iterate these steps as often as necessary, making changes as you go, until acceptable performance is achieved.

 SQL Trace is not a program in itself. It's a capability built into the Oracle server software. The files generated by SQL Trace are not very readable, so Oracle provides the tkprof utility to format them. The tkprof utility summarizes the trace information and presents it in a useful format.

Parameters to Set

Before running SQL Trace, there are three initialization parameters that need to be checked:

    TIMED_STATISTICS
    MAX_DUMP_FILE_SIZE
    USER_DUMP_DEST

TIMED_STATISTICS

The TIMED_STATISTICS parameter needs to be TRUE for SQL Trace to be able to collect any timing information about the statements you're executing. You can set this parameter in your instance parameter *INIT.ORA* file, or you can set it using either the ALTER SYSTEM or ALTER SESSION statements. For example:

```
ALTER SYSTEM SET TIMED_STATISTICS = TRUE;
ALTER SESSION SET TIMED_STATISTICS = TRUE;
```

If you're attempting to trace a session created by a program that connects to the database, you'll have difficulty enabling timed statistics at the session level. You would need to modify your program to issue the necessary ALTER SESSION statement. If you can't do that, your only option is to enable timed statistics at the instance level using the ALTER SYSTEM statement. The overhead for collecting timed statistics is minimal, so there's no need to spend a lot of time worrying about the issue. Enable them for the instance, if that's what it takes.

MAX_DUMP_FILE_SIZE

The MAX_DUMP_FILE_SIZE parameter places a limit on the size of the trace files that Oracle generates. Trace files can become very large very quickly, especially if you are running a program that executes a large number of SQL statements in a short period of time. The size limit is specified as operating system blocks, and the default limit is operating system-specific. However, you can specify any limit using the MAX_DUMP_FILE_SIZE parameter. Here are some examples:

```
ALTER SYSTEM SET MAX_DUMP_FILE_SIZE = 100;
ALTER SESSION SET MAX_DUMP_FILE_SIZE = 100;
MAX_DUMP_FILE_SIZE = 100;
```

The first two statements set MAX_DUMP_FILE_SIZE at the instance and session levels, respectively. The third line shows how you would specify the limit in an instance parameter file. In all cases, the limit is set at 100 operating system blocks.

USER_DUMP_DEST

The USER_DUMP_DEST parameter controls where the trace files are written. It should point to a directory somewhere on your system. This parameter may only be modified at the instance level using the ALTER SYSTEM statement. You can't change it at the session level.

Enabling and Disabling SQL Trace

SQL Trace can be enabled for an entire instance or a single session. Enabling this capability for an instance is taking the shotgun approach: it targets everyone connected to that instance and it results in a lot of trace files. This is not usually a good approach.

The most useful approach is enabling SQL Trace for a specific session as follows:

1. Run a program that you want to test, and use it to establish a session.

2. Log in using SQL*Plus, and use the DBMS_SYSTEM built-in package to control the tracing of the statements executed by the tested program.

Enabling SQL Trace for an instance

To enable SQL Trace for an instance, place the following entry in the instance parameter file, then stop and restart the instance:

```
SQL_TRACE = TRUE
```

When tracing is enabled at the instance level, every session connected to the instance will generate a trace file. Trace information will be collected for each session until the size of a session's trace file exceeds the MAX_DUMP_FILE_SIZE.

When the trace file for a session hits the maximum size, tracing stops for that one session.

Enabling SQL Trace for your session

You can't issue an ALTER SYSTEM command to change the SQL_TRACE setting for the entire instance. However, you can use an ALTER SESSION statement to change it for a single session. For example:

```
ALTER SESSION SET SQL_TRACE=TRUE;
ALTER SESSION SET SQL_TRACE=FALSE;
```

Use this method if you want to collect trace information for SQL statements that you execute in your current session. For all SQL statements executed while SQL_TRACE=TRUE, trace information will be written to the session's trace file. When you finish tracing, simply issue an ALTER SESSION statement that sets SQL_TRACE to FALSE. Tracing will also stop if you hit the limit on trace file size.

Enabling SQL Trace for another session

The DBMS_SYSTEM built-in package contains a procedure named SET_SQL_TRACE_IN_SESSION that can be used to turn SQL tracing on and off for any session connected to the database. Use this approach to collect trace information for a session other than your own. The DBMS_SYSTEM.SET_SQL_TRACE_IN_SESSION procedure takes three parameters, and the formal definition looks like this:

```
DBMS_SYSTEM.SET_SQL_TRACE_IN_SESSION (sid IN NUMBER,
                                      serial# IN NUMBER,
                                      sql_trace IN BOOLEAN);
```

The V$SESSION view can be queried for a list of users, together with their sid and serial# values. Those values can then be used in a call to SQL_TRACE_IN_SESSION to enable and disable tracing for a specific user. In the following example, tracing is enabled and disabled for the user jeff:

```
SQL> SELECT username, sid, serial#
  2  FROM v$session;

USERNAME                        SID   SERIAL#
------------------------------ --------- ---------
...
JEFF                              8        31
SYS                              11        10

9 rows selected.

SQL> EXECUTE DBMS_SYSTEM.SET_SQL_TRACE_IN_SESSION(8,31,TRUE);

PL/SQL procedure successfully completed.
```

```
SQL> EXECUTE DBMS_SYSTEM.SET_SQL_TRACE_IN_SESSION(8,31,FALSE);

PL/SQL procedure successfully completed.
```

In this example, we query V$SESSION for a list of users. We find that jeff, the user we are interested in, has a sid of 8 and serial# of 31. These values are then used in two calls to DBMS_SYSTEM.SET_SQL_TRACE_IN_SESSION. The first call enables tracing. The second disables it again. Tracing will also stop if the trace file size limit is reached.

 Sometimes you'll have multiple sessions using the same username. If that's the case, you may have difficulty figuring out which is the session that you want to trace. One viable technique is to query V$SESSION, then start up the session you want to trace. Doing that usually involves running a program that connects to the database. Then query V$SESSION again. If you include the LOGON_TIME column with the second query, it's usually fairly easy to pick out the session that you just started.

Finding Trace Files

Finding trace files after they have been generated can be somewhat difficult. Trace files are all written to the USER_DUMP_DEST directory, but their names (e.g., *ora_ 815.trc*) are system-generated. When tracing a specific user session, a good way to find the associated trace file is to list all the files in the USER_DUMP_DEST directory and look at their timestamps. The timestamp will reflect the time when the file was last modified, which will correlate to the time tracing stopped. Remember that tracing can stop because the MAX_DUMP_FILE_SIZE was reached. If the maximum file size was reached, the timestamp will reflect when that occurred. Otherwise, the timestamp will reflect the time tracing was explicitly disabled, so keep close track of the time when you enable and disable tracing.

 On Linux and Unix systems, the number in the filename represents the ID number of the operating system process that created the file. Sometimes that number can be a useful aid in finding the correct file. Another method is to search the trace files for a specific SQL statement using a utility such as grep.

Formatting Trace Output with tkprof

Once the trace file is located, the tkprof utility can be used to summarize the trace data into a useful format. tkprof can sort the results so that queries are sorted based on the amount of CPU or I/O used. tkprof can also automatically execute an EXPLAIN PLAN statement for each SQL statement in the trace file.

The tkprof utility is command-line driven, which means that information is passed to it using command-line parameters. The syntax to use looks like this:

```
tkprof tracefile outputfile
       [EXPLAIN=username/password]
       [TABLE=[schema.]tablename]
       [PRINT=integer]
       [AGGREGATE={YES | NO}]
       [INSERT=filename]
       [SYS={YES | NO}]
       [RECORD={YES | NO}]
       [SORT=sort_options
```

Keywords

tracefile

    Is the name of a trace file.

outputfile

    Is the name of the file to which tkprof will write formatted trace output.

EXPLAIN

    Causes tkprof to generate an execution plan for each SQL statement in the trace file. It does this by connecting as the specified user and issuing an EXPLAIN PLAN statement. Typically, you should use the same username here that was used by the session creating the trace file in the first place. The tkprof utility will use a table named PROF$PLAN_TABLE to hold output from the EXPLAIN PLAN statement, and will create that table if necessary.

TABLE

    Allows you to specify the name of a plan table to use when executing EXPLAIN PLAN statements. The default name is plan_table, and the default schema is the one for the user specified by the EXPLAIN parameter. Use this parameter if you have multiple users executing tkprof simultaneously and using the same username for the EXPLAIN parameter. Use of tkprof by multiple users will conflict if all users try to use the same plan table.

PRINT

    Tells tkprof to generate output only for the first *integer* SQL statements in the trace file.

AGGREGATE

Controls whether or not tkprof summarizes the results from multiple executions of the same SQL statement. The default is YES. Thus, if you execute the same statement 1000 times, tkprof will summarize the statistics from all 1000 executions. If you set AGGREGATE=NO, each execution will be reported separately. It's usually more convenient to take the default and view the results in summary form.

INSERT

Causes tkprof to generate a file of INSERT statements that can later be used to save the trace information in a database table. The script file will also contain a CREATE TABLE statement to create the table referenced by the INSERT statements.

SYS

Indicates whether or not you want recursive SQL statements included in the output file. Recursive SQL statements are those that Oracle generates behind the scenes to parse or execute user-issued statements. To parse a SELECT statement, for example, Oracle might need to query the data dictionary. Those queries would be considered recursive SQL statements. The default is to include them.

RECORD

Causes tkprof to generate a SQL script consisting of all user-issued SQL statements found in the trace file. You can use this script later to replay the trace session. The script file will be named using the filename that you specify here. You may optionally include a path and an extension.

SORT

Causes tkprof to sort the output file according to the *sort_options* that you specify. Table 8-3 describes the available options. Specify multiple options by placing them in a comma-separated list.

A number of options are available when sorting tkprof output. Sorting is useful because it allows you to move the worst-performing statements to the top of the file, and it is not necessary to read the entire file to find the statements most in need of tuning. The sort options listed in Table 8-3 allow you to choose the performance metrics on which to sort.

Table 8-3. The tkprof Sort Options

Description/Phase	Parse	Execute	Fetch	Other
The number of times a statement was parsed, executed, or fetched	prscnt	execnt	fchcnt	N/A
CPU time spent parsing, executing, or fetching	prscpu	execpu	fchcpu	N/A

Table 8-3. The tkprof Sort Options (continued)

Description/Phase	Parse	Execute	Fetch	Other
Elapsed time spent parsing, executing, or fetching	prsela	exeela	fchela	N/A
Physical disk reads while parsing, executing, or fetching	prsdsk	exedsk	fchdsk	N/A
The number of buffers accessed for consistent read purposes while parsing, executing, or fetching	prsqry	exeqry	fchqry	N/A
The number of buffers accessed for a current read while parsing, executing, or fetching	prscu	execu	fchcu	N/A
The number of library cache misses while parsing or executing	prsmis	exemis	N/A	N/A
The total number of rows fetched	N/A	N/A	fchrow	N/A
The userid of the user who parsed the statement	N/A	N/A	N/A	userid

tkprof Example

The following command was issued from a Unix environment:

```
$ tkprof ora_718.trc ora_718.lst SORT=execpu EXPLAIN=scott/tiger

TKPROF: Release 8.1.5.0.2 - Production on Tue Mar 14 17:46:22 2000

(c) Copyright 1999 Oracle Corporation.  All rights reserved.
$
```

This command reads from a trace file named *ora_718.trc* and writes formatted output to a file named *ora_718.lst*. The trace file results are sorted by execution CPU time; statements consuming the most CPU during execution will be listed first. The EXPLAIN parameter causes tkprof to execute an EXPLAIN PLAN on each statement it encounters. To do this, tkprof will log in to the database as the user named scott.

There is one important caveat when using the tkprof EXPLAIN parameter to generate execution plans for the statements in a trace file. The execution statistics in a trace file are gathered while the statements are executing, but the execution plan that tkprof generates is generated when the tkprof utility is run. Things could change between the time you trace and format the results, and the execution plan generated by tkprof may not be the plan that was used when the statement was actually executed. To guard against this problem, run tkprof as soon as possible after a trace file is generated. Also avoid creating indexes, analyzing tables, or doing anything else that might affect execution plans for the traced statements.

Interpreting tkprof Output

The tkprof output file is a text file that contains a section of information for each SQL statement found in the trace file. For each SQL statement, the following information is provided:

- The text of the SQL statement itself

- Statistics from the execution of that SQL statement

- Information on library cache misses and the optimizer goal

- The execution plan for the statement

If you ran a trace on the SQL statement presented at the beginning of this chapter (the one that queried three tables in the scott schema to produce a report of employee salary levels), and then wanted tkprof to format the results, the output for that statement would resemble:

```
SELECT e.empno, e.ename, d.dname, e.sal, sg.grade
FROM emp e, dept d, salgrade sg
WHERE e.deptno = d.deptno
AND e.sal > sg.losal
AND e.sal < sg.hisal
ORDER BY sal DESC
```

call	count	cpu	elapsed	disk	query	current	rows
Parse	1	0.03	0.04	9	149	0	0
Execute	1	0.00	0.00	0	0	0	0
Fetch	2	0.02	0.03	6	3	12	12
total	4	0.05	0.07	15	152	12	12

```
Misses in library cache during parse: 1
Optimizer goal: CHOOSE
Parsing user id: 20  (SCOTT)
```

Rows	Row Source Operation
12	SORT ORDER BY
12	HASH JOIN
20	MERGE JOIN CARTESIAN
5	TABLE ACCESS FULL DEPT
20	SORT JOIN
5	TABLE ACCESS FULL SALGRADE
14	TABLE ACCESS FULL EMP

Rows	Execution Plan
0	SELECT STATEMENT GOAL: CHOOSE
12	SORT (ORDER BY)
12	HASH JOIN

```
 20      MERGE JOIN (CARTESIAN)
  5        TABLE ACCESS   GOAL: ANALYZED (FULL) OF 'DEPT'
 20        SORT (JOIN)
  5          TABLE ACCESS   GOAL: ANALYZED (FULL) OF 'SALGRADE'
 14      TABLE ACCESS   GOAL: ANALYZED (FULL) OF 'EMP'
```

The timed statistics are very helpful in identifying statements with performance problems. Once a problem statement is identified, the execution plan can be reviewed to determine if there is a better, more efficient approach to executing that statement.

The phases of statement execution

SQL statements are executed in the following three phases:

Parse phase
> In this phase, Oracle takes the original SQL statement, checks the syntax, determines which objects are involved, checks the security on those objects, and then generates an execution plan for the statement. Oracle stores execution plans and the parsed versions of SQL statements in the shared pool. In an ideal situation, each SQL statement should only need to be parsed once, after which it can be executed many times.

Execution phase
> In this phase, Oracle does the actual work of executing the statement. For INSERT, UPDATE, and DELETE statements, the execution phase represents the bulk of the work. For SELECT statements, the execution phase is when Oracle finds the rows that need to be returned as the result of the query. Any sorting and grouping will be done here.

Fetch phase
> This phase only applies to SELECT statements. In this phase, Oracle returns rows to the application that executed the SELECT statement.

SQL Trace captures statistics for each of these three phases. The tkprof utility reports these statistics and reports the combined totals for all three phases. The statistics for each phase include the items shown in Table 8-4.

Table 8-4. Statistic Descriptions

Statistic	Description
COUNT	Reports the number of times a statement was parsed or executed. In the case of SELECT statements, it also reports the number of fetches that the application made to retrieve data.
CPU	Reports the amount of CPU time used during each of the three phases.
ELAPSED	Reports the amount of elapsed time used during each of the three phases.
DISK	Reports the number of database blocks that were physically read from the disk during each of the three phases.

Table 8-4. Statistic Descriptions (continued)

Statistic	Description
QUERY	Reports the number of buffers that were retrieved in consistent mode. Buffers are usually retrieved in consistent mode when the SQL statement in question is a SELECT.
CURRENT	Reports the number of buffers that were retrieved in current mode. Buffers are usually retrieved in current mode when INSERT, UPDATE, or DELETE statements are executed.

Key elements to look for in a tkprof report

What you look for in a trace file somewhat depends on why you are running the trace in the first place, but here are some suggestions for results you might watch for:

- High CPU or elapsed times

- Parse counts that are significantly greater than 1

- High numbers of library cache misses

- A high ratio of physical disk reads to consistent and current buffer retrievals

If a trace was run in response to user complaints, those complaints are most often voiced in terms of the time needed to perform a certain task or run a certain job. It is thus reasonable to run a trace while the task is performed or while the job in question is running, look at the CPU and elapsed times, and determine which queries are using the most time. Those queries usually represent the greatest opportunity for a performance improvement.

> Be aware that a high CPU time, or elapsed time, itself is not always bad. You also need to consider the statement being executed together with the number of times that it is executed. Ask if the time for a single execution seems reasonable, given what the statement is doing.

Ideally, a statement should be parsed only once. Subsequently, the parsed version of the statement and the execution plan should remain in the shared pool for use next time the statement is executed. Parsing is expensive, so if the parse counts are high relative to the execution counts, the size of your shared pool may need to be increased.

A high number of overall library cache misses (not necessarily for a single statement) also indicates that the shared pool may be too small. Oracle caches data dictionary information in the shared pool. Library cache misses represent times when Oracle couldn't find needed data dictionary information in the shared pool and was forced to read it from disk instead.

A high number of physical reads relative to the number of consistent or current reads indicates that full table scans are taking place. Check the execution plan to be sure.

Full table scans are not always bad. Just be sure that they are happening intentionally and not because you forgot to create an index.

SQL*Plus Tuning Aids

SQL*Plus has two features that can be useful when testing and tuning SQL statements. The SET AUTOTRACE command can be used to place SQL*Plus into a mode in which it displays the execution plan and statistics for each SQL statement that is executed. SQL*Plus also implements commands that allow tracking of the elapsed time necessary to execute one or more SQL statements.

SET AUTOTRACE

The SET AUTOTRACE command causes SQL*Plus to display the execution plan and the following statistics for each statement that is executed:

- The number of recursive SQL statements executed
- The number of blocks retrieved in current mode (db block gets)
- The number of blocks retrieved in read consistent mode (consistent gets)
- The number of physical reads from disk
- The amount of redo used
- The number of bytes transmitted via Net8 to the client executing the statement
- The number of bytes received via Net8 from the client
- The number of Net8 messages (roundtrips) exchanged between the client and server
- The number of in-memory sorts
- The number of sorts performed using disk
- The total number of rows processed

Some of these statistics differ from what is provided with SQL Trace; others are the same. Unlike the statistics generated from SQL Trace, statistics from SET AUTOTRACE are not broken out into parse, execution, and fetch phases.

Prerequisites for using autotrace

Some prerequisites must be met before using SET AUTOTRACE. If execution plans are desired, a plan table must exist in the schema and the name of that plan table must be plan_table. SQL*Plus will automatically use that table when autotrace is enabled. The process for creating a plan table was described earlier in this chapter in the "Creating the Plan Table" section.

If you wish to produce autotrace statistics, the user for whom the statistics are generated must have access to the dynamic performance views that SQL*Plus uses to get those statistics. This access should normally be granted through the use of a role named PLUSTRACE. Oracle supplies a script named *plustrce.sql* to create this role. The script resides in the *sqlplus/admin* directory underneath the Oracle home directory.

 On older releases of Oracle for Windows NT, look for a directory named *plus80* or *plus73*.

To create the PLUSTRACE role, log in as the user SYS (this login is usually done by the DBA), and execute the *plustrce.sql* script as shown in this example:

```
SQL> CONNECT sys/change_on_install
Connected.
SQL> @$ORACLE_HOME/sqlplus/admin/plustrce
SQL>
SQL> DROP ROLE PLUSTRACE;
drop role plustrace
         *
ERROR at line 1:
ORA-01919: role 'PLUSTRACE' does not exist

SQL> CREATE ROLE PLUSTRACE;

Role created.

SQL>
SQL> GRANT SELECT ON v_$sesstat TO PLUSTRACE;

Grant succeeded.

SQL> GRANT SELECT ON v_$statname TO PLUSTRACE;
```

```
Grant succeeded.

SQL> GRANT SELECT ON v_$session TO PLUSTRACE;

Grant succeeded.

SQL> GRANT PLUSTRACE TO DBA WITH ADMIN OPTION;

Grant succeeded.

SQL>
SQL> SET ECHO OFF
```

Don't worry about the error shown in the previous example—it is
normal if the role has not been created before. Oracle attempts to
drop the role prior to creating it (in case it already exists), and the
error results when there is no role to drop.

Once the script has been executed, a database role named PLUSTRACE will exist,
and this role can be granted to users who need to use SET AUTOTRACE.

Showing statistics and the plan

To see both statistics and the execution plan for statements that are executed, you
must use the command SET AUTOTRACE ON. Then you can issue any SQL statement for which testing is desired.

Example

```
SQL> SET AUTOTRACE ON
SQL> SELECT e.empno, e.ename, d.dname, e.sal, sg.grade
  2  FROM emp e, dept d, salgrade sg
  3  WHERE e.deptno = d.deptno
  4  AND e.sal > sg.losal
  5  AND e.sal < sg.hisal
  6  ORDER BY sal DESC;
```

EMPNO	ENAME	DNAME	SAL	GRADE
7839	KING	ACCOUNTING	5000	5
7566	JONES	RESEARCH	2975	4
7698	BLAKE	SALES	2850	4
7782	CLARK	ACCOUNTING	2450	4
7499	ALLEN	SALES	1600	3
7844	TURNER	SALES	1500	3
7934	MILLER	ACCOUNTING	1300	2
7521	WARD	SALES	1250	2
7654	MARTIN	SALES	1250	2
7876	ADAMS	RESEARCH	1100	1

```
        7900  JAMES      SALES              950          1
        7369  SMITH      RESEARCH           800          1

12 rows selected.

Execution Plan
-------------------------------------------------------------
    0       SELECT STATEMENT Optimizer=CHOOSE (Cost=9 Card=1 Bytes=75)
    1   0     SORT (ORDER BY) (Cost=9 Card=1 Bytes=75)
    2   1       HASH JOIN (Cost=7 Card=1 Bytes=75)
    3   2         MERGE JOIN (CARTESIAN) (Cost=5 Card=20 Bytes=700)
    4   3           TABLE ACCESS (FULL) OF 'DEPT' (Cost=1 Card=4 Bytes=8
          8)

    5   3           SORT (JOIN) (Cost=4 Card=5 Bytes=65)
    6   5             TABLE ACCESS (FULL) OF 'SALGRADE' (Cost=1 Card=5 B
          ytes=65)

    7   2           TABLE ACCESS (FULL) OF 'EMP' (Cost=1 Card=14 Bytes=560
          )

Statistics
-------------------------------------------------------------
        922  recursive calls
         13  db block gets
        152  consistent gets
         16  physical reads
          0  redo size
       1689  bytes sent via SQL*Net to client
        809  bytes received via SQL*Net from client
          4  SQL*Net roundtrips to/from client
         17  sorts (memory)
          0  sorts (disk)
         12  rows processed
```

When testing is complete, issue the SET AUTOTRACE OFF command to turn off the autotrace feature.

Showing only the plan or statistics

The output of autotrace can be limited to only the execution plan or only the statistics. To see only the plan, enable autotrace using the following command:

```
SET AUTOTRACE ON EXPLAIN
```

To limit autotrace to display only the statistics, use this command:

```
SET AUTOTRACE ON STATISTICS
```

 When you run autotrace in this limited manner, it may not be necessary to meet all the prerequisites. No plan table is needed if you do not display the execution plan, and no PLUSTRACE role is necessary if you do not display the statistics.

Suppressing the query's output

If you want to see the autotrace information for a query but not the query's results, use:

```
SET AUTOTRACE TRACEONLY
```

The TRACEONLY keyword replaces ON, so the following commands are also valid:

```
SET AUTOTRACE TRACEONLY EXPLAIN
SET AUTOTRACE TRACEONLY STATISTICS
```

The TRACEONLY option can save you from having to watch a lot of data scroll by on the screen. Realize though, that the SQL statement is still executed. In fact, the query's results are even transmitted back to the client. The only difference TRACE-ONLY makes is that SQL*Plus doesn't display those results.

Timers

SQL*Plus has two built-in facilities that can measure the elapsed time when executing SQL statements. The SET TIMING command functions similarly to SET AUTOTRACE, but reports the elapsed time after each statement. The TIMING command allows a timer to be started and stopped at any time.

SET TIMING

The SET TIMING ON command causes SQL*Plus to report the elapsed time for each SQL statement executed, as shown in the following example.

The SET TIMING OFF command is used to turn off the timing feature:

```
SQL> SET TIMING ON
SQL> SELECT e.empno, e.ename, d.dname, e.sal, sg.grade
  2  FROM emp e, dept d, salgrade sg
  3  WHERE e.deptno = d.deptno
  4  AND e.sal > sg.losal
  5  AND e.sal < sg.hisal
  6  ORDER BY sal DESC;

    EMPNO ENAME      DNAME                  SAL     GRADE
--------- ---------- --------------- --------- ---------
     7839 KING       ACCOUNTING            5000         5
     7566 JONES      RESEARCH              2975         4
     7698 BLAKE      SALES                 2850         4
     7782 CLARK      ACCOUNTING            2450         4
     7499 ALLEN      SALES                 1600         3
     7844 TURNER     SALES                 1500         3
     7934 MILLER     ACCOUNTING            1300         2
     7521 WARD       SALES                 1250         2
```

```
7654 MARTIN       SALES            1250         2
7876 ADAMS        RESEARCH         1100         1
7900 JAMES        SALES             950         1
7369 SMITH        RESEARCH          800         1

12 rows selected.

Elapsed: 00:00:00.01
```

 This example was run on a Linux system. On Linux and Unix, SQL*Plus reports the elapsed time in hours, minutes, seconds, and hundredths of a second. In a Windows environment, time is reported in milliseconds.

TIMING

The SQL*Plus TIMING command may be used to arbitrarily start and stop a timer. Use the command TIMING START to start a timer and TIMING STOP to stop the timer. When a timer is stopped, the elapsed time is displayed. For example:

```
SQL> TIMING START
SQL>
SQL> TIMING STOP
Elapsed: 00:00:05.15
```

Normally SQL statements would be run between the two TIMING commands so that timings are meaningful.

To display the time without stopping the timer, use the TIMING SHOW command:

```
SQL> TIMING START
SQL> TIMING SHOW
Elapsed: 00:00:03.40
SQL> TIMING SHOW
Elapsed: 00:00:06.93
```

Multiple timers may be run simultaneously by issuing more than one TIMING command, as shown below:

```
SQL> TIMING START
SQL> TIMING START
SQL> TIMING STOP
Elapsed: 00:00:05.46
SQL> TIMING STOP
Elapsed: 00:00:15.66
```

When multiple timers are used, they are always stopped in reverse of the order in which they were started. Consider each timer nested inside the other. To stop the outermost timer, you must stop all the innermost timers.

Improving Query Performance

If your query performance is unsatisfactory, remember that methods are available to help you improve it. You may want to:

- Modify the database structure
- Gather up-to-date statistics
- Rewrite the query
- Use optimizer hints to control the execution plan

Modifying Database Structure

Database structure modifications usually involve the creation of indexes. It's important to have the proper indexes to support your queries, but indexes aren't always the answer to poor performance. Other structural changes include separating table data and index data onto separate disks, spreading data over multiple disks, partitioning the data, and clustering data. However, these changes aren't likely to improve performance dramatically if you have a poorly written query to begin with.

Gathering Statistics

If the cost-based optimizer is in use, then table and index statistics play a large role in determining the execution plan that Oracle will use for any given statement. It's important that there be a set of statistics that results in the generation of good execution plans. In theory, up-to-date statistics that reflect the data accurately would always result in the best execution plans. In practice, occasional performance drops have been experienced after analyzing tables. Oracle8*i* actually includes a feature that allows the import of an arbitrary set of statistics to serve as the basis for optimizer-generated execution plans.

Rewriting Queries

Rewriting a query can sometimes have a big impact on performance. Consider the following query, which retrieves a list of employees located in cities other than Boston, New York, and Chicago:

```
SELECT empno, ename
FROM emp, dept
WHERE emp.deptno = dept.deptno
AND dept.loc NOT IN ('NEW YORK', 'BOSTON', 'CHICAGO');
```

The execution plan for this query looks like this:

```
SELECT STATEMENT    Cost = 3
  NESTED LOOPS
    TABLE ACCESS FULL DEPT
    TABLE ACCESS FULL EMP
```

Notice that the estimated query cost is 3. It's possible to rewrite this query using a NOT EXISTS predicate instead of joining the emp and dept tables. Here's how that query would look:

```
SELECT empno, ename
FROM emp
WHERE NOT EXISTS (
  SELECT *
  FROM dept
  WHERE emp.deptno = dept.deptno
  AND dept.loc IN ('NEW YORK', 'BOSTON', 'CHICAGO'));
```

The execution plan for this version of the query looks like this example:

```
SELECT STATEMENT    Cost = 1
  FILTER
    TABLE ACCESS FULL EMP
    TABLE ACCESS BY INDEX ROWID DEPT
      INDEX UNIQUE SCAN PK_DEPT
```

The second version of the query has a cost of 1, as opposed to a cost of 3 for the first, so the second query is likely the better choice. You can't depend totally on the optimizer's cost estimate though, because it's just that—an estimate. To be sure of which query performs best, perform some trial runs to collect some real performance. You could use SQL Trace for that purpose, allowing you to compare CPU time, elapsed time, and I/O between the two choices.

Using Optimizer Hints

The use of optimizer hints can also yield significant performance benefits, since they allow the execution plan to be modified and tuned based on knowledge of the actual data in the database.

Rather than allow Oracle total control over how a query is executed, specific directions can be provided to the optimizer through the use of hints. A *hint*, in Oracle, is an optimizer directive that is embedded in an SQL statement as a comment. For example:

```
SELECT /*+ FULL(dept) */
       empno, ename, dname
FROM emp, dept
WHERE emp.deptno = dept.deptno;
```

The hint in this case is FULL(dept); it tells Oracle to do a full table scan of the dept table. Oracle will honor this hint and perform a full table scan of dept when joining the tables, even if it appears that doing so will degrade performance.

The only time that Oracle does not honor a hint is when it is physically or logically impossible to do so.

Hint syntax

A hint applies to a single SQL statement, and hints may only be specified for SELECT, INSERT, UPDATE, and DELETE statements. The hint takes the form of a specially formatted comment and must appear immediately after the keyword that begins the statement:

```
keyword /*+ [hint|comment...] */
```

keyword

> The SQL command, which must be SELECT, UPDATE, or DELETE. The hint must immediately follow the keyword that begins the statement.

hint

> The hint itself, sometimes with one or more arguments enclosed in parentheses. Tables 8-5 through 8-10 provide a complete list of possible hints. Hints are not case-sensitive. A single comment may contain more than one hint, as long as the hints are separated by at least one space.

comment

> A user-specified comment. Oracle allows comments to be interspersed with hints.

Note that the table name in the second example below is emp, but an alias of e has been specified. The hint for the table uses the same alias, and is specified as FULL(e). Whenever an alias is used, the alias name must be used in any hints for the table:

```
SELECT /*+ FULL(emp) */ empno, ename
  FROM emp
 WHERE sal < 4000;

SELECT /*+ FULL(e) do a full tablescan on the emp table, because
              most employees do have billing rates < 4000. */
        empno, ename
  FROM emp e
 WHERE sal < 4000;
```

If multiple hints are supplied for a statement, they must all appear in the same comment, as shown below:

```
SELECT /*+ FULL(emp) FIRST_ROWS */ empno, ename
  FROM emp
  WHERE sal < 4000;
```

When subqueries are used, they are allowed to have their own hints. The hint for a subquery follows the keyword that starts the query, as shown in the following:

```
SELECT /*+ FIRST_ROWS */ empno, ename
FROM emp
WHERE NOT EXISTS (
  SELECT /*+ FULL(dept) */ *
  FROM dept
  WHERE emp.deptno = dept.deptno
  AND dept.loc IN ('NEW YORK', 'BOSTON', 'CHICAGO'));
```

When using hints, be careful to get the syntax exactly right. Because hints are embedded in the statements as comments, Oracle can't do any syntax checking. Oracle regards any incorrectly specified hint as a comment. In addition, you should always do an EXPLAIN PLAN after you code your hints, just to ensure that the optimizer really does what you think you told it to do.

Hints are always honored when possible

Hints are always honored if it is physically and logically possible to honor them. If one hint conflicts with others, or if it cannot possibly be implemented, Oracle will simply ignore the hint altogether. In the following example, the USE_CONCAT hint makes no sense because the query does not contain an OR condition. This query cannot be broken into two queries (with the results subsequently UNIONed together), so Oracle will ignore the hint. A bad hint is honored, however, whenever it is possible to implement:

```
SELECT /*+ USE_CONCAT */
       empno, ename
  FROM emp
  WHERE ename = 'SCOTT';
```

In the next example, the query contains a hint to do an index scan on the primary key index for the emp table. The primary key for emp is the empno column, and consequently there is an index on that column. This query seeks one record based on the employee name:

```
SELECT /*+ INDEX(emp pk_emp) */
       ename
  FROM emp
  WHERE ename = 'SCOTT';
```

Although it makes no sense to use the index on empno to retrieve an employee by name, Oracle will honor the request to use the primary key index with the following execution plan:

```
SELECT STATEMENT    Cost = 2
   TABLE ACCESS BY INDEX ROWID EMP
      INDEX FULL SCAN PK_EMP
```

Oracle will read every entry in the primary key index, retrieve the associated row from the employee table, and check the name to see if it has a match. This is worse than doing a full table scan! Oracle implements this plan because the hint requested it and because it is physically possible.

Types of Hints

Oracle hints can be divided loosely into the following categories:

- Optimizer goal hints
- Access method hints
- Join order hints
- Join operation hints
- Parallel execution hints
- Other hints

The next few sections describe the hints available in each category.

Optimizer goal hints

Optimizer goal hints allow you to influence the optimizer's overall goal when formulating an execution plan. For example, the hint can specify that the plan should be optimized to return the first record as quickly as possible. Table 8-5 gives a list of these hints.

Table 8-5. Optimizer Goal Hints

Hint	Description
ALL_ROWS	Tells the optimizer to produce an execution plan that minimizes resource consumption.
FIRST_ROWS	Tells the optimizer to produce an execution plan with the goal of getting to the first row as quickly as possible.
CHOOSE	Allows the optimizer to choose between the rule-based and the cost-based mode. If statistics are present for tables in the query, the cost-based approach will be taken.
RULE	Forces the optimizer to use a rule-based approach for the statement.

Avoid the RULE hint whenever possible. That hint causes the rule-based optimizer to be used. The rule-based optimizer uses a fixed set of rules when determining the execution plan for a statement and does not attempt to factor in the ultimate cost of executing that plan. The cost-based optimizer, on the other hand, bases its decision on the estimated I/O and CPU overhead required by various alternative plans. While Oracle still supports the rule-based optimizer, it hasn't been enhanced in years, won't be enhanced in the future, and may be desupported at some point. Oracle is putting its development effort into the cost-based optimizer.

Access method hints

Access method hints allow control of how data is accessed. For example, Oracle can be directed to perform a full table scan or to use an index when accessing a table, and the name of the specific index to be used can be specified. All access method hints take at least a table name as an argument because different access methods may be specified for different tables in the query.

Some access method hints are index-related and allow identification of indexes to be used. In many cases, such as with the INDEX hint, the index name may or may not be specified. The following hint tells Oracle to perform an index scan on the emp table, but that it's up to Oracle to pick the index:

```
/*+ INDEX(emp) */
```

This hint is useful if Oracle is expected to make the correct choice, or if hardcoding an index name into the hint is not desirable. You have the option however, of specifying the exact index to use. Here's an example:

```
/*+ INDEX(emp pk_emp) */
```

In this example, the exact index name is specified. A list of indexes may be specified, and Oracle will choose from the indexes in that list; for example:

```
/*+ INDEX(emp pk_emp, emp_dept_indx) */
```

In this example, assume that seven indexes exist for the emp table, but only two would be useful for the query in question. The hint provided tells Oracle to use an index scan to access the emp table, using either the index named pk_emp or the index named emp_dept_indx.

 The AND_EQUAL hint is special because it *requires* at least two indexes to be specified. That's because the hint causes Oracle to merge the results of two index scans. You can't do that unless you have two indexes to scan.

Table 8-6 lists the access method hints.

Table 8-6. Access Method Hints

Hint	Description
FULL(*table_name*)	Requests a full table scan of the specified table, regardless of any indexes that may exist.
ROWID(*table_name*)	Tells Oracle to perform a scan of the specified table based on ROWIDs.
CLUSTER(*table_name*)	Tells Oracle to do a cluster scan of the specified table. This hint is ignored if the table is not clustered.
HASH(*table_name*)	Tells Oracle to perform a hash scan of the specified table. This hint is ignored if the table is not clustered.
HASH_AJ(*table_name*)	Tells Oracle to do a hash anti-join of the specified table.
INDEX(*table_name* [*index_name*...])	Tells Oracle to access the specified table via an index scan. You may specify which index to use; otherwise Oracle chooses the index. You may also specify a list of indexes to choose from, and Oracle will choose from that list.
INDEX_ASC(*table_name* [*index_name*...])	Similar to the INDEX hint, but tells Oracle to scan the index in ascending order.
INDEX_COMBINE(*table_name* [*index_name*...])	Tells Oracle to use some combination of two indexes. You may specify which indexes to choose from or let Oracle make the choice.
INDEX_DESC(*table_name* [*index_name*...])	Similar to INDEX_ASC, but forces Oracle to scan the index in descending order.
INDEX_FFS(*table_name* [*index_name*...])	Tells Oracle to do a fast full index scan.
MERGE_AJ(*table_name*)	Turns a NOT IN subquery into a merge anti-join.
AND_EQUAL(*table_name index_name index name*...)	Tells Oracle to scan two or more indexes and merge the results. You must specify at least two index names.
USE_CONCAT	Turns a query with OR conditions into two or more queries unioned together with a UNION ALL.

Join order hints

Join order hints allow control over the order in which Oracle joins tables. There are only three of these hints, listed in Table 8-7.

Table 8-7. Join Order Hints

Hint	Description
ORDERED	Tells Oracle to join tables from left to right, in the same order in which they are listed in the FROM clause.
STAR	Tells Oracle to use a star query execution plan, if at all possible. This step can only work if at least three tables are joined, and the largest table has a concatenated index on columns that reference the two smaller tables. The two smaller tables are joined first, then a nested-loop join is used to retrieve the required rows from the largest table.
STAR_TRANSFORMATION	Tells Oracle to transform the query into a star query, if possible, and then use the best plan for that query.

Join operation hints

Join operation hints allow control of the way two tables are joined. Oracle uses three basic methods whenever two tables are joined:

Merge join

>   This type of join is performed by sorting rows from each table by the join columns. Once the two rowsets have been sorted, Oracle reads through both and joins any matching rows. A merge join often uses fewer resources than the other options, but all records must be sorted before the first row is returned. It also requires sufficient memory and temporary disk space to handle the sort.

Nested loops join

>   The method used for this type of join corresponds to the image most people have when they think of joining tables. Oracle picks one table as the driving table and reads through that table row by row. For each row read from the driving table, Oracle looks up the corresponding rows in the secondary table and joins them. Because no sort is involved, a nested loops join will usually get you the first record back more quickly than a merge join. For the same reason, a nested loops join also does not require large amounts of disk space and memory. However, a nested loops join may result in a considerably greater number of disk reads than a merge join.

Hash join

>   This type of join is similar to a merge join, but a sort is not required. A hash table is built in memory to allow quick access to the rows from one of the tables to be joined. Then rows are read from the other table. As each row is read from the second table, the hash function is applied to the join columns and the result used to find the corresponding rows from the first table.

Along with the hints used to specify the join method, other hints are lumped into the join operation category. Table 8-8 lists all the join operation hints.

Table 8-8. Join Operation Hints

Hint	Description
USE_NL(*table_name*)	Tells Oracle to use a nested loop when joining this table. The table specified by this hint is the one accessed by the innermost loop. The other table is the driving table.
USE_MERGE(*table_name*)	Tells Oracle to use the sort merge method when joining this table.
USE_HASH(*table_name*)	Tells Oracle to use a hash join for the specified table.
NO_MERGE	Applies to queries that contain joins on one or more views. It prevents Oracle from merging the query from a view into the main query.
DRIVING_SITE(*table_name*)	This hint applies when executing a distributed join, one that joins tables from two or more databases. Without a hint, Oracle chooses which database actually collects the tables and does the join. By using the hint, you tell Oracle that you want the join performed by the database containing the specified table.

Parallel execution hints

Parallel execution hints influence the way Oracle executes a query in a parallel processing environment. When running with a single CPU or when parallel processing has been disabled, parallel processing is not possible and these hints will be ignored. Parallel execution hints are illustrated in Table 8-9.

Table 8-9. Parallel Execution Hints

Hint	Description
PARALLEL(*table_name* [, *degree* [, *num_instances*]])	Tells Oracle to access data from the indicated table in parallel processing mode. You can optionally specify the degree of parallelism to use and the number of instances that will be involved. The keyword DEFAULT may be used for both arguments, in which case Oracle decides the values based on parameters in the *INIT.ORA* file and the table definition. Using the PARALLEL hint in an INSERT statement automatically turns on APPEND mode. See the APPEND and NO_APPEND hints.
NO_PARALLEL(*table_name*)	Tells Oracle not to access the specified table in parallel.
APPEND	Applies only to INSERT statements. It tells Oracle not to attempt to reuse any free space that may be available in any extents currently allocated to the table.
NOAPPEND	This hint is the opposite of APPEND and tells Oracle to use any free space in extents currently allocated to the table. The hint exists because APPEND becomes the default behavior whenever a PARALLEL hint is used in an INSERT statement.

Table 8-9. Parallel Execution Hints (continued)

Hint	Description
PARALLEL_INDEX (*table_name, index_name* [, *degree* [, *num_instances*]])	Tells Oracle to access data from the indicated table by scanning the specified index in parallel processing mode. The index must be a partitioned index. You can optionally specify the degree of parallelism to use and the number of instances that will be involved. The keyword DEFAULT may be used for both arguments, in which case Oracle decides the values based on parameters in the *INIT.ORA* file and the table definition.

Other hints

A few hints don't fit neatly into one of the other categories. These hints are listed in Table 8-10.

Table 8-10. Other Hints

Hint	Description
CACHE (*table_name*)	Applies only when a full table scan is performed on the specified table. It tells Oracle to place blocks for that table at the most recently used end of the buffer cache so they will remain in memory as long as possible. This can be useful for small lookup tables that you expect to access repeatedly.
NOCACHE (*table_name*)	This hint is the opposite of CACHE and tells Oracle to place blocks at the least recently used end of the buffer cache, where they will be cleared out as soon as possible.
PUSH_SUBQ	Tells Oracle to evaluate nonmerged subqueries as soon as possible during query execution. If you expect the subquery to eliminate a large number of rows, this hint can improve performance.

A

SQL Resources

In this appendix, I have listed some useful resources, both online and offline, that may help you with SQL, SQL*Plus, and PL/SQL. I hope you find them helpful!

Books

There are many excellent Oracle books on the market today. This section lists some that I find particularly helpful:

Aronoff, Eyal, Kevin Loney, and Noorali Sonawalla. *Advanced Oracle Tuning and Administration.* Osborne McGraw-Hill, 1997. This book includes the most comprehensive discussion and explanation of the EXPLAIN PLAN facility available anywhere.

Feuerstein, Steven, and Bill Pribyl. *Oracle PL/SQL Programming, Second Edition.* O'Reilly & Associates, 1997. Hands down, the definitive guide to PL/SQL. If it's about PL/SQL (through Oracle8), it's in this book!

Feuerstein, Steven. *Oracle PL/SQL Programming: Guide to Oracle8i Features.* O'Reilly & Associates, 1999. This book contains a very nice summary of all the new PL/SQL features available in Oracle8*i*. It's a great supplement to *Oracle PL/SQL Programming, Second Edition.*

Feuerstein, Steven. *Advanced Oracle PL/SQL Programming with Packages.* O'Reilly & Associates, 1996. This book provides all the information you will ever need about developing your own PL/SQL packages.

Feuerstein, Steven, Charles Dye, and John Beresniewicz. *Oracle Built-in Packages.* O'Reilly & Associates, 1998. Once you've mastered PL/SQL programming, this book takes you to the next level by explaining how to leverage the built-in packages Oracle provides with the database.

Gennick, Jonathan. *Oracle SQL*Plus: The Definitive Guide*. O'Reilly & Associates, 1999. A complete guide to all the nuances of SQL*Plus. This book has a wealth of information for both the beginner and the experienced SQL programmer.

Kreines, David and Brian Laskey. *Oracle Database Administration: The Essential Reference*. O'Reilly & Associates, 1999. Sure, I'm biased, but this book has all the information you need to effectively manage an Oracle database.

Lomasky, Brian, and David Kreines. *Oracle Scripts*. O'Reilly & Associates, 1998. This book is full of utilities and routines that function as excellent tools for day-to-day development and administration and that are excellent learning examples of complex SQL programming techniques.

Niemiec, Richard *Oracle Performance Tuning Tips & Techniques*. Osborne McGraw-Hill, 1999. If you want access to the collective tuning experience of some real SQL experts, this book has it.

Other Publications

Select

This publication, produced as a membership benefit by the International Oracle Users Group—Americas (IOUG-A), contains a variety of articles and columns on Oracle programming and articles containing SQL-related tips, techniques, and practices.

Oracle Magazine

This magazine, which is published by Oracle Corporation, is primarily a marketing tool, but it also carries articles (often by Oracle technical staff or experienced developers) on SQL and PL/SQL development.

Many Oracle user groups and special interest groups also publish newsletters containing useful information for SQL programmers.

Organizations

International Oracle Users Group—Americas (IOUG-A)
401 North Michigan Avenue
Chicago, IL 60611 USA
Voice: (312) 245-1579
fax: (312) 527-6785
email: *ioug@ioug.org*

European Oracle Users Group (EOUG)
Brigittenauer Lände 50-54, A-1203
Vienna, Austria
Voice: +43 1 33777 870
fax: +43 1 33777 873
email: *eoug@at.oracle.com*

Asia-Pacific Oracle Users Group (APOUG)
PO Box 3046
The Pines, Doncaster East
VIC 3109, Australia
Voice: +61 3 9842 3246
fax: +61 3 9842 3050
email: 100242.1746@compuserve.com

Australian Oracle User Group (AUSOUG)
PO Box 16
Wilston QLD 4051 Australia
Voice: +61 7 3352 7985
fax: +61 7 3352 7135

Web Sites

http://www.oracle.com

Oracle Corporation's web site. Contains a wide variety of information on almost any Oracle-related topic and links to other sites, including the Oracle Support site.

http://www.ioug.org

Operated by the IOUG-A. Contains technical articles from *Select* magazine, papers from IOUG-A conferences, a technical repository, and a technical discussion forum.

http://www.eoug.com

The web site for the EOUG. Contains information of general interest to Oracle developers, including information on conferences and educational events for Europe, the Middle East, and Africa.

http://www.ausoug.org

The web site for the AUSOUG. Contains information of general interest to Oracle developers, including information on conferences and educational events for Australia.

http://www.revealnet.com

This site hosts the PL/SQL "Pipeline," a free online discussion community for PL/SQL topics that attracts some of the best and most experienced Oracle talent from around the world. Beginners are welcome. The atmosphere is very cordial, and participants are tolerant of all levels of questions.

http://technet.oracle.com

Oracle Technology Network's (OTN) web site, which is operated by Oracle Corporation. Contains a wide variety of technical resources for Oracle developers. Provides access to the full Oracle documentation set, code samples, and white papers.

http://www.ixora.com.au

This site is definitely not for the faint of heart or beginner, but it does contain an unmatched depth of information on Oracle tuning and internals.

http://www.primarykey.com

If you are looking for a book about any aspect of Oracle, this is the place to find it. This site is operated by people who actually know about Oracle and who can help you find the resources you need.

Index

About the Author

David C. Kreines is the Manager of Database Services for Rhodia, Inc., a subsidiary of Rhone-Poulenc S.A., and the coauthor of *Oracle Database Administration: The Essential Reference* (O'Reilly & Associates, 1999) and *Oracle Scripts* (O'Reilly & Associates, 1998). Dave has worked with Oracle as a developer and database administrator since 1985, on a wide variety of platforms, from PCs to mainframes. He is an Oracle Certified Professional, is certified as a DBA, and has been a frequent contributor to Oracle conferences, user groups, and publications, both in the United States and in Europe. Dave served two terms as president of the International Oracle Users Group–Americas (IOUG-A), and spent ten years on the board of directors.

Colophon

Our look is the result of reader comments, our own experimentation, and feedback from distribution channels. Distinctive covers complement our distinctive approach to technical topics, breathing personality and life into potentially dry subjects.

The animal on the cover of *Oracle SQL: The Essential Reference* is a scorpion. Fossil records indicate that scorpions were among the first arachnids, and the presence of gills in some fossil specimen may indicate that the scorpion evolved from a sea-dwelling ancestor. Today, scorpions dwell in desert habitats, where they sleep under rocks or in sand burrows during the day, and come out at night to hunt insects. Scientists know of approximately 1,300 species of scorpions, ranging in size from one to eight inches, and ranging in color from yellow-brown to green to black.

The scorpion locates its prey by detecting air-born vibrations through the sensory hairs on its pedipalps (claws). The scorpion then uses its pedipalps to grasp the prey while injecting it with paralyzing venom from the aculeus (stinger) on the end of its tail. A scorpion also uses its venomous sting for defense against would-be devourers, which include fellow arachnids, centipedes and spiders, as well as lizards, birds, and small mammals.

The scorpion's mating ritual involves an elaborate courtship dance, during which the male and female grasp claws; the male secretes spermatophore on a rock or twig over which the female crosses, drawing in the sperm. Gestation can last up to one and a half years for some species, after which the female gives birth to numerous live young, who spend their first week or two traveling around on their mother's back.

Scorpions produce venom that is deadly to humans. Don't walk barefoot in the desert at night, or, if you must, shine a black light before you—scorpions fluoresce in ultraviolet light!

Darren Kelly was the production editor, Ann Schirmer was the copyeditor, and Maureen Dempsey was the proofreader for *Oracle SQL: The Essential Reference*. Claire Cloutier, Linley Dolby, Sarah Jane Shangraw, and Mary Sheehan provided quality control. Judy Hoer wrote the index. Interior composition was done by James Carter, Deborah Smith, and Nancy Williams.

Ellie Volckhausen designed the cover of this book, based on a series design by Edie Freedman. The cover image is a 19th-century engraving from the Dover Pictorial Archive. Emma Colby produced the cover layout with QuarkXPress 4.1 using Adobe's ITC Garamond font.

Alicia Cech and David Futato designed the interior layout based on a series design by Nancy Priest. Mike Sierra implemented the design in FrameMaker 5.5.6. The text and heading fonts are ITC Garamond Light and Garamond Book; the code font is Constant Willison. The illustrations that appear in the book were produced by Robert Romano using Macromedia FreeHand 8 and Adobe Photoshop 5. This colophon was written by Sarah Jane Shangraw.

Whenever possible, our books use a durable and flexible lay-flat binding. If the page count exceeds this binding's limit, perfect binding is used.

More Titles from O'Reilly

Oracle

Advanced Oracle PL/SQL Programming with Packages

By Steven Feuerstein
1st Edition October 1996
690 pages, Includes diskette
ISBN 1-56592-238-7

This book explains the best way to construct
packages, a powerful part of Oracle's PL/SQL
procedural language that can dramatically
improve your programming productivity and
code quality, while preparing you for object-oriented development
in Oracle technology. It comes with PL/Vision software, a library of
PL/SQL packages developed by the author, and takes you behind
the scenes as it examines how and why the PL/Vision packages
were implemented the way they were.

Oracle Built-in Packages

By Steven Feuerstein,
Charles Dye & John Beresniewicz
1st Edition April 1998
956 pages, Includes diskette
ISBN 1-56592-375-8

Oracle's built-in packages dramatically
extend the power of the PL/SQL language,
but few developers know how to use them
effectively. This book is a complete reference to all of the built-ins,
including those new to Oracle8. The enclosed diskette includes an
online tool that provides easy access to the many files of source
code and documentation developed by the authors.

Oracle PL/SQL Programming Guide to Oracle8i Features

By Steven Feuerstein
1st Edition October 1999
272 pages, Includes diskette
ISBN 1-56592-675-7

This concise and engaging guide will give
you a jump start on the new PL/SQL features
of Oracle8i (Oracle's revolutionary "Internet
database"). It covers autonomous transactions,
invoker rights, native dynamic SQL, bulk binds and collects, system-
level database triggers, new built-in packages, fine-grained access
control, calling Java methods from within PL/SQL, and much more.
Includes a diskette containing 100 files of reusable source code and
examples.

Oracle Web Applications: PL/SQL Developer's Introduction

By Andrew Odewahn
1st Edition September 1999
256 pages, ISBN 1-56592-687-0

This book is an easy-to-understand guide
to building Oracle8i (Oracle's "Internet
database") Web applications using a variety
of tools – PL/SQL, HTML, XML, WebDB,
and Oracle Application Server (OAS). It
also covers the packages in the PL/SQL toolkit and demonstrates
several fully realized Web applications. This book provides the
jump-start you need to extend relational concepts to Web content
and to make the transition from traditional programming to the
development of useful Web applications for Oracle8i. Also covers
Web development for Oracle8 and Oracle7.

Oracle PL/SQL Programming, 2nd Edition

By Steven Feuerstein with Bill Pribyl
2nd Edition September 1997
1028 pages, Includes diskette
ISBN 1-56592-335-9

The first edition of Oracle PL/SQL
Programming quickly became an
indispensable reference for PL/SQL
developers. The second edition focuses on
Oracle8, covering Oracle8 object types, object views, collections,
and external procedures, as well as new datatypes and functions
and tuning, tracing, and debugging PL/SQL programs. The
diskette contains an online Windows-based tool with access
to more than 100 files of source code.

Oracle PL/SQL Language Pocket Reference

By Steven Feuerstein,
Bill Pribyl & Chip Dawes
1st Edition April 1999
104 pages, ISBN 1-56592-457-6

This pocket reference boils down the
most vital information from Oracle PL/SQL
Programming into an accessible quick
reference that summarizes the basics of
PL/SQL: block structure, fundamental
language elements (e.g., identifiers,
declarations, defaults), data structures (including Oracle8
objects), control statements, and use of procedures, functions,
and packages. It includes coverage of PL/SQL features in the
newest version of Oracle, Oracle8i.

Oracle

Oracle SQL*Plus: The Definitive Guide

By Jonathan Gennick
1st Edition March 1999
526 pages, ISBN 1-56592-578-5

This book is the definitive guide to SQL*Plus, Oracle's interactive query tool. Despite the wide availability and usage of SQL*Plus, few developers and DBAs know how powerful it really is. This book introduces SQL*Plus, provides a syntax quick reference, and describes how to write and execute script files, generate ad hoc reports, extract data from the database, query the data dictionary tables, use the SQL*Plus administrative features (new in Oracle8i), and much more.

Oracle SQL*Plus Pocket Reference

By Jonathan Gennick
1st Edition April 2000
94 pages, ISBN 1-56592-941-1

This quick reference is an excellent, portable resource for every Oracle administrator and developer. It summarizes the syntax of SQL*Plus, Oracle's ubiquitous interactive query tool, including new Oracle8i release 8.1.6 features. It also summarizes how to interact with SQL*Plus and presents the basics of selecting data, formatting reports, and tuning SQL.

Oracle Essentials: Oracle8 & Oracle8i

By Rick Greenwald, Robert Stackowiak & Jonathan Stern
1st Edition October 1999
374 pages, ISBN 1-56592-708-7

This concise guide explains what's important about Oracle8 (the "object-relational database") and Oracle8i (the "Internet database"). It covers overall system products, architecture, and data structures; installation, management, security, networking, backup and recovery, and tuning issues; and specific technologies such as data warehouses, online transaction processing (OLTP), distributed systems, high availability, Oracle8 and Oracle8i extensions, and Oracle's interfaces to the Web.

Oracle Database Administration: The Essential Reference

By David Kreines & Brian Laskey
1st Edition April 1999
580 pages, ISBN 1-56592-516-5

This book provides a concise reference to the enormous store of information Oracle8 or Oracle7 DBAs need every day. It covers DBA tasks (e.g., installation, tuning, backups, networking, auditing, query optimization) and provides quick references to initialization parameters, SQL statements, data dictionary tables, system privileges, roles, and syntax for SQL*Plus, Export, Import, and SQL*Loader.

Oracle8i Internal Services for Waits, Latches, Locks and Memory

By Steve Adams
1st edition October 1999
132 pages, ISBN 1-56592-598-X

Based on Oracle8i, release 8.1, this concise book contains detailed, hard-to-find information about Oracle internals (data structures, algorithms, hidden parameters, and undocumented system statistics). Main topics include waits, latches, locks (including instance locks used in parallel server environments), and memory use and management. Aimed especially at readers doing advanced performance tuning.

Oracle SAP Administration

By Donald K. Burleson
1st Edition September 1999 (est.)
200 pages (est.), ISBN 1-56592-696-X

This book provides tried-and-true advice for administrators and developers who use the SAP business system and the Oracle database system (Oracle8 or Oracle7) in combination. It covers SAP's SAPDBA and SAPGUI utilities and describes effective data file placement, initialization parameters, and monitoring techniques, as well as high-performance table reorganization, backup, recovery, tuning, and parallel processing.

Oracle

Oracle Design

By Dave Ensor & Ian Stevenson
1st Edition March 1997
546 pages, ISBN 1-56592-268-9

This book looks thoroughly at the field of Oracle relational database design, an often neglected area of Oracle, but one that has an enormous impact on the ultimate power and performance of a system. Focuses on both database and code design, including such special design areas as data models, denormalization, the use of keys and indexes, temporal data, special architectures (client/server, distributed database, parallel processing), and data warehouses.

Oracle8 Design Tips

By Dave Ensor & Ian Stevenson
1st Edition September 1997
130 pages, ISBN 1-56592-361-8

The newest version of the Oracle DBMS, Oracle8, offers some dramatically different features from previous versions, including better scalability, reliability, and security; an object-relational model; additional datatypes; and much more. To get peak performance out of an Oracle8 system, databases and code need to be designed with these new features in mind. This small book tells Oracle designers and developers just what they need to know to use the Oracle8 features to best advantage.

Oracle Performance Tuning, 2nd Edition

By Mark Gurry & Peter Corrigan
2nd Edition November 1996
964 pages, Includes diskette
ISBN 1-56592-237-9

The first edition of this book became a classic for developers and DBAs. This edition offers 400 pages of updated material on Oracle features, including parallel server, parallel query, Oracle Performance Pack, disk striping and mirroring, RAID, MPPs, SMPs, distributed databases, backup and recovery, and much more. Includes a diskette containing the SQL and shell scripts described in the book.

Oracle Scripts

By Brian Lomasky & David C. Kreines
1st Edition May 1998
204 pages, Includes CD-ROM
ISBN 1-56592-438-X

A powerful toolset for Oracle DBAs and developers, these scripts will simplify everyday tasks – monitoring databases, protecting against data loss, improving security and performance, and helping to diagnose problems and repair databases in emergencies. The accompanying CD-ROM contains complete source code and additional monitoring and tuning software.

Oracle Security

By Marlene Theriault & William Heney
1st Edition October 1998
446 pages, ISBN 1-56592-450-9

This book covers the field of Oracle security from simple to complex. It describes basic RDBMS security features (e.g., passwords, profiles, roles, privileges, synonyms) and includes many practical strategies for securing an Oracle system, developing auditing and backup plans, and using the Oracle Enterprise Manager and Oracle Security Server. Also touches on advanced security features, such as encryption, Trusted Oracle, and Internet and Web protection.

Oracle PL/SQL Developer's Workbook

By Steven Feuerstein
with Andrew Odewahn
1st Edition May 2000
592 pages, ISBN 1-56592-674-9

A companion to Feuerstein's other bestselling Oracle PL/SQL books, this workbook contains a carefully constructed set of problems and solutions that will test your language skills and help you become a better developer. Exercises are provided at three levels: beginner, intermediate, and expert. It covers the full set of language features: variables, loops, exception handling, data structures, object technology, cursors, built-in functions and packages, PL/SQL tuning, and the new Oracle8i features (including Java and the Web).

Oracle

Oracle PL/SQL Built-ins Pocket Reference

By Steven Feuerstein,
John Beresniewicz & Chip Dawes
1st Edition October 1998
78 pages, ISBN 1-56592-456-8

This companion quick reference to
Steven Feuerstein's bestselling *Oracle PL/SQL
Programming* and *Oracle Built-in Packages*
will help you use Oracle's extensive set of
built-in functions and packages, including
those new to Oracle8. You'll learn how to
call numeric, character, date, conversion, large object (LOB), and
miscellaneous functions, as well as packages like DBMS_SQL and
DBMS_OUTPUT.

How to stay in touch with O'Reilly

1. Visit Our Award-Winning Web Site

http://www.oreilly.com/

★ "Top 100 Sites on the Web" —*PC Magazine*
★ "Top 5% Web sites" —*Point Communications*
★ "3-Star site" —*The McKinley Group*

Our web site contains a library of comprehensive product information (including book excerpts and tables of contents), downloadable software, background articles, interviews with technology leaders, links to relevant sites, book cover art, and more. File us in your Bookmarks or Hotlist!

2. Join Our Email Mailing Lists

New Product Releases
To receive automatic email with brief descriptions of all new O'Reilly products as they are released, send email to:
listproc@online.oreilly.com
Put the following information in the first line of your message (*not* in the Subject field):
subscribe oreilly-news

O'Reilly Events
If you'd also like us to send information about trade show events, special promotions, and other O'Reilly events, send email to:
listproc@online.oreilly.com
Put the following information in the first line of your message (*not* in the Subject field):
subscribe oreilly-events

3. Get Examples from Our Books via FTP

There are two ways to access an archive of example files from our books:

Regular FTP
- ftp to:
  ftp.oreilly.com
  (login: anonymous
  password: your email address)
- Point your web browser to:
  ftp://ftp.oreilly.com/

FTPMAIL
- Send an email message to:
  ftpmail@online.oreilly.com
  (Write "help" in the message body)

4. Contact Us via Email

order@oreilly.com
To place a book or software order online. Good for North American and international customers.

subscriptions@oreilly.com
To place an order for any of our newsletters or periodicals.

books@oreilly.com
General questions about any of our books.

software@oreilly.com
For general questions and product information about our software. Check out O'Reilly Software Online at **http://software.oreilly.com/** for software and technical support information. Registered O'Reilly software users send your questions to: **website-support@oreilly.com**

cs@oreilly.com
For answers to problems regarding your order or our products.

booktech@oreilly.com
For book content technical questions or corrections.

proposals@oreilly.com
To submit new book or software proposals to our editors and product managers.

international@oreilly.com
For information about our international distributors or translation queries. For a list of our distributors outside of North America check out:
http://www.oreilly.com/www/order/country.html

5. Work with Us

Check out our website for current employment opportunites:
www.jobs@oreilly.com
Click on "Work with Us"

O'Reilly & Associates, Inc.
101 Morris Street, Sebastopol, CA 95472 USA
TEL   707-829-0515 or 800-998-9938
         (6am to 5pm PST)
FAX   707-829-0104

International Distributors

UK, EUROPE, MIDDLE EAST AND AFRICA (EXCEPT FRANCE, GERMANY, AUSTRIA, SWITZERLAND, LUXEMBOURG, LIECHTENSTEIN, AND EASTERN EUROPE)

INQUIRIES
O'Reilly UK Limited
4 Castle Street
Farnham
Surrey, GU9 7HS
United Kingdom
Telephone: 44-1252-711776
Fax: 44-1252-734211
Email: information@oreilly.co.uk

ORDERS
Wiley Distribution Services Ltd.
1 Oldlands Way
Bognor Regis
West Sussex PO22 9SA
United Kingdom
Telephone: 44-1243-779777
Fax: 44-1243-820250
Email: cs-books@wiley.co.uk

FRANCE

INQUIRIES
Éditions O'Reilly
18 rue Séguier
75006 Paris, France
Tel: 33-1-40-51-52-30
Fax: 33-1-40-51-52-31
Email: france@editions-oreilly.fr

ORDERS
GEODIF
61, Bd Saint-Germain
75240 Paris Cedex 05, France
Tel: 33-1-44-41-46-16 (French books)
Tel: 33-1-44-41-11-87 (English books)
Fax: 33-1-44-41-11-44
Email: distribution@eyrolles.com

GERMANY, SWITZERLAND, AUSTRIA, EASTERN EUROPE, LUXEMBOURG, AND LIECHTENSTEIN

INQUIRIES & ORDERS
O'Reilly Verlag
Balthasarstr. 81
D-50670 Köln
Germany
Telephone: 49-221-973160-91
Fax: 49-221-973160-8
Email: anfragen@oreilly.de (inquiries)
Email: order@oreilly.de (orders)

CANADA (FRENCH LANGUAGE BOOKS)

Les Éditions Flammarion ltée
375, Avenue Laurier Ouest
Montréal (Québec) H2V 2K3
Tel: 00-1-514-277-8807
Fax: 00-1-514-278-2085
Email: info@flammarion.qc.ca

HONG KONG

City Discount Subscription Service, Ltd.
Unit D, 3rd Floor, Yan's Tower
27 Wong Chuk Hang Road
Aberdeen, Hong Kong
Tel: 852-2580-3539
Fax: 852-2580-6463
Email: citydis@ppn.com.hk

KOREA

Hanbit Media, Inc.
Chungmu Bldg. 201
Yonnam-dong 568-33
Mapo-gu
Seoul, Korea
Tel: 822-325-0397
Fax: 822-325-9697
Email: hant93@chollian.dacom.co.kr

PHILIPPINES

Global Publishing
G/F Benavides Garden
1186 Benavides Street
Manila, Philippines
Tel: 632-254-8949/637-252-2582
Fax: 632-734-5060/632-252-2733
Email: globalp@pacific.net.ph

TAIWAN

O'Reilly Taiwan
No. 3, Lane 131
Hang-Chow South Road
Section 1, Taipei, Taiwan
Tel: 886-2-23968990
Fax: 886-2-23968916
Email: taiwan@oreilly.com

CHINA

O'Reilly Beijing
Room 2410
160, FuXingMenNeiDaJie
XiCheng District
Beijing, China PR 100031
Tel: 86-10-66412305
Fax: 86-10-86631007
Email: beijing@oreilly.com

INDIA

Computer Bookshop (India) Pvt. Ltd.
190 Dr. D.N. Road, Fort
Bombay 400 001 India
Tel: 91-22-207-0989
Fax: 91-22-262-3551
Email: cbsbom@giasbm01.vsnl.net.in

JAPAN

O'Reilly Japan, Inc.
Yotsuya Y's Building
7 Banch 6, Honshio-cho
Shinjuku-ku
Tokyo 160-0003 Japan
Tel: 81-3-3356-5227
Fax: 81-3-3356-5261
Email: japan@oreilly.com

ALL OTHER ASIAN COUNTRIES

O'Reilly & Associates, Inc.
101 Morris Street
Sebastopol, CA 95472 USA
Tel: 707-829-0515
Fax: 707-829-0104
Email: order@oreilly.com

AUSTRALIA

Woodslane Pty., Ltd.
7/5 Vuko Place
Warriewood NSW 2102
Australia
Tel: 61-2-9970-5111
Fax: 61-2-9970-5002
Email: info@woodslane.com.au

NEW ZEALAND

Woodslane New Zealand, Ltd.
21 Cooks Street (P.O. Box 575)
Waganui, New Zealand
Tel: 64-6-347-6543
Fax: 64-6-345-4840
Email: info@woodslane.com.au

LATIN AMERICA

McGraw-Hill Interamericana
Editores, S.A. de C.V.
Cedro No. 512
Col. Atlampa
06450, Mexico, D.F.
Tel: 52-5-547-6777
Fax: 52-5-547-3336
Email: mcgraw-hill@infosel.net.mx

O'REILLY®

O'Reilly & Associates, Inc.
101 Morris Street
Sebastopol, CA 95472-9902
1-800-998-9938

Visit us online at:
www.oreilly.com
order@oreilly.com

O'REILLY WOULD LIKE TO HEAR FROM YOU

Which book did this card come from?

_____

Where did you buy this book?
❏ Bookstore   ❏ Computer Store
❏ Direct from O'Reilly   ❏ Class/seminar
❏ Bundled with hardware/software
❏ Other _____

What operating system do you use?
❏ UNIX   ❏ Macintosh
❏ Windows NT   ❏ PC(Windows/DOS)
❏ Other _____

What is your job description?
❏ System Administrator   ❏ Programmer
❏ Network Administrator   ❏ Educator/Teacher
❏ Web Developer
❏ Other _____

❏ Please send me O'Reilly's catalog, containing
a complete listing of O'Reilly books and
software.

Name _____ Company/Organization _____

Address _____

City _____ State _____ Zip/Postal Code _____ Country _____

Telephone _____ Internet or other email address (specify network)

Nineteenth century wood engraving
of a bear from the O'Reilly &
Associates Nutshell Handbook®
Using & Managing UUCP.

POST CARD

PLACE
STAMP
HERE

NO POSTAGE
NECESSARY IF
MAILED IN THE
UNITED STATES

BUSINESS REPLY MAIL
FIRST CLASS MAIL   PERMIT NO. 80   SEBASTOPOL, CA

Postage will be paid by addressee

O'Reilly & Associates, Inc.
101 Morris Street
Sebastopol, CA 95472-9902